# FAMILY VIDEO GUIDE

## TO RECOMMENDED MOVIES

New Updated/Enlarged Edition

Edited By
John H. Evans

**MOVIE MORALITY MINISTRIES, INC.**

FAMILY VIDEO GUIDE TO
RECOMMENDED MOVIES
New Updated/Enlarged Edition

Edited by John H. Evans

COPYRIGHT © 1996 by John H. Evans

All rights reserved. No part of this book may be reproduced or transmitted in any form or by any means, electronic or mechanical, including photocopy, recording, or by any information storage retrieval system, without permission from the publisher.

Printed in the United States of America

First Printing - 1996

Published by

Movie Morality Ministries, Inc.
1309 Seminole Drive
Richardson, Texas 75080-3736

ISBN 0-9628497-1-5

# Table of Contents

Introduction . . . . . . . . . . . . . . . . . . . . . . . . . . . . . . . . . . . . . . v
Guidelines for Recommending Movies . . . . . . . . . . . . . . . . . vii
Explanation of Terms . . . . . . . . . . . . . . . . . . . . . . . . . . . . . . ix
Recommended Secular Movies . . . . . . . . . . . . . . . . . . . . . . . . 1
Recommended Christian Movies . . . . . . . . . . . . . . . . . . . . . 103
Sources of Christian Videos . . . . . . . . . . . . . . . . . . . . . . . . 131
APPENDIX
   Listing of Secular Movies by Age Group . . . . . . . . . . . . . 135
   Listing of Christian Movies by Age Group . . . . . . . . . . . 144

# INTRODUCTION

## PURPOSE AND CONTENT

Like the 1991 edition of this book, this updated and enlarged version is designed to help readers select high quality movies on video for their families. Since 1991, we have reviewed most of the films coming to the theaters and have been able to increase the number of recommended secular films from 618 to 801 in this edition. We have also added a number of outstanding, entertaining Christian video movies bringing the total to 218 Christian movies.

John H. Evans, Editor

## MORE G/PG MOVIES BEING RELEASED

Entertaining, wholesome movies are almost as scarce today as they were five years ago. However, according to official MPAA statistics, some progress has been made in the number of G and PG movies released. They increased from 100 in 1991 to 128 in 1995. At the same time, though, the combined total of PG-13, R and NC-17 movies has increased from 514 to 571. As a percentage, the combined total of G and PG films released has increased two percentage points, while the total of PG-13, R and NC-17 films has given up a comparable amount.

## PORTION OF RECENT MOVIES INCREASING

Since we are constantly adding more recent movies, the overall portion of new films in the book has been increased. Approximately 60% of the recommended movies were released during 1970-95, while the remaining ones are from the 1940's, 1950's and 1960's. The moral quality of films produced prior to the 1970's was more carefully maintained so this period continues to be a rich source of high quality, outstanding films. We continue to urge families to give these older motion pictures a try, for we believe they will be pleased.

## VARIETY OF MOVIES RECOMMENDED

This family video guide is not limited to films suitable for young children or even the whole family. Instead, we have selected movies for different age levels. For example, some are sufficiently complex or sophisticated that only teenagers and adults would understand them. We also continue to recommend a wide assortment of dramas, adventures, comedies, fantasies, mysteries, musicals and westerns. These are mostly theatrical movies, but some made-for-TV movies have also been included.

## REVIEW FORMAT

The format for the reviews has remained the same. For each film, we have given its year of release, MPAA classification (classification began in 1968), type, age of the youngest person to whom the film will appeal, running time, color or black and white, and about a 70 word description of its story line and cast. We've also included an entertainment rating for each film. For secular films, this rating is the average of the entertainment ratings given in three of four prominent movie review publications, depending on their availability: Leonard Maltin's *TV Movies and Video Guide*, Steven Scheurer's *Movies on TV and Vidocassette*, Martin and Porter's *Video Movie Guide* and Blockbuster Video's *Guide to Movies and Videos*. We again acknowledge these publications as excellent sources of information on secular movies. In the case of Christian videos, the entertainment ratings were assigned by our own reviewers based on their evaluation of the videos.

## CHRISTIAN ENTERTAINMENT FILMS DECLINING

The production of Christian dramas, adventures and comedies has been declining in recent years. Instead, there has been more emphasis on teaching films, musicals and documentaries, as well as films oriented toward young children. This poses a challenge for us since our mission is to identify Christian films with strong entertainment values which can serve as alternates to undesirable secular entertainment films. However, there have been some notable exceptions, and we have added a number of new Christian videos with strong entertainment values to this new edition. At the same time, we have retained most of the films in the 1991 Family Video Guide, except for some older ones which have become difficult to obtain.

## SOURCE OF VIDEOS

All of the recommended films are available on videocassette, but it may be necessary to contact more than one video store to find the movie you want. Also, Christian dramas, adventures and comedies are becoming more difficult to find at Christian book stores. So, at the end of each review we have given information on mail order sources for the video.

## APPENDIX

As in previous editions, we have included a listing in the appendix which arranges the movie titles by age levels and types of movie. This appendix will be of particular value to parents, teachers and ministers.

## ACKNOWLEDGMENTS

We acknowledge the able assistance of a number of persons who contributed to this updated, enlarged edition of the *Family Video Guide*. We are particularly indebted to Greg Wilson and Fran Smith for writing most of the new reviews added to the book, and to Paul Bicking for proof reading and related services. The brief summary reviews in the book are based on more lengthy reviews prepared by a number of reviewers, including the following: Alice Anderson, Paul Bicking, Krista Kay Bontrager, Mary Draughon, Frank Dunbar, John Evans, Bonnie Harvey, Bob Liparulo, Sherry Oswald, Margaret Reid, Fran Smith, Joe Walters, Greg Wilson and Pete Zimowski.

We trust these reviews will help readers select movies which will permit them to think on those things which are "true, honest, just, pure, lovely, and of good report"(Phil. 4:8)

Happy viewing!

*John H. Evans, Editor*

# GUIDELINES FOR RECOMMENDING MOVIES

## GENERAL

### TRADITIONAL VALUES AND BIBLICAL PRINCIPLES

To a large extent, we have used the same guidelines in this new edition of the Family Video Guide as we did in 1991. These guidelines are based on traditional moral values and Biblical principles. Also, we give preference to those movies whose principal characters and story line exhibit positive values and lifestyles. However, we don't reject films with degenerate characters if these characters and their actions are a legitimate part of the story and their behavior is not condoned, glorified or exploited to entertain.

### ENTERTAINMENT APPEAL OF CHRISTIAN FILMS

The Christian films were selected on the basis of their strong entertainment appeal and professional quality. While most are dramas, comedies, concerts or docudramas, a few especially appealing educational videos are also included. These entertaining Christian videos teach Biblical values and some have a straightforward Christian salvation message. No conventional teaching or preaching videos are included.

## SPECIFIC CRITERIA FOR OFFENSIVE ELEMENTS

### FOUL LANGUAGE

Films with some mild crude words, such as "hell" and "damn," plus a limited number of moderately crude language, such as "bastard" or "ass," can be acceptable in some otherwise quality videos for mature audiences. But we draw the line at obscene words such as slang and crude words referring to excretion, sexual intercourse or genitals. We have made an occasional exception to this guideline, but in these cases have mentioned it in the review. The most common argument for including these offensive terms in a film is that they are "realistic." However, just because these words are used in real life doesn't make them appropriate for films. Bombarding viewers with such dialogue will only de-sensitize them, which can affect their own speech. As a result, our culture will become more vulgar over time.

### PROFANITY

We feel strongly that the Lord's name should always be held in reverence, both in real life and on the movie screen. Thus, we rarely recommend a film with this type of irreverence, which we call regular profanity. The most common form of regular profanity in movies is the g-d word or the words "Jesus" or "Christ" used irreverently as an exclamation. When the expressions "My God," "Oh Lord" or "God!" are used, we consider these a milder form of exclamatory profanity since they usually are not meant to be irreverent. A few of our recommended movies include some mild exclamatory profanities, and we have noted this in the text.

## **VIOLENCE**
We feel violence in a film is justified if it is a legitimate part of the story and does not become prolonged, gory or sadistic. We have not included films that use violence only to entertain or thrill, nor those with a message that problems can be solved through murder, inflicting injuries or property destruction. It is well documented that a society exposed to excessive violence through the media becomes increasingly violent themselves. Children are especially in danger of developing aggressive, anti-social behavior from such exposure.

## **NUDITY/SEXUAL CONTENT**
Pornographic material such as explicit sex scenes, frontal and breast nudity or any sexual material which erotically stimulates the viewer is not acceptable. These elements contribute to promiscuous sex, sexual abuse of women and children and other crimes. Implied sex between married couples will not disqualify a film for mature audiences if it is not explicit. We also reject movies that have a significant amount of crude sexually suggestive dialogue or action.

## **ALCOHOL/DRUG USE**
Alcohol drinking occurs in most modern films and the use of hard drugs is not uncommon. We do not rule out movies with alcohol drinking or other drug abuse unless it is glamorized or encouraged.

## **OCCULTIC CONTENT**
If a film portrays occultic phenomena, demons, witches, or other evil supernatural beings, acceptability depends on the way they are portrayed. If the phenomena or beings are portrayed in a straightforward, objective manner and not in a favorable light, they may be considered acceptable. However, if their portrayal tends to encourage occult practices or treats them lightly or comically, we are likely to see this as unacceptable.

## **NEW AGE PHILOSOPHY**
New Age philosophies have been subtly incorporated in a number of recent films. Since these conflict with Biblical theology, we consider very carefully how it is presented. Any hint of encouraging New Age beliefs, or presenting them as truth, would disqualify a film for this book.

## **RELIGION**
It is fairly common for religious persons in general, and Christians in particular, to be portrayed unfavorably in the newer films. Often Christians are portrayed as cruel, bigoted, greedy, stupid or comical. If a film demeans sincere religious persons in any way, it is not considered acceptable.

# EXPLANATION OF TERMS

Some abbreviations, ratings, and other terms used in the reviews are explained below.

**RATING** - Entertainment rating [1 = Poor; 2 = Fair; 3 = Good; 4 = Excellent]

    For secular movies, the entertainment rating of a film is the average of the ratings given by three prominent secular movie critics (Maltin, Scheuer, Martin/Porter, and Blockbuster Video).

    Most Christian movies do not have a Motion Picture Association of America (MPAA) classification, such as G, PG, etc., and secular movie critics normally do not give entertainment ratings to unclassified films. Therefore, the entertainment ratings for Christian movies were determined by the editor of this book working with reviewers who had screened the films. If a Christian movie has an MPAA classification, its entertainment rating is the average of the ratings given by three prominent secular movie critics.

**(e)** = Secular entertainment rating estimated. Estimate based on ratings of less than three secular movie critics.

**YEAR** = Year film released

**CLASSIFICATION** [G, PG, PG-13] = MPAA classification

**NR** = Not Rated [Not classified by the MPAA]

    Films made prior to 1968 were not classified by the MPAA, so are also designated "NR."

**TVM** = Made-for-TV movie

**TYPE** = Overall nature of the film (drama, comedy, etc.)

**AGE** = Age of youngest person to whom the film would appeal

**MIN.** = Running time of film

**COLOR or B&W** = Designates if film is in color or in black and white

**LANGUAGE TERMS:**

    Mild crude = Hell and damn only
    Moderate crude = All other crude language (e.g., "bastard," "ass")
    Obscene = Slang denoting excretion, intercourse or genitals
    Profanity = Irreverent use of the words "Jesus," "Christ," or "God."

# RECOMMENDED SECULAR MOVIES

# Secular Movies

### ABSENT MINDED PROFESSOR, THE — RATING 3.2
**1961  NR  Comedy  Age 06+  97 min.  B&W**

This delightful Disney comedy features Fred MacMurray as a scientist who accidentally discovers "flubber" (flying rubber) and makes his ancient Model T fly. No one believes in his invention, except Keenan Wynn who attempts to steal the mysterious formula. Enjoyable comedy and interesting special effects make this production fun for the whole family.

### ACCOMPANIST, THE — RATING 2.3(e)
**1994  PG  Drama  Age 12+  111 min.  Color**

To escape the poverty of occupied France during WWII, a young conservatory pianist auditions for an operatic star. Tensions escalate when the Germans threaten to kidnap the singer. The two defect, seeking refuge in England. English subtitles for French dialogue are fairly easy to follow. This intriguing coming of age story is appropriate for teens and adults. Two moderate crude words and an implied affair, but it is not condoned.

### ACROSS THE GREAT DIVIDE — RATING 2.5
**1976  G  Adventure  Age 06+  100 min.  Color**

A surprisingly well-crafted children's film *Across The Great Divide* presents two courageous orphan children who encounter adventure and trouble on the way to their new home in Oregon. They run into a conniving rogue along the way and ultimately join with him to survive the trek across the mountains. From the producers of the *Wilderness Family* films.

### ADAM — RATING 3.5
**1983  TVM  Drama  Age 12+  99 min.  Color**

Based on a true story, this film centers around a Florida couple whose six-year-old child has disappeared from a department store. This riveting drama describes the traumatic months spent in searching for the boy and the parents' feelings of anguish as well as hope. Because of this massive effort, the government formed the Missing Children's Bureau. A timely piece.

### ADVENTURES OF THE GREAT MOUSE DETECTIVE — RATING 3.5
**1986  G  Adventure  Age 06+  74 min.  Color**

"The game's afoot" in this animated Disney adaptation of Eve Titus' book. A perceptive mouse, Basil of Baker Street, solves puzzling crimes in a mouse-sized world of his own beneath Sherlock Holmes' residence. Features the voice of Vincent Price as the evil archenemy Professor Ratigan. A delightful, fun-filled treat for the whole family. From the directors of *The Little Mermaid*.

### ADVENTURES OF MILO AND OTIS — RATING 3.3
**1990  G  Adventure  Age 06+  76 min.  Color**

A mischievous kitten named Milo and his pug-nosed puppy friend, Otis, have many exciting adventures in this live action film narrated by Dudley Moore. One day Milo is swept down a roaring river with Otis in frantic pursuit. Once rescued, they discover it's not easy to find their way home. Some very funny and scary moments occur before they return. Young and old will enjoy the beautiful scenery, lively musical score and lovable animals.

### ADVENTURES OF THE WILDERNESS FAMILY — RATING 3.2
**1975  G  Adventure  Age 06+  101 min.  Color**

This Swiss Family Robinson-like human interest story features a disgruntled construction worker who takes his unhappy family away from a smog-ridden urban setting to the Rocky Mountain wilderness. They construct a cabin and contend with the dangers that surround them. Modern audiences of all ages will enjoy this intriguing tale, along with the breathtaking scenery.

### ADVENTURES OF THE WILDERNESS FAMILY-PART II — RATING 3.0
**1976  G  Adventure  Age 06+  104 min.  Color**

This look-alike sequel to *Adventures Of The Wilderness Family* details further adventures of a modern family who, tired of the urban rat race, escape to the tranquility and dangers of the Rocky Mountain wilderness. Adventuresome story and spectacular scenery make this good family entertainment.

### ADVISE AND CONSENT
**RATING 3.3**
1962　　　NR　　　Drama　　　Age 17+　　　140 min.　　　B&W

A spellbinding adaptation of Allen Drury's novel. It focuses on the political wheeling and dealing occurring when the President asks for a confirmation of his controversial appointment for the Secretary of State. Notable performances by Henry Fonda, Walter Pidgeon, Charles Laughton, and Burgess Meredith enhance this well-oiled production. Laughton steals the show as a sophisticated, conniving southern senator.

### AFRICAN QUEEN, THE
**RATING 4.0**
1951　　　NR　　　Adventure　　　Age 12+　　　105 min.　　　Color

In this all-time great film classic, Humphrey Bogart plays a worldly old boat captain who must transport Katharine Hepburn, a spinster sister of a murdered missionary, up the Congo River. Along the way they fight insufferable conditions as well as the Germans just as World War I has broken out. John Huston's remarkable direction enhances the story and allows the main characters to give memorable performances.

### AGAINST A CROOKED SKY
**RATING 2.0**
1975　　　G　　　Adventure-Western　　　Age 06+　　　89 min.　　　Color

A familiar remake of John Ford's classic *The Searchers*. *Against A Crooked Sky* presents a frightened boy looking for his sister who's been kidnapped by Indians. Veteran actor Richard Boone plays the part of Old Trapper. This film will appeal to the diehard Western fan. It contains some violence characteristic of western films.

### AGE OF INNOCENCE
**RATING 3.2**
1993　　　PG　　　Drama　　　Age 17+　　　133 min.　　　Color

Elegant adaptation of Edith Wharton's classic novel, set in New York City during the 1800's. Michelle Pfieffer plays the worldly young woman who doesn't fit the mold of refined society. An interesting look at the social customs of that period. Oscar-winner for best costume design and cinematography. This remarkable film tells a passionate love story without the usual Hollywood sexual content, but it's definitely for adults only.

### AIRPORT
**RATING 3.5**
1970　　　G　　　Drama-Adventure　　　Age 12+　　　137 min.　　　Color

This suspenseful film features Helen Hayes as an unlikely stowaway who is being tracked down by a metropolitan airport. The drama intensifies when it's discovered that an irate passenger on the same plane is carrying a bomb in his briefcase. All this takes place on a cold winter night. An all-star cast includes such notables as Dean Martin, Jacqueline Bisset, and Burt Lancaster.

### ALAMO, THE
**RATING 2.7**
1960　　　NR　　　Docudrama　　　Age 12+　　　161 min.　　　Color

John Wayne stars in this fictionalized real life narrative about events surrounding the fall of the Alamo in Texas. Striking and memorable, this period war film hosts a number of well-known faces, including Richard Widmark, Laurence Harvey, Frankie Avalon, and Richard Boone. History buffs will particularly enjoy this action packed realistic film.

### ALAN AND NAOMI
**RATING 2.3**
1992　　　PG　　　Drama　　　Age 12+　　　96 min.　　　Color

A young Jewish girl, traumatized by her father's murder at the hands of the Nazis before her very eyes, escapes to New York. There, she meets Alan, a young boy who patiently befriends her in order to bring her back to reality. This poignant, heartwarming story demonstrates the redeeming value of love and commitment. One muffled obscenity, a few racist slurs and some fist fighting.

### ALIEN FROM LA
**RATING 1.8**
1988　　　PG　　　Adventure　　　Age 17+　　　87 min.　　　Color

Wanda Saknussemm travels to Africa to determine the cause of her father's death. She falls into the same huge hole as her father did and ends up in the legendary world of Atlantis. As she searches for her dad, she's befriended by two rough and ready men who fight endless battles to keep her from being arrested. Lots of action, humor and fighting.

*Secular Movies*

### ALL CREATURES GREAT AND SMALL — RATING 3.3
1974     NR     Drama     Age 06+     92 min.     Color

Adapted from James Herriot's novels, this charming and delightful period piece features a young British veterinarian (Simon Ward) apprenticed to an older vet (Anthony Hopkins). Poignant character portrayals along with the slice-of-life plot will tug at everyone's heartstrings. Beautiful story of rural life in England with magnificent scenes of the English country.

### ALL GOD'S CHILDREN — RATING 2.7
1980     TVM     Drama     Age 12+     97 min.     Color

The Montpelier School District is struggling with the issue of forced busing. Two sixteen-year-old boys—one white and the other black—get entangled in this sticky social issue. The boys steal a school bus to protest the new law. Their families and the town discover things about themselves as a result of this crisis.

### ALL I WANT FOR CHRISTMAS — RATING 2.2
1991     G     Drama     Age 12+     89 min.     Color

A precocious seven-year-old has a special Christmas wish; she wants to see her divorced parents back together. She and her brother ask a department store Santa (Leslie Nielsen) to help with the reunion. An enchanting film that reinforces the virtues of family life, the innocence of childhood, and the magic of Christmas. One regular profanity and the delicate subject of divorce may make this film inappropriate for younger children.

### AMAZING PANDA ADVENTURE — RATING 2.5(e)
1995     PG     Adventure     Age 06+     92 min.     Color

Suspenseful cat-and-mouse adventure film between Steve Tyler, an American naturalist, and greedy Chinese poachers who have captured a mother panda and her cub. After Tyler is injured, his son, Ryan, and a couple of Chinese guides track the bears, forcing them into a confrontation with the poachers. A unique look at the importance of a good father-son relationship. One mild crude word and a regular profanity.

### AMERICAN CHRISTMAS CAROL, AN — RATING 2.8
1979     TVM     Fantasy-Drama     Age 06+     98 min.     Color

Henry Winkler ("The Fonz") portrays an aged Mr. Slade, a Depression-period Scrooge, in this unique remake of the Dickens classic set in a quaint New England town. Flashbacks presented by the ghosts of Christmases past, present and future brighten up the plot. Good entertainment for the family.

### AMERICAN DREAM — RATING 3.8
1985     TVM     Drama     Age 06+     90 min.     Color

Danny and Donna are a typical American couple in Chicago attempting to raise three children. Donna discovers she is pregnant, which poses a problem since their current home is too small. They begin their search for a bigger home, but find that a "fixer-up" is the best they can afford. Entertaining presentation of family issues and how they are resolved in a mature manner.

### AMERICAN IN PARIS, AN — RATING 3.7
1951     NR     Musical     Age 06+     113 min.     Color

Gene Kelly trips the light fantastic with brilliant flair in this Oscar-winning musical. In this picture, an American ex-GI who stays in Paris to become an artist falls in love with two women. Although the plot is simple, the dazzling combination of Gershwin music and elaborate choreography makes the film great fun.

### AMERICAN TALE: FIEVEL GOES WEST, AN — RATING 2.8
1991     G     Fantasy-Adventure     Age 06+     85 min.     Color

Fievel the mouse's dream of being a cowboy comes true when his Russian immigrant family moves west at the urging of an evil cat. Little do they know what exciting dangers and adventures await them. Features distinctive voices of John Cleese, Jimmy Stewart, and Dom DeLuise. Children of all ages will enjoy this entertaining, hilarious piece of animated work from Steven Spielberg. Some mild cartoon slapstick violence.

### AMY
**RATING 3.2**
1981　　　G　　　Drama　　　　　　Age 12+　　　100 min.　　　Color

Amy Medford (Jenny Agutter) flees her wealthy and domineering husband, Elliot, to take a job at a school for the blind and deaf. Amy teaches the deaf children to speak despite much criticism from people and teachers who say that the deaf are unable to learn this skill. Amy falls in love with Dr. Ben Cochran (Barry Newman), who shows her that romance can once again be a part of her life. Touching, inspiring film.

### AND BABY MAKES SIX
**RATING 3.0**
1979　　　TVM　　　Drama　　　　　　Age 17+　　　93 min.　　　Color

A 46 year old woman is planning a long awaited second honeymoon when her world starts to fall apart. When her oldest son drops out of college, she faces the difficult task of telling her husband about their son's actions. Then she discovers she is pregnant, and the family must deal with an unwanted late-in-life pregnancy. Dramatic depiction of all sides of the abortion issue.

### ANDRE
**RATING 3.5(e)**
1994　　　PG　　　Comedy-Drama　　　Age 06+　　　94 min.　　　Color

A true story about a lovable pet seal in Maine in the 1960's. Toni Whitney, a little girl, and Andre the seal become inseparable. After an appearance on the Ed Sullivan show, Toni and her seal become famous as tourists flock to see them. This film has breathtaking scenery, a mischievous seal that watches TV, and a humorous, uplifting story for the whole family. Several mild and a few moderate crude words.

### ANDROMEDA STRAIN, THE
**RATING 3.3**
1971　　　G　　　Science Fiction　　　Age 17+　　　130 min.　　　Color

This popular science-fiction thriller tells of a satellite that crashes in New Mexico and the subsequent leak of a deadly virus. It's a race against time as four brilliant scientists try to isolate the organism so an antidote can be found. To make matters worse, there's a possibility of nuclear war. Very intriguing. Many hells and damns.

### ANGEL AND THE BADMAN
**RATING 3.5**
1947　　　NR　　　Western　　　　　　Age 12+　　　100 min.　　　B&W

John Wayne plays an infamous outlaw who experiences a dramatic change of heart because of the gentle love of a Quaker girl. Exciting action, enthralling scenery, a fast-moving plot, and a poignant theme should interest audiences everywhere. Finely crafted for a low-budget film. Also available in computer colored version.

### ANGEL ON MY SHOULDER
**RATING 3.3**
1946　　　NR　　　Drama-Fantasy　　　Age 12+　　　102 min.　　　B&W

A murdered gangster makes a bargain with the devil to come back to earth in human form and do his bidding. He becomes a respected judge, however, and attempts to outwit his evil master. This film, featuring Paul Muni and Anne Baxter, is a delightful fantasy that has been remade for television.

### ANGELS IN THE OUTFIELD
**RATING 3.3**
1994　　　PG　　　Comedy-Drama　　　Age 06+　　　103 min.　　　Color

A young boy named Roger, an avid baseball fan, hopes that the worst team in baseball, the California Angels, wins the pennant. His prayers are answered when some comical but real angels come to the rescue and help out the team. Another wonderful Disney film, full of positive messages and belief in the supernatural. Some moderate crude comments along with some slapstick violence.

### ANNE OF AVONLEA
**RATING 3.6**
1988　　　TVM　　　Drama　　　　　　Age 06+　　　200 min.　　　Color

This truly heartwarming movie follows the grown-up adventures of Anne Shirley, a precocious orphan raised by Marilla Cuthbert and her husband. In this well-made sequel to *Anne of Green Gables*, Anne leaves the Cuthberts to become a schoolteacher, but love and duty may bring her back to Green Gables. A wonderfully wholesome story with positive messages about love and honesty.

### ANNE OF GREEN GABLES                                                    RATING 3.3
1985        TVM         Drama-Romance              Age 06+        197 min.            Color

This moving romantic tale describes the life of a young orphan girl from her adoption by a bachelor farmer and his austere sister to her flourishing love for Gilbert Blythe. Anne grows from a gangly little girl into a mature young woman, capturing the affection of all who know her. The simple charm of the title character and the magnificent Canadian scenery will enchant audiences of all ages. Brilliantly directed.

### ANOTHER WOMAN                                                           RATING 3.0
1989        PG          Drama                      Age 17+        81 min.             Color

Woody Allen is responsible for this somber, introspective story of Ken and Marian, a fifty-year-old married couple. Both have been involved in adulterous affairs, but they are not condoned. Flashbacks reveal intimate events in Marian's life. She is struggling with inner conflicts, but has no spiritual strength. Gena Rowlands portrays this sensitive, perceptive woman. Some explicit sexual discussions and one profanity.

### APPLE DUMPLING GANG RIDES AGAIN, THE                                    RATING 1.7
1979        G           Comedy-Western             Age 04+        88 min.             Color

Don Knotts and Tim Conway play inept outlaws in this Disney slapstick comedy sequel. Although the cast is chock-full of innovative comic actors who do well on a solo basis, it lacks the right mix for a good ensemble performance. Although it lacks originality, kids are likely to enjoy it anyway.

### APPLE DUMPLING GANG, THE                                                RATING 2.0
1975        G           Comedy-Western             Age 04+        100 min.            Color

A trio of kids inherited by a gambler (Bill Bixby) find gold nuggets in a depleted 1870 mine. Tim Conway and Don Knotts give hilarious performances as outlaws who just can't get it all together. Young children will be delighted by this innocent, clean, simple-minded Disney fare.

### APPOINTMENT WITH DEATH                                                  RATING 1.8
1988        PG          Mystery-Drama              Age 12+        108 min.            Color

Based on Agatha Christie's spine-tingling novel, this film follows an impeccable Belgian detective Hercule Poirot as he tracks down a murderer of a shrewish widow at an archaeological dig in Jerusalem. Peter Ustinov's lively and competent character portrayal of Poirot brightens this marvelous old fashioned murder mystery. The complex murder puzzle keeps the audience guessing. One profanity.

### AROUND THE WORLD IN 80 DAYS                                             RATING 3.3
1956        NR          Adventure                  Age 06+        170 min.            Color

This all-star spectacular, based on Jules Verne's tale, features Phineas Fogg (David Niven) betting his club that he can travel around the world in eighty days. Although somewhat dated, this Mike Todd version still offers exciting entertainment, including forty cameo appearances of well known stars. Earned three Oscars for musical score, cinematography, and editing.

### AUNTIE MAME                                                             RATING 3.5
1958        NR          Comedy-Drama               Age 06+        143 min.            Color

Rosalind Russell masterfully portrays an eccentric aunt whose young nephew is placed in her care. She's a barrel of laughs and believes that "life is a banquet and most poor suckers are starving to death". Adapted from Patrick Dennis' novel, this one-woman show is an episodic but highly amusing piece of work. Broadway took this film and turned it into the musical 'Mame'.

### AURORA ENCOUNTER                                                        RATING 3.5
1986        PG          Science Fiction-Adventure  Age 06+        90 min.             Color

Veteran actor Jack Elam stars in this easygoing science-fiction tale about a small friendly alien from outer space who visits a rural town in Texas in the late 1800's. A local newspaper man begins an investigation when the alien makes a few public appearances. Children of all ages will likely enjoy this fantasy. It contains one vulgarity and a few rough words.

### AUTOBIOGRAPHY OF MISS JANE PITTMAN — RATING 3.8
1974     TVM     Docudrama     Age 17+     110 min.     Color

This fascinating story describes in emotional detail the history of the blacks from their slavery experiences during the Civil War to the civil rights movement in the 60's. The story is told through the eyes of the 110-year-old ex-slave Jane Pittman. A superb performance by Cicely Tyson in the title role and a moving script make this one of the best TV movies ever made. Some graphic killings and beatings.

### BABAR: THE MOVIE — RATING 2.8
1989     G     Fantasy-Drama     Age 06+     75 min.     Color

This animated film for children is clever, fun, and enlivened with some sprightly musical numbers. Its action, however, contains a great many battles, much hand to hand fighting, harrowing chases and cartoon style injuries. It presents the struggle of Babar, a young elephant king, to save his kingdom from the attack of a hoard of ferocious rhinos.

### BABE — RATING 3.8(e)
1995     G     Comedy     Age 04+     89 min.     Color

Babe, the only pig on an Australian farm, is adopted by a mother sheepdog. Babe, thinking he is a dog, learns to herd sheep. The live-action farm animals talk to each other, and we discover they are jealous of the precocious pig. But Babe's heroic deeds win the hearts of the other animals. A truly funny and delightful fable about fitting in and the power of love. One moderate crudity.

### BABES IN TOYLAND — RATING 2.3
1961     NR     Musical     Age 06+     105 min.     Color

A technicolor Disney rendition of Victor Herbert's operetta, this musical fairy tale stars Ray Bolger (Scarecrow in *Wizard of Oz*), and Annette Funicello. When Bolger kidnaps Tom the Piper's son, the action gets underway. Features well known songs such as "Toyland" and "March of the Wonder Soldiers". Children will enjoy the magical adventures of the folks in Toyland.

### BABETTE'S FEAST — RATING 4.0
1987     G     Drama     Age 17+     102 min.     Color

Moving story about two daughters of a pastor who forego personal fulfillment in order to serve the needy in their small Danish village. Babette, a young French woman, devotes herself to the sisters so they can carry out their ministry. The film concludes with an elegant, though sometimes humorous feast which Babette prepares for the daughters and their pious associates. Marvelous, European style film. English subtitles.

### BABYSITTERS CLUB — RATING 3.0(e)
1995     PG     Comedy     Age 12+     85 min.     Color

Based on the popular book series, this film tells the adventures of seven young girls who sponsor a babysitting camp one summer in a small town. Everything is going smoothly until the leader gets distracted by her divorced dad's return and another girl falls in love. The girls, however, remain close friends through thick and thin. This is a must-see for your daughters. One slang reference to sex.

### BACHELOR AND THE BOBBYSOXER, THE — RATING 3.0
1947     NR     Comedy     Age 12+     95 min.     B&W

A lady judge (Myrna Loy) orders a swinging bachelor (Cary Grant) to date her kid sister (Shirley Temple) to get rid of her "crush" on him. Grant seems to be much more interested in Myrna Loy than her kid sister. The witty exchanges between Loy and Grant carry the show and Grant's charm will appeal to all. Sidney Sheldon's light and witty screenplay earned him an Oscar.

### BACHELOR MOTHER — RATING 3.3
1939     NR     Comedy     Age 12+     81 min.     B&W

This sparkling Norman Crasna comedy features Ginger Rogers as a single woman who becomes the recipient of an abandoned baby and is subsequently mistaken for its mother. An understanding store owner's son (David Niven) tries to reform the "fallen woman". The confusion that breaks out makes for hilarious comedy.

## BAD DAY AT BLACK ROCK — RATING 3.8
1954　　NR　　Drama　　Age 12+　　82 min.　　Color

WW II army veteran John McCree (Spencer Tracy) returns to the town of Black Rock to find his Japanese friend Kokomo. He learns that Kokomo and a friend discovered water on their land immediately following the Pearl Harbor attack. Unfortunately, he finds they are victims of foul play. McCree's searching proves to be a problem for the town in general and the guilty in particular.

## BALTO — RATING 3.5(e)
1995　　G　　Adventure　　Age 04+　　70 min.　　Color

An exciting animated adventure story about Balto, an outcast dog in Nome, Alaska, who becomes a hero. When a little girl becomes deathly ill, Balto braves a blizzard and travels 600 miles for medicine. Based on a true story set in 1925, brave Balto faces danger and attacks by other dogs, but also meets some hilarious friends during his long journey. Strong messages about heroes coming in different shapes and sizes.

## BAMBI — RATING 3.5
1942　　NR　　Adventure-Fantasy　　Age 04+　　72 min.　　Color

Walt Disney's classic animated picture tells the gentle, poignant story of a fawn growing up to be a mighty stag. It shows how the stages of its life directly correspond to the life cycles in the forest. The clever plot includes a tragedy brought about by hunters, but has some refreshing comic relief supplied by Thumper the rabbit. Enjoyable.

## BAND WAGON, THE — RATING 4.0
1953　　NR　　Musical　　Age 06+　　112 min.　　Color

Dashing and debonair Fred Astaire teams up with Cyd Charisse in this hard-luck story about a has-been actor who tries to get back into show biz. Musical favorites such as "Dancing in the Dark", "Shine on Your Shoes", and "That's Entertainment" highlight the film. Excellent direction and finely tuned dance numbers

## BARABBAS — RATING 3.0
1962　　NR　　Drama-Biblical　　Age 17+　　134 min.　　Color

An elaborate biblical spectacle presents the life of the thief who was released in Jesus' place from death on the cross. The majority of the plot deals with his victories as a gladiator and his life in the mines. A veteran cast consists of Anthony Quinn, Jack Palance, and Ernest Borgnine. This production ranks far above others in the biblical genre.

## BAREFOOT IN THE PARK — RATING 3.5
1967　　NR　　Comedy-Drama　　Age 17+　　105 min.　　Color

In this bittersweet Neil Simon comedy, Robert Redford and Jane Fonda play a newlywed couple trying to adjust to married life in New York. Unfortunately, they have more dreams than money. There is a running gag about climbing the stairs in the five floor walk-up apartment. Their mother-in-laws and a zany, unconventional neighbor (Charles Boyer) add to the humor. Overall the story is quite clever and entertaining.

## BARNUM — RATING 2.5(e)
1987　　TVM　　Docudrama　　Age 06+　　94 min.　　Color

P.T. Barnum is the ultimate American showman. This film is adapted from his autobiography and stars Burt Lancaster as Barnum. It starts with his humble beginnings in 1810 and shows a life time of accomplishments, schemes and promotions. Particular attention is given to his successful career as an entertainer. Circus enthusiasts will appreciate this fine drama.

## BATTLESTAR GALACTICA — RATING 2.2
1978　　PG　　Science Fiction-Adventure　　Age 06+　　125 min.　　Color

President Adar has conceived a peace treaty that would stop a thousand years of war between mankind and the subhuman Cylons. Now it's the spaceship commander's (Lorne Greene) responsibility to take the survivors of a destroyed planet to a new home. Well done special effects. Will appeal to young persons and science fiction fans.

### BEAR, THE
**RATING 2.5**
1989     PG     Adventure-Nature     Age 12+     95 min.     Color

A huge Kodiak bear adopts a cub orphaned in a natural disaster. Tension mounts when two hunters stalk the Kodiak, wound it, and it strikes back in defense. Unable to get the Kodiak, they manage to trap the cub. The enraged bear returns to rescue the cub and one of the hunters finds himself in a very dangerous trap. Breathtaking British Columbia scenery and brilliant classical music score. Outstanding film for adults and young persons.

### BEAUTY AND THE BEAST
**RATING 3.8**
1991     G     Fantasy     Age 04+     85 min.     Color

Extravagant, animated Disney classic based on the enchanting fairy tale. A young maiden is held prisoner by the Beast in his castle. She charms him with her grace and beauty, and learns to love and accept him, despite his grotesque appearance. Viewers will enjoy this moving story of unconditional love, coupled with an Oscar-winning score and amusing characters. Perfect for the whole family.

### BEETHOVEN
**RATING 2.5**
1992     PG     Comedy     Age 06+     87 min.     Color

A typical middle-class family adopts a lovable St. Bernard dog that ends up wreaking havoc in the house. The no-nonsense, dog-hating father finally learns to love Beethoven the dog despite the messes he makes. Unfortunately, an evil veterinarian wants to use the dog for experimental purposes. A predictable, but entertaining story for the entire family. Two regular profanities.

### BEETHOVEN'S 2ND
**RATING 2.6**
1993     PG     Comedy     Age 06+     86 min.     Color

Beethoven, the big lovable dog, is back, this time with four adorable puppies. The Newton family's adventures continue as they try to keep the puppies from being captured by the mother's mean owner. Their escapades take them to a lake resort where they meet up with the villainous owner. The fun and action never slow down. Two moderate crude words and two moderate obscenities.

### BEETHOVEN LIVES UPSTAIRS
**RATING 2.8(e)**
1994     NR     Drama     Age 12+     52 min.     Color

A young boy named Christoph discovers the wonders of music as he becomes friends with his neighbor upstairs, Ludwig Beethoven. We see all of Beethoven's idiosyncrasies and his genius for music from the boy's perspective, including Beethoven's struggle with deafness near the end of his life. A moving film even for those not familiar with the famous composer's music.

### BELIZAIRE THE CAJUN
**RATING 3.0**
1985     PG     Drama     Age 12+     113 min     Color

Armand Assante gives an impressive performance in the title role of this lush drama, set in the 1850's in Louisiana. Belizaire must endure the effects of mob justice and prejudice as he tries to romance his childhood sweetheart. One effect of mob justice portrayed is a little bloody, but overall the good values of courage and honesty in this movie win out over the prejudices of the mob. Several mild crude words.

### BELLS ARE RINGING
**RATING 2.8**
1960     NR     Musical-Comedy     Age 12+     127 min.     Color

In this film version of the Broadway musical, a meddlesome telephone operator eavesdrops on conversations between callers and gives them friendly advice. She falls in love with a songwriter whom she meets over the telephone. Memorable tunes like "Just in Time" and "The Party's Over" along with good acting will appeal to all.

### BELLS OF ST. MARY'S
**RATING 3.3**
1945     NR     Drama-Comedy     Age 06+     126 min.     B&W

In this excellent sequel to *Going My Way*, Bing Crosby returns as Father O'Malley, a priest relegated to a run-down parish. He and Mother Superior (Ingrid Bergman) attempt to persuade a wealthy miser to donate money for new buildings. Bing croons the song "Aren't You Glad You're You?" in his inimitable style. Warm, rich viewing entertainment.

## Secular Movies

**BEN-HUR**                                                                   RATING 3.8
1959     NR     Drama-Biblical         Age 12+         217 min.         Color

The ultimate film of epic proportions, *Ben Hur* concentrates on the intense Roman persecution of the Jews during the lifetime of Jesus. Specifically, two ex-friends (Judah Ben-Hur and Messala) are set in conflict. The setting is Palestine biblical times. A nine-time Oscar winner, this magnificent film has some exceptional scenes, including the famous chariot race and the sea battle.

**BEND OF THE RIVER**                                    RATING 3.3
1952     NR     Western               Age 12+         91 min.         Color

Jimmy Stewart plays an ex-gunman who leads a wagon train of settlers over the mountains to Oregon. He's joined by a former outlaw played by Arthur Kennedy. They travel through Indian territory to Portland where they continue their trip aboard a river boat on the Colombia River. They endure Indian attacks, gunfights, food shortages and a treacherous double-cross. Action, adventure and spectacular scenery.

**BENIKER GANG, THE**                                    RATING 2.8
1985     G     Drama-Comedy        Age 06+         87 min.         Color

This pleasurable family movie presents Arthur Beniker, a disgruntled 18-year-old orphanage resident who stages a break-out with four other kids. They set up housekeeping on their own and have their problems, but a lot of fun and adventure also. The acting is believable and the unique personality of each orphan is interestingly portrayed.

**BENJI**                                                                                  RATING 3.5
1974     G     Adventure            Age 06+         87 min.         Color

Benji, a rather unlikely canine hero, comes to the rescue of two kidnapped children and earns a home with the grateful parents. The kids are held in a scary old house, but Benji leads the way to them. Like his predecessors, Lassie and Rin Tin Tin, the little mutt knows exactly what to do at just the right time. Perfect family entertainment. After all, how could anyone resist this lovable dog?

**BENJI THE HUNTED**                                         RATING 2.3
1987     G     Adventure           Age 06+         90 min.         Color

Braving the Pacific Northwest wilderness, our favorite canine hero shines with more feats of derring-do as he protects some defenseless orphaned cougar cubs from life-threatening situations. The humans are practically overlooked, and the animals provide most of the drama. Benji's irresistible charm would win over any animal lover (or hater). Great family film. Contains some mild violence.

**BEST CHRISTMAS PAGEANT EVER, THE**              RATING 3.0(e)
1986     TVM     Drama                Age 06+         60 min.         Color

Six children with bad reputations decide to take part in a local church Christmas pageant in this delightful feature. Most people think they belong in jail. Although the choir director meets with opposition from some of the church members, she is determined to put on the best Christmas pageant ever. When the curtain finally goes up, everyone is in for a surprise. Good family fun. Some small acts of violence may disturb very young children.

**BEST LITTLE GIRL IN THE WORLD, THE**                RATING 3.5
1981     TVM     Drama                Age 12+         95 min.         Color

The parents of two daughters are beset with two severe family problems. One daughter is pregnant out of wedlock, while the other suffers from anorexia and bulimia. Most of the film portrays the traumatic struggle of the daughter with anorexia-bulimia to triumph over the disease. The drama is intense, the acting outstanding and the story powerful.

**BEST YEARS OF OUR LIVES**                          RATING 4.0
1946     NR     Drama                Age 12+         172 min.         B&W

Touching, well-acted story about three veterans of World War II who return home and try to readjust to civilian life. They discover they have changed and struggle through emotional problems relating to their families and jobs.

## BEYOND RANGOON                                                                 RATING 3.5(e)
1995         R          Adventure-Drama              Age 17+       97 min.             Color

Compelling story about a young American physician's adventures in modern Burma. She sees first-hand the injustice perpetrated by the government when her pro-democracy guide is wounded. Their journey is a series of hardships and challenging obstacles that they learn to overcome. A daring film that teaches courage and respect for other cultures. Severe violent scenes are too intense for young children.

## BIG GREEN, THE                                                                   RATING 3.0(e)
1995         PG         Drama-Comedy                 Age 06+       100 min.            Color

A feel-good movie about a rag-tag soccer team of boys and girls in rural Texas. The team is organized and coached by the pretty new school teacher from England. Helped by the local sheriff, she inspires the kids to develop a champion soccer team that energizes the whole town. Suspense and excitement build as they meet the challenge of larger and more experienced competition. A great family film.

## BIG RED                                                                              RATING 2.8
1962         NR         Adventure                    Age 04+       89 min.             Color

Walter Pidgeon plays a wealthy dog fancier who grooms a sleek Irish setter for professional shows. The boy he hires to take care of Red becomes attached to him and finds it hard to let go. While at a show, the dog escapes to find the boy he also loves. Moving story for all ages.

## BILL                                                                                 RATING 3.7
1981         TVM        Docudrama                    Age 12+       100 min.            Color

Mickey Rooney superbly portrays Bill Sackter, a retarded adult who is forced to leave an institution he has lived in for 45 years. A compassionate filmmaker reaches out to Bill, providing him with employment and a feeling of belonging. Based on a true story, this film warms the heart and renews love for the less fortunate.

## BILL: ON HIS OWN                                                                     RATING 3.2
1983         TVM        Docudrama                    Age 12+       97 min.             Color

The continuing story of Bill Sackter, a mentally handicapped adult who is trying to make it in the world. Mickey Rooney again portrays Bill who just wants to become a "regular good man." A student social worker tries to help by enrolling Bill into school. It's not very often a film can be as entertaining as this one and still teach about the value of compassion and perseverance. Hooray for Bill.

## BILL COSBY-HIMSELF                                                                   RATING 3.0
1983         PG         Comedy-Monologue             Age 12+       105 min.            Color

In this one-man show, Cosby pokes fun at human feelings and foibles in the areas of family life, child-rearing, drinking and drug-taking, and going to the dentist. As usual, he is at the top of his form with brilliant true-to-life stories. This video is both funny and thought provoking.

## BILL COSBY: 49                                                                       RATING 3.5
1988         NR         Comedy-Monologue             Age 17+       67 min.             Color

In a recorded stage performance, Bill Cosby, one of the most popular comedians of our time, describes humorous characteristics he's developed as a middle-ager. Unlike most comics of our day, Cosby doesn't resort to tasteless "blue humor". He just tells wacky, hilarious stories to which everyone can relate. Entertaining and insightful.

## BIRDS OF PREY                                                                        RATING 3.5
1973         TVM        Adventure                    Age 06+       81 min.             Color

A former Air Force pilot (David Janssen) now flies a Salt Lake City radio station traffic helicopter. He witnesses a bank robbery taking place and pursues the villains in an exciting copter-after-copter aerial chase. He manages to rescue a female hostage from the robbers and the suspense chase continues. Well-done footage involving some fancy flying and a surprise ending.

## BISHOP'S WIFE, THE                                                                                       RATING 3.0
**1947        NR         Comedy                        Age 06+         108 min.              B&W**
This delightful Christmas comedy-fantasy features a sophisticated angel (Cary Grant) coming to earth to help a bishop (David Niven) and his wife (Loretta Young). His assignment is to help them raise funds for a new cathedral. Light-hearted, entertaining performances and a wholesome story line make this a perfect family treat

## BITTER HARVEST                                                                                            RATING 3.5
**1981        TVM        Docudrama                     Age 12+         100 min.              Color**
Ron Howard plays a young dairy farmer who is desperately trying to find out what is poisoning his cattle and his little son in this frightening TV drama. Based on a true story, the film deals with the small farmer fighting big government bureaucracy. Outstanding performance of Howard keeps viewers on the edge of their seats. Fairly graphic calf birth and cattle slaughter.

## BLACK BEAUTY                                                                                              RATING 3.5(e)
**1994        G          Drama                         Age 04+         88 min.               Color**
This sensitive adaptation of a timeless classic presents the horse's point of view. A young colt on a wealthy country estate courts the affections of his rambunctious stable mate. Life changes dramatically for them when they are sold. Black Beauty endures much rough treatment, which may upset some younger viewers, until he is cared for by a young boy. A film for horse lovers of all ages.

## BLACK HOLE, THE                                                                                           RATING 1.8
**1979        PG         Sci-Fi-Adventure              Age 12+         97 min.               Color**
An intrepid group of American space explorers encounter a "mad scientist" who's controlled a team of robots on his giant spacecraft for 20 years. He is now on the verge of entering and exploring a black hole. The space explorers try to take control of his spaceship and stop him. Some are drawn into the black hole in a dramatic, violent sequence. Ingenious special effects. Will appeal to science fiction buffs.

## BLACK STALLION, THE                                                                                       RATING 3.7
**1979        G          Adventure                     Age 06+         103 min.              Color**
In one of the best children's films ever made, a young boy (Kelly Reno) shipwrecked on a desert island befriends and later adopts an Arabian stallion he affectionately calls "The Black". Once they are rescued, the boy realizes the stallion has potential as a race horse. Mickey Rooney delivers a realistic performance as a veteran horse trainer. Breathtaking scenery. The whole family will thoroughly enjoy this one.

## BLACK STALLION RETURNS, THE                                                                               RATING 2.8
**1983        PG         Adventure                     Age 06+         93 min.               Color**
Famous Black Stallion is stolen by Arabians who take him to Casa Blanca for an important race. His owner, a boy, manages to follow the thieves to Casablanca in order to recover the horse. Numerous adventures ensue, culminating in an exciting horse race. The boy must decide whether to return the stallion to the United States or allow it to roam free in Casablanca with other horses. Good entertainment.

## BLIND SPOT                                                                                                RATING 3.8(e)
**1993        TVM        Drama                         Age 17+         100 min.              Color**
Nell Harrington (Joanne Woodward), a successful state representative, has a wonderful daughter and son-in-law expecting their first child. When her children have a car accident, it's discovered that her son-in-law was using drugs. Nell learns her pregnant daughter is also using drugs. A well-acted Hallmark Hall of Fame presentation about a mother's love and perseverance. A few mild crude words and two regular profanities. Drug abuse shown once, but not condoned.

## BLUE KNIGHT, THE                                                                                          RATING 2.3
**1975        TVM        Drama                         Age 12+         73 min.               Color**
George Kennedy plays an L.A. streetwise officer searching for the murderer of an aging fellow cop. In his sleuthing, Kennedy confronts some rough, seamy characters and gets himself into some precarious predicaments. He's obsessed with finding the killer and never lets up. Kennedy gives a sturdy portrayal of his character. Later a TV series, this film is a well done, realistic police story.

## BLUE YONDER, THE — RATING 3.5
1985   NR   Fantasy-Adventure   Age 06+   89 min.   Color

A sentimental Disney fantasy, this picture features a young boy who goes back in time with the aid of a time travel machine. His mission is to stop his late aviator grandfather from making an unsuccessful transatlantic flight. In the process, he changes the course of history. Fine acting performances overshadow a predictable plot. Renamed *Time Flyer*, this cable movie appeals to audiences of all ages.

## BOATNIKS — RATING 2.5
1970   G   Comedy   Age 06+   100 min.   Color

This lighthearted Disney comedy features a gallant young Coast Guard officer trying to chase down a trio of inept jewel thieves. All the while he's fanning a hot romance with a sweet, young thing. The bumbling crooks are played by veteran funnymen Phil Silvers and Norman Fell. As usual, Disney has provided fun-filled, simple-minded fare for the whole family.

## BON VOYAGE, CHARLIE BROWN — RATING 3.2
1980   G   Adventure   Age 04+   76 min.   Color

In this animated *Peanuts* feature, Charlie Brown and the gang travel to France on a student exchange program. The lovable cartoon characters of Charles Schulz charm audiences young and old alike. *Bon Voyage, Charlie Brown* is a world travel guide, complete with down-to-earth *Peanuts*.

## BOOMERANG — RATING 4.0
1947   NR   Drama   Age 12+   88 min.   B&W

An innocent man is arrested and put on trial for the murder of a priest in this tightly-paced courtroom drama. The prosecuting attorney doesn't believe in the soundness of his case, so he hunts down the real facts. An all-star cast features Karl Malden and Jane Wyatt. Based on a true story.

## BORN FREE — RATING 3.5
1966   NR   Drama-Adventure   Age 06+   96 min.   Color

A timeless wildlife classic for all ages, *Born Free* tells the heart-rending story of Elsa, a lioness turned loose into the wild after years of captivity in the compound. A Kenya game warden and his wife retrain their pet to fend for herself after learning she might be shipped off to a zoo. Inspiring.

## BORN YESTERDAY — RATING 3.7
1950   NR   Comedy   Age 12+   103 min.   B&W

A former junk dealer hires a college professor (William Holden) to teach his "dumb blonde" girlfriend how to be sophisticated. Judy Holliday won an Oscar for her hilarious performance as Billie, the dizzy blonde. Witty dialogue and a good story makes this a genuine crowd-pleaser.

## BOY NAMED CHARLIE BROWN — RATING 3.2
1970   G   Drama-Comedy   Age 04+   85 min.   Color

This is a full length motion picture, not just a cartoon. "Good ole wishy-washy Charlie Brown" gets a chance for fame in a national spelling bee in this animated Peanuts film debut. A tuneful piano score combined with clever visual effects gives the production a charming flavor. A perfect film for kids.

## BRAVE LITTLE TOASTER — RATING 3.2
1991   G   Fantasy   Age 04+   90 min.   Color

Cute Disney animated film about a toaster and his appliance friends who leave their deserted house in search of their master. On the way, they encounter life-threatening dangers and learn the value of teamwork. Some nice songs by Van Dyle Parks and a suspense-filled storyline makes this film a must-see. Maybe a little scary for the younger ones, but overall it's very enjoyable.

*Secular Movies*

### BREATHING LESSONS — RATING 3.8
1994     TVM     Drama     Age 12+     98 min.     Color

Ira (James Garner) and Maggie (Joanne Woodward), on their way to a funeral, meet an assortment of colorful characters. Outgoing Maggie talks about marriage and divorce. Maggie's son, Jesse, divorced and it broke her heart. Maggie persuades Ira to visit Jesse's ex-wife hoping she will patch things up with Jesse. Maggie may be a little too hopeful. Wonderful Hallmark presentation, full of warmth, off-beat humor and good drama.

### BRIAN'S SONG — RATING 3.8
1970     TVM     Docudrama     Age 12+     73 min.     Color

Based on a true story, this film describes the caring, unique friendship between two Chicago Bears football players. Gayle Sayers, a black running back, and Brian Piccolo, a fellow teammate become roommates and great friends. When Brian is stricken with terminal cancer, Gayle supports and encourages him to the end. James Caan and Billy Dee Williams give fine portrayals as Piccolo and Sayers. One of the best.

### BRIDGE ON THE RIVER KWAI, THE — RATING 4.0
1957     NR     Adventure     Age 12+     161 min.     Color

A tough, determined British officer (Alec Guiness) and his men are captured by the Japanese. Together they build a long hanging bridge for psychological therapy. One prisoner, however, rebels and tries to destroy the bridge. Intense action-packed episodes along with a battle of wills makes this tremendous film worth watching. Oscar winning performance by Alec Guiness. Some beatings and battle violence.

### BRIEF HISTORY OF TIME, A — RATING 3.5
1992     NR     Documentary     Age 12+     84 min.     Color

World-renowned physicist Stephen Hawking, who's afflicted with a progressive muscular disorder and communicates with a voice synthesizer, discusses black holes and the origin of the universe in this engrossing documentary. Even non-students will appreciate Hawking's findings, told in an intriguing, understandable way. Admirably, Hawking links God with the creation of the universe. Produced by Errol Morris, creator of *The Thin Blue Line*.

### BRIGADOON — RATING 3.3
1954     NR     Musical-Fantasy     Age 12+     108 min.     Color

Gene Kelly and Van Johnson play Americans who discover a Scottish village that comes to life once every century in this enchanting Lerner & Loewe musical. Kelly and Cyd Charisse team up for some unforgettable dance numbers. Although lacking originality, an ethereal charm and a beautiful score make it enjoyable entertainment.

### BRIGHTY OF THE GRAND CANYON — RATING 2.2
1985     G     Adventure-Drama     Age 06+     90 min.     Color

Brighty is a likable trail burro living in the Grand Canyon. When an old prospector is murdered, Brighty leads the government ranger to him. The ranger's investigation is interrupted when he and Brighty accompany President Teddy Roosevelt on a lion hunt in the canyon. But they both resume their determined effort to track down the murderer. Colorful seasonable changes in the canyon add to the film's appeal.

### BUCK ROGERS IN THE 25TH CENTURY — RATING 1.7
1979     PG     Science Fiction-Drama     Age 06+     89 min.     Color

The comic strip hero awakens from a blissful state after years of suspended animation. Buck (Gil Gerard) finds himself on a planet under attack by a power-hungry princess and her evil henchmen. As usual, he must come to the rescue of the helpless citizens. Originally a TV pilot, this film may not appeal to adults. Young people, though, will probably like the special effects. Many battles, explosions and property destruction.

### BUGS BUNNY-ROAD RUNNER — RATING 3.2
1979     G     Comedy     Age 04+     92 min.     Color

This memorable collection of Warner Brothers cartoons consists of the hilarious antics of Porky Pig, Daffy Duck, Elmer Fudd and Bugs, Pepe Le Pew, and the Roadrunner. New episodes of Bugs Bunny are also included. THE BUGS BUNNY-ROAD RUNNER MOVIE is vintage stuff for the cartoon connoisseur. Enjoyable and fun for the family too.

### BUNDLE OF JOY                                                    RATING 2.5
**1956        NR        Musical-Comedy        Age 12+        98 min.        Color**
A musical remake of the old Ginger Rogers comedy BACHELOR MOTHER, this engaging film features a department store clerk (Debbie Reynolds) who adopts an abandoned baby. Just about everybody thinks her boyfriend ( Eddie Fisher) is the father and a scandal results. Audiences will enjoy the lovely tunes by Eddie and the charming story.

### BURNING SECRET                                                   RATING 2.5
**1988        PG        Drama        Age 17+        107 min.        Color**
Set against the elegance and beauty of Vienna in 1919, an Austrian lady (Faye Dunaway) finds herself drawn into an illicit love affair with a charming middle-aged baron. They meet in a hotel near a sanatorium where the woman's young son is under treatment. To win her over, he befriends her innocent, asthmatic twelve-year-old son. She comes to realize how tragic her involvement in the affair could be. Acting is superb.

### BYE, BYE BIRDIE                                                  RATING 2.8
**1963        NR        Musical        Age 06+        112 min.        Color**
Dick Van Dyke amiably portrays the manager of a drafted teen rock 'n roll idol returning to a small town to bid his adoring fans a fond farewell. Enamored with the star, a high school girl played by Ann-Margaret abandons her old boyfriend. Reminiscent of the furor surrounding Elvis Presley's military departure, this version of the Broadway musical sparkles with an enjoyable cast and upbeat music. The whole family will love it.

### CAINE MUTINY                                                     RATING 3.7
**1954        NR        Drama        Age 12+        125 min.        Color**
An adaptation of Herman Wouk's classic novel, this superb film deals with a mutiny organized by two naval officers against their mentally unstable captain (Humphrey Bogart). The film portrays the mutiny as well as the courtroom drama which follows. Brilliantly filmed and well-acted by a famous cast, *Caine Mutiny* is a definite must-see. Because of its brilliance, a made-for TV movie followed in 1988.

### CALL TO GLORY                                                    RATING 3.0
**1984        TVM        Drama        Age 12+        97 min.        Color**
This captivating film offers a personal look at the inner life of an Air Force officer and his family. It takes place during the 1962 Cuban missile crisis while the officer and his fellow pilots are flying secret aerial missions over Cuba. A well-written script and war-time tension enhance the film. In one scene, father and daughter have a tender but explicit discussion of sex.

### CAMELOT                                                          RATING 2.2
**1967        NR        Musical        Age 06+        181 min.        Color**
The legend of King Arthur and the knights of the Round Table is reborn in this beautiful Lerner and Loewe musical. It follows Arthur's first encounter with Guinevere to the fall of Camelot. Richard Harris and Vanessa Redgrave deliver extraordinary performances in their mythical roles of Arthur and Guinevere. Good escape musical.

### CANDLESHOE                                                       RATING 2.5
**1977        G        Comedy        Age 06+        101 min.        Color**
A slick swindler tries to pass off a street urchin (Jodie Foster) as Helen Hayes' heiress in order to find hidden family treasure. The young girl is duped into hunting through an English estate for the treasure. This delightful Disney comedy filmed in England contains quite a bit of rough treatment, kicking, slapping, fighting and property destruction. Overall, however, it is standard Disney family fare.

### CAROLINE?                                                        RATING 3.2
**1990        TVM        Mystery-Suspense        Age 12+        100 min.        Color**
This absorbing movie follows the struggle of a woman who was supposedly killed 15 years earlier in a plane crash. She returns home, claiming to be Caroline, the long-lost daughter. Her father has no doubts about who she is, but his new wife is not sure. Is this really Caroline or an impostor? This suspenseful, well-acted Hallmark Hall of Fame production won an Emmy. A few moderate crude words.

## Secular Movies

### CAROUSEL
**RATING 3.3**
1956    NR    Musical    Age 06+    128 min.    Color

Billy Bigelow, a boisterous carnival barker, turns over a new leaf in order to win the love of a shy girl (Shirley Jones) in this romantic musical. After the birth of their first child, Billy takes drastic steps to provide for its welfare. Immortal Rodgers and Hammerstein musical score adds a wistful charm. Features such delightful songs as "If I Loved You" and "You'll Never Walk Alone".

### CASABLANCA
**RATING 4.0**
1943    NR    Drama-Adventure    Age 12+    102 min.    B&W

Humphrey Bogart and Ingrid Bergman display their acting prowess in this timeless Hollywood blockbuster. Setting is an intriguing nightclub in World War II Casablanca, Morocco. The owner (Bogart) lets it serve as a haven for wartime refugees. When his old flame (Bergman) from Paris appears on the scene, he becomes entangled in a drama with her and her husband. Classic lines and lovely music, including "As Time Goes By", enhance this glorious film.

### CASE OF LIBEL, A
**RATING 3.5**
1984    TVM    Docudrama    Age 17+    92 min.    Color

One of the finest courtroom dramas ever made, *A Case Of Libel* details the true story of the Pegler-Reynolds libel suit. Pegler, a newspaper columnist, maliciously attempts to destroy the reputation of Reynolds, a war correspondent, through a series of vicious lies. Ed Asner plays a very astute trial attorney. Two or three profanities.

### CASE OF THE LOGICAL i RANCH, THE
**RATING 3.0(e)**
1994    NR    Mystery-Musical    Age 06+    30 min.    Color

The adventures of Mary-Kate and Ashley are a series of video mysteries for children starring the Olsen twins. Usually the twins sing three or four songs as they unravel a mystery. In this one, the girls find the source of the mysterious rumbling sounds and gas fumes coming from the ground at the ranch. Some fear that a dragon lives underground, but the Olsens prove that rumor wrong.

### CASE OF THE SEA WORLD ADVENTURE, THE
**RATING 3.0(e)**
1995    NR    Mystery    Age 06+    30 min.    Color

Super sleuths Mary-Kate and Ashley Olsen believe they have discovered a dead man in the Sea World Park in Orlando, Florida. The twins start following the person they believe responsible for the crime, which leads them to a cruise ship. Sure enough, the "crime" was a clever plot to get the twins and their parents on a much-needed vacation together.

### CASE OF THE THORN MANSION, THE
**RATING 3.0(e)**
1994    NR    Mystery-Musical    Age 06+    30 min    Color

The Olsen and Olsen detective agency, headed by Mary-Kate and Ashley, gets a mysterious call that Thorn Mansion is haunted. The twins investigate and hear strange buzzing noises and see someone dressed in white walking around. They discover the strange noises and mysterious figure are easily explained. The girls sing an unfriendly song about their younger sister called "Butt-Out," adding a crude element to this otherwise entertaining and acceptable video.

### CASTAWAY COWBOY, THE
**RATING 2.8**
1974    G    Adventure    Age 06+    91 min.    Color

James Garner plays a Texan cowboy shipwrecked in Hawaii during the late 1850's in this simple Disney western. He meets a widow (Vera Miles) who wants him to help turn her farm into a cattle ranch. Problems arise when a land-hungry villain tries to interfere. Pleasant Disney fun for the whole family and beautiful Hawaiian scenery.

### CAT FROM OUTER SPACE, THE
**RATING 2.3**
1978    G    Comedy-Sci-Fi    Age 06+    104 min.    Color

A mysterious cat from another planet has accidentally landed on Earth and its supernaturally powered collar wreaks havoc among the earthly citizens. The cat seeks help from American scientists to rebuild his spaceship, but military bureaucracy and enemies stand in the way. Hilarious Disney comedy for kids featuring Ken Berry and Sandy Duncan.

## CHARADE  RATING 3.8
**1963   NR   Mystery-Comedy   Age 17+   114 min.   Color**

In this Hitchcock flavored mystery, a courtly Cary Grant helps a desperate widow (Audrey Hepburn) locate a fortune that her late husband has stashed away. He hid the money before he was murdered by the same pals he had swindled. The "friends" believe the widow knows where the loot is hidden. Exciting and suspenseful thriller for mystery buffs.

## CHARIOTS OF FIRE  RATING 3.7
**1981   PG   Drama   Age 06+   123 min.   Color**

An awe-inspiring tale of great emotional depth. Acclaimed the best picture of 1981, it focuses on the inner struggles of two English runners competing in the 1924 Olympics. One is a devout Scottish missionary and the other an ambitious Jewish student at Cambridge. Their ambitions and convictions are explored in extraordinary detail. Captivating film with Christian overtones.

## CHARLIE BROWN'S ALL STARS  RATING 4.0(e)
**1966   NR   Adventure-Drama   Age 06+   26 min.   Color**

After an opening loss of 123-0, Charlie Brown's baseball team threatens a walkout. Our good old friend tries to win the team back by promising them uniforms, but then is unable to deliver. When his sponsor finds out he has girls and a dog on his team, Charlie is really in trouble. Good, clean animated fun.

## CHARLIE THE LONESOME COUGAR  RATING 2.8
**1967   NR   Adventure-Comedy   Age 04+   75 min.   Color**

A friendly cougar comes into a logging camp, searching for some food and affection. After adopting the big cat into their "family", the men debate whether or not they should return it to the wild. This humorous Disney animal film has a surprisingly believable story and good acting. Entertaining.

## CHARLOTTE'S WEB  RATING 3.0(e)
**1973   G   Adventure-Drama   Age 04+   85 min.   Color**

A clever barnyard spider spells encouraging messages in her web to save a piglet from being turned into bacon in this animated delight. The marvelous voices of Debbie Reynolds, Paul Lynde, and Henry Gibson add to the charming flavor of the film. Based on E. B. White's classic children's tale, this is good children's entertainment.

## CHASING DREAMS  RATING 2.5
**1981   PG   Drama   Age 12+   96 min.   Color**

This coming-of-age drama tells the story of a college-aged farm boy who trains for the school's baseball team, while also caring for his handicapped younger brother. Of course, he also must find time to help out his father on the farm. A warm-hearted story showing the value of commitment and perseverance. A few moderate crude words and one fight scene.

## CHEETAH  RATING 3.0
**1989   G   Adventure-Nature   Age 06+   83 min.   Color**

Walt Disney production about a family who moves to Kenya so that the father can continue his scientific work. His children, Ted and Susan, befriend a native boy who shows them the area. They discover an orphaned cheetah cub and take it upon themselves to raise it. Once the animal achieves adulthood, a villager steals it and enters it in a race with some greyhounds. The children insist on finding the cheetah and an exciting adventure ensues.

## CHIEFS  RATING 3.8(e)
**1985   TVM   Drama   Age 12+   200 min.   Color**

The first black police chief of a small town is determined to solve a series of unexplained murders in this intriguing TV drama. He wonders why an eerie spell has been cast over the townspeople and the town's political boss (Charlton Heston). Contains severe treatment of blacks and whites, including whipping, striking and shooting.

## CHINA RUN                                                                    RATING 3.0(e)
**1988        NR          Docudrama              Age 12+         90 min.         Color**
An enjoyable documentary featuring Stan Cockrell, a country boy from Kentucky, who goes to China to participate in a 3,000 mile solo marathon. All along the way, he mixes and mingles with the Chinese people and learns much about their everyday life and feelings. Stan's cheerful friendliness and interesting encounters give this docudrama a unique appeal.

## CHITTY CHITTY BANG BANG                                                       RATING 2.2
**1968        G           Musical-Fantasy        Age 04+         142 min.        Color**
Based on Ian Fleming's story for children, this fantasy musical features a magical race car that can fly and sail over the water. Dick Van Dyke plays a "crackpot" inventor who takes his children on some exciting adventures. Children will enjoy the fun special effects.

## CHOSEN, THE                                                                   RATING 3.5
**1982        PG          Drama                  Age 12+         108 min.        Color**
Set in Brooklyn during World War II, this unusually profound film deals with the friendship of two Jewish boys from completely different environments and backgrounds. A conflict between friendship and family loyalty erupts when the boys' families disagree about setting up a Jewish nation in Israel. Both families display a respect for God. Wholesome, enjoyable film. However, at a party for Jewish young people, sex between a Jewish boy and girl is implied.

## CHRISTMAS IN JULY                                                             RATING 3.7
**1940        NR          Comedy                 Age 06+         70 min.         B&W**
A poverty-stricken young man mistakenly thinks he has won a coffee slogan contest and runs up a gigantic bill in a wild shopping spree at a department store. In this rib-tickling comedy, Dick Powell delivers an excellent performance as the overeager pauper. A touch of bitterness runs throughout the comedy. Delightful treat, however.

## CHRISTMAS LILIES OF THE FIELD                                                 RATING 3.0
**1979        TVM         Drama                  Age 06+         100 min.        Color**
In this joyful sequel, compassionate black Homer Smith (Billy Dee Williams) returns to the chapel in Arizona he had built 15 years ago for some German nuns. Now, Mother Mary wants him to build an orphanage and a kindergarten. The spirited interplay between Homer and Mother Maria is fun just as it was in the original. This lovely piece will charm audiences everywhere.

## CHRISTMAS TO REMEMBER, A                                                      RATING 3.7
**1978        TVM         Drama                  Age 06+         100 min.        Color**
This nostalgic, Depression-era film features an elderly couple who take their grandson in for the holidays. Angered at God for his son's death in World War I, the grandfather resents the presence of the lad until his wife scolds him for his cruelty. Moving performances by Jason Robards and Eva Marie Saint.

## CHRISTMAS WITHOUT SNOW                                                        RATING 3.3
**1980        TVM         Drama                  Age 12+         96 min.         Color**
A divorced schoolteacher from Nebraska moves to San Francisco to start afresh. At her new church, the demanding choir director insists on singing "The Messiah" using their mediocre talents. To make matters worse, the pastor's son vandalizes the organ. Will this motley group of singers be able to band together in time to sing? An entertaining movie about one of the greatest pieces of Christian music ever written.

## CHRISTY                                                                       RATING 3.5(e)
**1994        TVM         Drama                  Age 06+         95 min.         Color**
Christy is a devout and courageous young woman who gives up city life in 1912 to teach at a missions school in the heart of the Smoky Mountains. Life there is harsh and the people unaccepting, except for handsome Rev. Grantland and short-tempered Doctor McNeil. Christy must fight the adults' ignorance and bitter feuding as she begins teaching their children. The inspiring TV movie that started the series, *Christy*.

### CHRONICLES OF NARNIA, THE
**RATING 3.0(e)**
1991     NR     Fantasy     Age 06+     174 min.     Color

A delightful three-part set of English-produced videos based on C.S. Lewis' tales for children. Children accidentally stumble into the mythical world of Narnia, changing their lives forever! They encounter adventures and fantasy creatures that stagger their imaginations. Christian symbolism in the series explores themes of truth, faith, redemption, and good versus evil. The stories will challenge viewers to think and discuss the inherent messages.

### CINDERELLA
**RATING 4.0(e)**
1985     TVM     Fantasy-Drama     Age 04+     60 min.     Color

The romantic tale of the forgotten sister with the missing glass slipper comes to life in this modern remake. Jennifer Beale plays a beautiful, sweet Cinderella and Matthew Broderick plays the love-struck Prince Henry. One of the best in the Faerie Tale Theatre series, *Cinderella* will appeal to children of all ages.

### CINDERELLA
**RATING 3.5(e)**
1964     TVM     Musical-Fantasy     Age 06+     100 min.     Color

Wonderful Rodgers and Hammerstein musical featuring Leslie Ann Warren as Cinderella. When a charming prince throws a ball, Cinderella's wicked stepmother and three sisters prepare to go, but intentionally leave her out. A woman with magical powers appears and provides Cinderella with a beautiful dress, shoes, and dazzling escorts. A charming musical.

### CITIZEN KANE
**RATING 4.0**
1941     NR     Drama     Age 17+     119 min.     B&W,

Touted as one of the finest American movies ever made, this Orson Welles masterpiece parallels the story of wealthy newspaper magnate William Randolph Hearst and his turbulent rise to power. A determined reporter diligently uncovers information on this tycoon. Shows how a powerful individual can influence the media and government. Modern audiences will appreciate the imaginative camera work of this innovative film.

### CIVIL WAR, THE
**RATING 4.0(e)**
1994     NR     Documentary     Age 17+     80min.each     B&W

This ten-tape series, originally produced for PBS, tells the story of the American Civil War. Ken Burns has done an outstanding job of telling the complex events of the war through first-hand journal accounts. The music, images and stories of the Americans involved in this momentous war will remain firmly etched in your mind. Spend some time and watch this first-rate series.

### CLOAK AND DAGGER
**RATING 3.0**
1984     PG     Drama-Adventure     Age 12+     101 min.     Color

An over imaginative boy who plays fantasy espionage video games with his make-believe friend accidentally obtains a video tape with top secret information. Some criminal opportunists want the tape and pursue him with deadly intentions. The problem is, no one believes he is in trouble, not even his own family. Contains some intense violence including shootings and two obscured beatings. An exciting adventure.

### CLOSE ENCOUNTERS OF THE THIRD KIND
**RATING 4.0**
1977     PG     Sci-Fi-Fantasy     Age 06+     132 min.     Color

Stephen Spielberg wrote and directed this intelligent story about a childlike extra-terrestrials' meeting with earthlings. Richard Dreyfuss plays an average man completely baffled by the situation. However, he and others violate government orders and rendezvous with the aliens in their spectacular space ship. The climatic landing by the alien space ship is awesome. Breathtaking special effects and a hauntingly beautiful musical score.

### COCAINE: ONE MAN's SEDUCTION
**RATING 3.0**
1983     TVM     Drama     Age 12+     104 min.     Color

Dennis Weaver brilliantly plays a well-to-do real estate agent who uses cocaine to handle his job related stress. The habit almost destroys his life, his marriage, and his career. This engrossing, well done TV drama convincingly portrays the destructiveness of this drug. Definitely worth watching.

### COLD SASSY TREE — RATING 3.3
**1989**    **TVM**    **Drama**    Age 12+    100 min.    Color

This romantic tearjerker is about a small-town widower who marries a young spinster soon after his wife's death. The people of the small Georgia town are scandalized by this behavior and a storm of gossip surrounds the couple. Only the courage and love of his new wife can show the town and his family what a good choice he has made. Several mild crudities and some prolonged kissing scenes are included.

### COLONEL CHABERT — RATING 3.3(e)
**1995**    **NR**    **Drama**    Age 17+    111 min.    Color

After one of the Napoleonic Wars, Colonel Chabert is declared dead. Miraculously, 10 years later, someone who claims to be Chabert shows up in town to find that his wife has remarried and now owns his large estate. His battle to prove that he is Chabert may be more difficult than fighting for Napoleon. A good film with some war violence not for the queasy and a few moderate crude words.

### COMPUTER WORE TENNIS SHOES — RATING 2.2
**1969**    **NR**    **Comedy-Fantasy**    Age 06+    87 min.    Color

This light, nonsensical Disney comedy features a forgetful college student (Kurt Russell) who accidentally plugs himself into a computer and becomes a genius. Some gangsters get wind of this and try to exploit his mind for their purposes. The plot lacks substance, but kids will enjoy the fast-paced action.

### CORRINA, CORRINA — RATING 3.5
**1994**    **PG**    **Comedy**    Age 06+    135 min.    Color

Corrina (Whoopi Goldberg), a black college graduate, is hired as a maid for a recent widower and his daughter, Molly. Corrina wins her way into their hearts, and racial barriers are overcome as Corrina and the widower fall in love. With her compassion and fun loving spirit, Corrina brings life and fun back into their lives. A heartwarming movie about racial tolerance. Two regular profanities, along with some brief sexual references.

### COUNTRY GIRL — RATING 3.5
**1954**    **NR**    **Drama**    Age 12+    104 min.    B&W

Bing Crosby plays a recovering alcoholic singer who tries to get back into the business with the help of a sympathetic director (William Holden). Grace Kelly won an Oscar for her compassionate portrayal as his supportive wife. Although this production is often overlooked by movie fans, the masterful performances are worth a look.

### COURAGE MOUNTAIN — RATING 3.2
**1990**    **PG**    **Drama**    Age 06+    90 min.    Color

During WW1, a Swiss girl named Heidi is sent to an Italian girls' school. Her simple ways are mocked by her peers. When Austrian troops invade the school, Heidi and several others manage to escape, and Heidi takes it upon herself to lead them over the Swiss Alps. Good acting, action and spectacular scenery make for an entertaining film.

### COURTSHIP — RATING 3.0(e)
**1987**    **TVM**    **Drama**    Age 12+    85 min.    Color

Playwright Horton Foote wrote this engrossing drama set in 1915 in America. The film follows the lives of two young women forbidden from enjoying courtship by their domineering father. Will the women ignore their father's wishes and seek out romance? A marvelous PBS presentation that brings to life the high morals and elegant manners of the turn of the century. A romantic story without the usual traces of suggestive dialogue.

### CRISIS AT CENTRAL HIGH — RATING 3.5
**1981**    **TVM**    **Docudrama**    Age 12+    125 min.    Color

This shocking recreation of events surrounding the racial integration of an Arkansas high school features JoAnne Woodward as the determined administrator who speeds up the process. She must contend with irate parents and threatening mobs on a day-to-day basis. Working with her staff, she calmly but resolutely deals with the very volatile situation. The teleplay is based on Mrs. Huckaby's actual journal. Excellent.

### CRY THE BELOVED COUNTRY — RATING 3.0(e)
1995  PG-13  Drama  Age 17+  112 min  Color

Noted actor James Earl Jones plays a Zulu Christian pastor in South Africa during the 1940s. He leaves his village to search for his son in Johannesburg. There he finds him jailed for the murder of a white man. The pastor also finds out that the victim's father is a white man from the same village. A very thought-provoking drama of a black man and a white man sharing a common tragedy.

### CYRANO DE BERGERAC — RATING 3.8
1991  PG  Drama  Age 12+  138 min.  Color

Sweeping French adaptation of Rostand's classic novel about a romantic swordsman who fears nothing, except telling his cousin Roxanne of his love for her. He fears rejection because of his large nose, so he uses a young cadet to do his wooing for him. This fast-paced drama will keep viewers' attention in spite of its French dialogue and English subtitles. A few moderately violent scenes involving swordplay.

### D2: THE MIGHTY DUCKS — RATING 2.5
1994  PG  Comedy-Drama  Age 12+  107 min  Color

This fun-filled Disney sequel features a young championship hockey team bound for the International Junior Goodwill Games. Both the coach and the team get caught up in the false glamor of commercial sports. Can the coach pull them through to victory? The whole family will enjoy this energetic, wholesome film that affirms the human spirit. Some hockey game violence.

### DAD — RATING 2.0
1989  PG  Drama  Age 17+  116 min.  Color

Jake and Betty Tremont are an aging couple with health problems. John, their affluent son in New York, has not seen them for quite some time. He comes home to be with his ill mother only to have to take care of his father who suffers a heart attack. *Dad* is a deeply reflective drama that stresses the value of family relationships. Vulgar language is used once and regular profanity twice. One frank discussion of sex between Jake and Betty.

### DAKOTA — RATING 2.3
1988  PG  Drama  Age 12+  100 min.  Color

Lou Diamond Phillips (of *La Bamba* fame) portrays a troubled youth trying to run away from a disturbing past. After taking a job at a Texas ranch, he begins to develop a sense of responsibility and learns to deal with his brother's death. All the while, trouble is brewing with two of the town bullies. He also develops a romantic interest in the rancher's attractive daughter. Phillip's fine performance greatly enhances the film.

### DANNY — RATING 3.0
1977  G  Drama  Age 06+  90 min.  Color

A young girl acquires a horse that has been injured and sold by the pampered daughter of wealthy stable owners. Through the little girl's tender care and dedication, the horse becomes a champion jumper. Children and adults will love this simple but poignant story.

### DARBY O'GILL AND THE LITTLE PEOPLE — RATING 3.2
1959  NR  Comedy-Fantasy  Age 06+  90 min.  Color

An Irish storyteller becomes involved with the title characters in his wild yarns of leprechauns and banshees. Foolishly, he tricks King Brian of the Leprechauns into granting him three wishes. He later regrets his move. Magnificent special effects along with a touch of suspense will thrill viewers of this Disney classic. Features a young Sean Connery.

### DARK HORSE — RATING 3.0
1992  PG  Drama  Age 12+  98 min.  Color

Allison is devastated when her father moves the family to the country after the death of her mother. Allison cuts school, lies to her father and sneaks out to a dance. She gets arrested for drunk driving and is sentenced to ten weekends of community service at a horse ranch. There, Allison may just be able to learn to help others instead of hurting herself. One fight scene.

### DAVID COPPERFIELD                                                                                   RATING 2.5
**1970        TVM        Drama                          Age 06+          100 min.              Color**
A modern TV production of Charles Dickens' classic novel, made in Great Britain, has a top notch cast and first class production quality. David, an orphan, is disliked by his cruel stepfather, but is helped by his eccentric aunt. He grows up to be an author and marries his childhood sweetheart. Could have greater appeal for contemporary audiences than the original produced in 1935.

### DAVY CROCKETT, KING OF THE WILD FRONTIER                                                             RATING 3.2
**1955        NR         Adventure                      Age 06+          93 min.               Color**
Taken from three Disney TV episodes, this fun adventure story tells about Davy's courageous exploits - from rousting out some local bad guys to his never-say-die acts of valor during the Battle of the Alamo. Fess Parker, a hero for many boys during the 1950's, plays Crockett. Kids will be thrilled by these inspiring stories of bravery.

### DAY AFTER, THE                                                                                       RATING 3.5
**1983        TVM        Drama                          Age 17+          126 min.              Color**
In this thought-provoking TV drama, a nuclear blast devastates the small town of Lawrence, Kansas, leaving the survivors with critical problems. The depiction of the bomb blast destroying the town and stark scenes of makeshift medical facilities filled with wounded and dying victims instill memorable impressions. Intensity of subject matter makes this inappropriate for young children. Controversial and disturbing.

### DAY THE EARTH STOOD STILL, THE                                                                       RATING 3.8
**1951        NR         Sci-Fiction-Drama              Age 06+          92 min.               B&W**
A visitor from outer space lands in Washington, D.C. and warns the earthly citizens about the dangers of nuclear warfare in this fascinating sci-fi tale. He learns that most of the humans agree with his views - but not everyone. A philosophical treatise, this film contains many subtle cuts against fascism. Audiences will appreciate the timeliness of this outstanding work.

### DEAD, THE                                                                                            RATING 3.5
**1987        PG         Drama                          Age 17+          82 min.               Color**
Set in 1904 Dublin, Ireland, a group of ladies host a vibrant feast with food and spirits for several friends and family members. Gabriel (Donald McCann) and Gretta Conroy (Anjelica Huston) seem to have everything for which to be grateful. However, a song sung that night revives old memories of Gretta's former love who died suddenly. This film lacks real spiritual insights and hope, but will appeal to sophisticated movie goers.

### DEAR AMERICA: LETTERS HOME FROM VIETNAM                                                              RATING 3.8
**1988        PG-13      Documentary                    Age 17+          86 min.               Color**
Pathos of the Vietnam War and the feelings of the soldiers who struggled through it are presented in this moving documentary. Film footage, coupled with readings from real letters written to family and friends bring out the stark reality of the war. Moderately crude and vulgar language are each used a few times. Comical frontal and rear nudity occur a few times. It is appropriate for mature young adults and adults.

### DECORATION DAY                                                                                       RATING 3.3
**1990        TVM        Drama                          Age 12+          96 min.               Color**
Another Hallmark Hall of Fame winner starring James Garner as an ex-judge who attempts to discover why his World War II buddy refuses to accept the Congressional Medal of Honor 30 years after his heroic actions. He becomes caught up in the sensitive area of race relations and learns about forgiveness. A few violent scenes of flashbacks to the war may be too intense for young children.

### DEERSLAYER, THE                                                                                      RATING 2.3
**1978        TVM        Adventure                      Age 17+          98 min.               Color**
During the French and Indian War, Hawkeye and Chingachgook are trying to save the life of a kidnapped Mohican princess as well as avenge the death of Chingachgook's son. They meet a trapper and his daughter who are in danger from the warring tribes. A French officer comes to their aid. Based on James Fenimore Cooper's classic novel.

### DENNIS THE MENACE                                                      RATING 2.8
1993        PG          Comedy                Age 12+        94 min.            Color

Hank Ketcham's lovable, mischievous comic strip character comes to life on the big screen. Dennis still likes to bug his irritable next door neighbor, Mr. Wilson. He runs into a thief and is taken hostage. A hilarious comedy for kids of all ages. Several moderately violent slapstick scenes, along with one moderate crude word and three implied regular profanities never actually spoken.

### DESERT BLOOM                                                            RATING 3.2
1986        PG          Drama                 Age 17+        106 min.           Color

In a modest income family, Rose must deal with living in the same house with her emotionally disturbed stepfather. Her good friend, Aunt Starr, moves in and they develop a close relationship. A loving family is depicted in spite of the stepfather's conduct. The dialogue contains a few instances of regular profanity. Set in Las Vegas, Nevada, during the atomic bomb testing period of the 1950's. Unique, enjoyable drama.

### DESTRY RIDES AGAIN                                                      RATING 4.0
1939        NR          Western               Age 06+        94 min.            B&W

It's up to Sheriff Destry (Jimmy Stewart) to reform a boisterous town in this Western satire. The only problem is that the mild-mannered sheriff doesn't believe in using guns to keep the peace. Not only that he is chased by Frenchie, a flirtatious saloon girl (Marlene Dietrich). Rip-roaring action coupled with good laughs make this film a real delight for Western fans.

### DIARY OF ANNE FRANK                                                     RATING 3.5
1959        NR          Docudrama             Age 12+        170 min.           B&W

A carefully produced adaptation of the hit Broadway drama, this film captures the trauma experienced by a family of Jewish refugees in Amsterdam during World War II. They must hide in the attic of a sympathizer to escape capture by the Nazis. Anne Frank encourages the others not to lose hope in spite of the troubles they face. Shelly Winters plays the panicky Mrs. Van Daan, who shares with the Frank family. A sobering, but inspiring picture.

### DISORDERLY ORDERLY, THE                                                 RATING 2.7
1964        NR          Comedy                Age 12+        90 min.            Color

Jerry Lewis plays a bumbling orderly who turns a psychiatric sanitarium into a chaotic disaster in this outrageous comedy. Hilarious sight gags along with clever slapstick antics provide some wild fun. If you love the silliness of Jerry Lewis, you will enjoy this film.

### DOCTOR DOLITTLE                                                         RATING 2.0
1967        NR          Fantasy-Musical       Age 06+        152 min.           Color

This version of Hugh Lofting's tale for children features Rex Harrison as the eccentric animal doctor who prefers the company of his patients to that of people. Kids will enjoy the amusing story and the great visual effects. The whimsical song, "Talk to the Animals", won an Academy Award.

### DOG OF FLANDERS                                                         RATING 3.2
1959        NR          Adventure-Drama       Age 04+        96 min.            Color

This heartwarming tale features a Dutch boy who adopts a lost dog and nurses it back to health. He then uses the dog to pull a milk delivery cart. Theodore Bikel and Donald Crisp deliver convincing performances, but the boy (David Ladd) and the adorable dog steal the show. Get the Kleenex out for this one.

### DOLLMAKER, THE                                                          RATING 3.7
1984        TVM         Drama                 Age 06+        104 min.           Color

Jane Fonda plays a Kentucky country mother of five who must uproot her family because of her husband's job transfer to Detroit in the 1940's. She and her family endure many hardships as they live in crowded makeshift housing for defense workers. She has a talent for whittling and discovers a satisfying and profitable use for it. Fonda won an Emmy for her sensitive portrayal. Fine family film.

*Secular Movies*

### DR. SEUSS: THE CAT IN THE HAT                                         RATING 4.0(e)
**1984        NR        Fantasy                    Age 04+        30 min.        Color**
A little different from the book, this delightful cartoon still has the Cat in the Hat entertaining two bored children on a rainy day. The fish, Mr. Crinklestein, gets very upset and the house is in shambles by the time their mother gets home, but rest assured that the Cat in the Hat has everything under control. Dr. Seuss' famous rhymes and fast-paced action are evident here.

### DR. ZHIVAGO                                                           RATING 3.8(e)
**1965        *R         Drama                      Age 17+        176 min.       Color**
The epic story of Yuri Zhivago as he struggles to survive during the momentous Bolshevik revolution in Russia. The hardships of this terrible time are wonderfully captured in a heartbreaking story against a backdrop of gorgeous scenery. The adult theme includes very graphic scenes of war and violence, along with an adulterous affair which is not condoned. *Originally released in 1965, the 1995 re-release carries an R rating because of the violence.

### DRAGNET                                                              RATING 3.2
**1954        NR        Drama                      Age 06+        89 min.        Color**
In this feature film of the popular TV series, Detective Joe Friday (Jack Webb) and his partner track down the murderer of a mobster. They don't hesitate to violate civil liberties in the process. All clues point to the former business associates of the gangster. Webb gives a cool portrayal of the unflappable detective, and does a fine job of directing as well.

### DREAM FOR CHRISTMAS, A                                              RATING 2.8
**1973        TVM       Drama                      Age 06+        100 min.       Color**
Black Arkansas pastor and his family leave their peaceful lifestyle for the big city of Los Angeles. Their mission is to help save a church from a developer's bulldozer. Though the children have some problems adjusting to their new environment, it isn't long before they begin to have a positive impact on the community. Christian morals exemplified. Good acting. Will appeal to youth groups.

### DRIVING MISS DAISY                                                  RATING 3.8
**1989        PG        Drama                      Age 12+        99 min.        Color**
Delightful story about ornery Jewish matriarch Daisy Werthan (Jessica Tandy) and her black Christian chauffeur (Morgan Freeman). The movie explores their 30-year relationship as it progresses from wary apprehension to mutual respect and admiration. Interaction between the two is immensely entertaining. A charming film about growing older and wiser and the breakdown of racial barriers. Outstanding. One profanity.

### DUMBO                                                                RATING 4.0
**1941        NR        Adventure-Fantasy          Age 04+        64 min.        Color**
Timothy the mouse encourages Dumbo, a shy circus elephant with big ears, to fly in this charming Disney classic. Entertaining animals, a meaningful story, and a lighthearted ending will delight audiences of all ages. A brilliant "pink elephant" dream sequence tops it all off. This film won an Oscar for best musical score.

### EAGLE HAS LANDED, THE                                              RATING 3.0
**1976        PG        Drama-War                  Age 17+        123 min.       Color**
Eagle is the code name for a German plot to kidnap Winston Churchill and take him to Germany. Near the end of WW2, the Germans come to the realization that the war is lost and need a negotiating tool. Colonel Radl orchestrates a plan to get Churchill and engages Steiner and Lian to help him. Moderate crude language occurs several times and vulgar once. Some explicit killings. Action, romance and mystery.

### EAST OF EDEN                                                        RATING 4.0
**1955        NR        Drama                      Age 12+        115 min.       Color**
Based on Steinbeck's novel about two teenage brothers living with their father in a California farming valley in 1913. The story focuses on the brothers' rivalry for their father's love. Matters worsen when the 'rebellious son' (James Dean) discovers his mother, believed dead, operates a brothel. James Dean makes one of his first appearances in film. Director Elia Kazan presents some of his best visual work. Emotionally powerful drama.

### EASTER PARADE                                                    RATING 3.7
**1948          NR          Musical                    Age 06+        103 min.          Color**
Fred Astaire tries to forget his former dance partner while rising to the top with Judy Garland in this exhilarating Irving Berlin musical. Famous tunes include "Stepping Out With My Baby," "Shaking the Blues Away," and "Easter Parade". Sit back and enjoy excellent gala performances by an all-star cast.

### EFFICIENCY EXPERT                                                RATING 3.2
**1992          PG          Comedy                     Age 12+        85 min.           Color**
A failing Australian plant that manufactures leather moccasins hires a management consultant (Anthony Hopkins) to resolve its problems. Although appalled by the antiquated machinery and methods, he is quickly won over by the friendliness of the employees. This excellent film upholds many positive values, including dignity and concern for workers, loyalty, and friendship. The dialogue is marred, however, by one severe and two moderate obscenities and one regular profanity.

### EIGHTY-FOUR (84) CHARING CROSSROADS                              RATING 2.8
**1987          PG          Drama                      Age 12+        100 min.          Color**
A New York writer (Anne Bancroft) is enamored with old English literature works. She becomes close correspondence friends with the employees of a quaint book shop in London during the difficult post World War II days. She desperately wants to visit the London book shop, but for years various obstacles delay her journey. Eventually she does visit the shop in what proves to be a sad, but touching experience. A film with charm and wit.

### EL CID                                                            RATING 3.0
**1961          NR          Drama                      Age 12+        184 min.          Color**
Set in 1080 A.D., this magnificent restoration of the 1961 epic film follows the rise of the legendary Spanish hero, El Cid (Charlton Heston). El Cid rescues Muslim chiefs and overthrows cities in his fight for religious freedom. Sophia Loren plays Jimena, his beautiful and mysterious wife. An outstanding story with glorious music and colorful views of the Spanish countryside. Many violent war scenes may be too intense for youngsters.

### ELENI                                                             RATING 2.5
**1986          PG          Drama                      Age 17+        116 min.          Color**
A New York Times reporter joins an Athens news bureau to find the communist guerrillas who tortured and murdered his mother in the late 1940's during the civil war in Greece. Flashbacks present a very intense drama in which the Greek revolutionaries oppress the Greek peasants. Finally, the reporter confronts the judge who sentenced his mother to death. Two graphic torture scenes, beatings and killings. Outstanding, well done film.

### ELEPHANT MAN, THE                                                 RATING 3.8
**1980          PG          Drama                      Age 17+        124 min.          B&W**
John Hurt delivers an impressive performance as John Merrick, a hideously deformed man shunned by English society at the turn of the century. Merrick is befriended by a compassionate doctor played by Anthony Hopkins. Hopkins treats Merrick with dignity and attempts to reintroduce him to society. This unnerving story is for mature viewers who will appreciate its poignant and truthful moments. Some moderate violence and one scene of drunkenness.

### EMPIRE OF THE SUN                                                 RATING 2.7
**1987          PG          Adventure-War              Age 17+        152 min.          Color**
During the Japanese invasion of China, a British family gets separated, leaving young Jim Graham to survive on his own. An American befriends him, and they find themselves in an internment camp located next to a Japanese airfield. The film focuses on Jim's clever means of surviving in a ruthless environment. He and a young Japanese pilot develop a touching relationship. Regular profanity used a few times.

### ENCHANTED APRIL                                                   RATING 3.3
**1992          PG          Comedy-Drama               Age 12+        101 min.          Color**
Four English women escape their boring, lonely existence by renting a castle on the coast of Italy for a month. To their surprise, they quickly find themselves missing their husbands, so they invite them to come, and the fun begins. This film has it all—humor, romance, and gorgeous scenery. Also, the storyline is virtually free of any offensive elements. An excellent film for adults.

## Secular Movies

### ENEMY BELOW, THE — RATING 3.0
1957     NR     Adventure-War     Age 12+     98 min.     Color

This action packed World War II film features a suspenseful cat and mouse chase across the Atlantic involving an American destroyer and a German U boat. Interesting portrayal of the interaction between the commanders and crews of the two vessels. Good performances by Robert Mitchum and Curt Jergens, plus outstanding undersea photography. Enjoyable for war movie fans. The special effects won an Oscar.

### ENGLISHMAN WHO WENT UP A HILL, THE — RATING 3.3(e)
1995     PG     Comedy     Age 12+     98 min.     Color

Hugh Grant plays Reginald, an uptight young English cartographer who comes to Wales during World War II to measure mountains. While there, he meets a charming assortment of Welshmen and Betty, a pretty lass. While they become romantically involved, the townspeople come up with a way to make their hill into a mountain. First-rate, light-hearted movie with a few suggestive remarks and implications.

### ERNEST GOES TO JAIL — RATING 3.0
1990     PG     Comedy     Age 06+     82 min.     Color

Jim Varney again stars as zany Ernest P. Worrell. This time he is a bank custodian who accidentally gets involved in a prison escape plan and soon finds himself stuck in prison awaiting execution. Frantically, he searches for a way to "short circuit" his execution as well as to thwart a plan to rob the bank where he worked. As usual, this Ernest film has much slapstick fighting and rough treatment. Entertaining comedy.

### ERNEST RIDES AGAIN — RATING 1.8
1993     PG     Comedy     Age 06+     100 min.     Color

More slapstick antics from Ernest P. Worley, a fun-loving dimwit. This time, Ernest attempts to discover the hiding place of the crown jewels of England. He teams up with a history professor and soon gets caught up in a madcap chase. "Ernest" fans will love the clever impersonations and zany dialogue. A hilarious film with some slapstick kicking and punching.

### ERNEST SAVES CHRISTMAS — RATING 2.3
1988     PG     Comedy     Age 06+     95 min.     Color

Ernest is a taxi driver who is enamored with Christmas. Of all things, Santa comes to Orlando, Florida, on business and rides in Ernest's cab. Pamela, a teenage girl who has left home, joins Ernest and Santa Claus while they tour the town. When Ernest tries to help Santa persuade a local puppeteer showman to take on Santa's job, Ernest's bumbling slapstick antics seem to do more harm than good. Genuinely funny episodes.

### ERNEST SCARED STUPID — RATING 2.3
1991     PG     Comedy     Age 12+     91 min.     Color

Comical Halloween adventure featuring Ernest as a garbage collector who accidentally releases a grotesque troll from its tomb. He begins a hi-tech war against the troll with the help of some children. The fast-paced action and hysterical sight gags will keep the kids laughing! A few moderate crude words, slapstick violence, and some occultic figures are not portrayed positively or intended to be taken seriously.

### EXODUS — RATING 2.8
1960     NR     Docudrama     Age 12+     213 min.     Color

Paul Newman and Eva Marie Saint star in this spectacular historical film about the struggles encountered by Jewish refugees in the new Israel. Developed around the Palestinian war for liberation, *Exodus* features dramatic scenes such as Jews escaping from a Cyprus detention camp and running a blockade set up by the British. Stirring musical score. Audiences will benefit from the informative nature of this film.

### FAHRENHEIT 451 — RATING 3.5
1966     NR     Science Fiction     Age 17+     112 min.     Color

Outstanding futuristic study about a society that forbids the printing and ownership of books. Montag is a young fireman who secretly examines several titles to see what they contain. Once he has tasted the richness and value of good books, he begins to question the rationale for banning them. Man burned to death in one scene. Somewhat depressing, but overall an intriguing film.

**FAIL-SAFE** RATING 3.7
1964    NR    Adventure              Age 12+    111 min.    B&W
A U.S. strategic bomber is mistakenly ordered to drop a nuclear bomb on Moscow. Air Force and high-ranking government officials desperately try to persuade him to turn back. But his secret orders prevent him from obeying any radio commands beyond the "fail safe" point on his mission. The leaders of both the U.S. and Russia strive to avoid a crisis. Surprising, dramatic ending. Starring Henry Fonda and Walter Matthau. Very suspenseful drama.

**FALLEN IDOL** RATING 3.8
1949    NR    Drama                  Age 12+    94 min.     B&W
An ambassador's young son idolizes a crafty household servant whose wife is killed. The servant's wife was unpleasant and he was in love with an embassy employee. Without realizing it, the boy brings suspicion on the servant. Basically told through the eyes of the little boy, this outstanding adaptation of the Graham Greene novel will capture the imagination of audiences.

**FAMILY UPSIDE DOWN, A** RATING 3.2
1978    TVM   Drama                  Age 17+    100 min.    Color
Fred Astaire and Helen Hayes star as an elderly couple who become more and more dependent on their children in this realistic, honest drama. Astaire, a retired house painter devastated by heart attacks, ends up in a rest home, leaving his fretful wife to pick up the pieces. Tension builds and tempers flair sometimes, but they overcome their difficulties with love and patience. A thought provoking and enjoyable work.

**FANTASIA** RATING 4.0
1940    NR    Musical-Fantasy        Age 04+    120 min.    Color
Disney soars to new heights with this varied collection of animated classics. These include Stravinsky's "Rite of Spring" and "The Sorcerer's Apprentice" featuring Mickey Mouse. Most memorable is Tchaikovsky's "Nutcracker Suite" showing fairies decorating flowers. The classical music adds to the grandiose flavor. A few of the sequences could frighten small children.

**FANTASTIC VOYAGE** RATING 3.2
1966    NR    Adventure-Science Fiction   Age 06+    100 min.    Color
In this unusual futuristic film, a team of scientists are shrunk down to microscopic size. They explore the inner workings of the human body, starting with a ride through the blood stream. The body's immune system regards them as bacterial infections and attacks them. Intriguing action and an informative story will keep audiences on the edge of their seats. Cast includes Raquel Welch, Edmond O'Brien, Arthur Kennedy and James Brolin.

**FAR FROM HOME: THE ADVENTURES OF YELLOW DOG** RATING 3.2
1995    PG    Adventure              Age 12+    81 min.     Color
Think of this as *Old Yeller* with a happy ending. A courageous boy and his dog become lost when they are thrown overboard from a boat during a fierce storm. They must brave the wilderness, attacks by wolves and other adventures as they battle their way back home. A good family movie for all with a positive message. Two moderate obscenities. Also contains some violence that may scare younger children.

**FAREWELL TO ARMS, A** RATING 3.5
1932    NR    Drama                  Age 12+    78 min.     B&W
Helen Hayes shines in this truthful adaptation of Hemingway's classic World War I romance between an American ambulance driver assigned to the Italian Army and a British nurse. Their deep felt relationship comes to a sad, poignant ending. Adolphe Menjou flawlessly plays an Italian army officer and Gary Cooper offers his handsome "good guy" looks. Charles Lang won an Oscar for his lavish cinematography.

**FARMER'S DAUGHTER, THE** RATING 3.2
1947    NR    Comedy-Drama           Age 12+    97 min.     B&W
A stubborn Swedish girl runs for a Congressional seat against her lover in this enjoyable comedy. Loretta Young won an Oscar for her delightful performance. This film presents a combination of comedy and patriotism. Also starring Ethel Barrymore and James Arness, *The Farmer's Daughter* became a TV series.

## FATHER FIGURE — RATING 3.3
**1980 TVM Drama Age 12+ 94 min. Color**

Howard, a penitent widower (Hal Linden), attempts to be reconciled with his two young embittered sons whom he hasn't seen in five years. Howard is living with a woman when his sons come to visit him for the summer. The film emphasizes the relationship of Howard and his two sons with their conflicts as well as their impressions of love. Unfortunately, the film is accepting of Howard living with a woman out of wedlock.

## FATHER GOOSE — RATING 2.8
**1964 NR Comedy Age 06+ 115 min. Color**

Cary Grant trades his usual dapper wardrobe for the ragged clothes of a South Seas bum on a Pacific island during World War II. He is hired by the Australian navy to watch for enemy planes. However, during his mission, he reluctantly ends up guarding a stranded school teacher (Leslie Caron) and her school class who are fleeing from the Japanese. A fun family feature.

## FATHER OF THE BRIDE — RATING 3.3
**1991 PG Comedy Age 12+ 105 min. Color**

Enjoyable remake of the classic 1950 comedy about a father (Steve Martin) and his special relationship with his daughter Annie. When Annie comes home from college to inform him that she's engaged, he experiences some misgivings about the young man he's never met. This is a light-hearted, entertaining, romantic comedy suitable for older age groups. Two sexually oriented remarks and two homosexuals portrayed in a humorous light.

## FATHER OF THE BRIDE II — RATING 3.5(e)
**1995 PG Comedy Age 12+ 106 min. Color**

Steve Martin continues his role from the 1991 Father of the Bride. Now his daughter announces he will become a grandfather. A short time later his wife discovers that she too is pregnant. The idea of becoming a middle-aged father and a young grandfather simultaneously throws George Banks into a frenzy. Lots of laughs and good family fun with a few sexually suggestive remarks.

## FATHER'S LITTLE DIVIDEND — RATING 3.0
**1951 NR Comedy Age 12+ 82 min. B&W**

In this joyous sequel to FATHER OF THE BRIDE, Spencer Tracy again plays the father of Elizabeth Taylor who is now married and is going to have a baby. Tracy doesn't relish being a grandfather and becomes a bit indignant. He ends up playing babysitter, which is one of the funnier highlights of this show. This comedy will tickle audiences. Also available in the computer-colored edition.

## FIDDLER ON THE ROOF — RATING 3.3
**1971 G Musical-Drama Age 12+ 180 min. Color**

Tevye, a Jewish farmer, tries to preserve his Jewish heritage in spite of persecution in the small Russian-Jewish village of Anatevka. A rousing score includes such immortal songs as "Matchmaker, Matchmaker" and "Sunrise, Sunset". Based on the long-running Broadway smash, this film does justice to the brilliant characterizations and thoughtful story line.

## FIGHTING PRINCE OF DONEGAL, THE — RATING 3.0
**1966 NR Adventure Age 06+ 110 min. Color**

A young Irish prince escapes from an English prison and returns to Ireland to recapture his castle and girlfriend in a rousing battle. Dazzling, swashbuckling feature filmed on location, this Disney adventure film set in the 16th century is a must-see for audiences of all ages. A lively piece of fun.

## FIRE — RATING 2.3
**1977 TVM Adventure Age 12+ 98 min. Color**

Sam Brisbane (Ernest Borgnine) is the owner of a lumber mill in Silverton, Oregon. The town and its residents are threatened by a raging forest fire that is out of control. Peggy and Alex must set aside their marital differences in order to help care for the many victims of the fire. This is a suspenseful action movie which depicts people's willingness to pull together during a disaster.

### FIRST KNIGHT  RATING 3.5 (e)
1995　　PG-13　　Drama　　　　　　　Age 17+　　132 min.　　　　Color

An adaptation of King Arthur, Lancelot and Guinevere. King Arthur (Sean Connery) loves the young Guinevere and plans to marry her until she falls in love with handsome Lancelot (Richard Gere). The battle between the aging King Arthur and Lancelot for the love of Guinevere is one of the classic love stories of all time. Some violent battle scenes make this a film appropriate for older audiences.

### FLIGHT OF THE NAVIGATOR  RATING 3.0
1986　　PG　　Adventure-Drama　　　　Age 06+　　90 min.　　　　Color

A young boy is kidnapped by an alien space ship and whisked away for eight years. His return is difficult because his traveling through space kept him from aging. Because of scientific data implanted in his brain, both aliens and the local space authorities want access to the boy and his information. A thrilling adventure story, especially for science fiction fans. Some moderate crudities and two obscenities.

### FLINTSTONES, THE  RATING 2.8
1994　　PG　　Comedy　　　　　　　Age 06+　　92 min.　　　　Color

Amusing live-action film about that "modern Stone Age family" in Bedrock. Fred (John Goodman) gives his friend Barney all of his savings so that he and his wife Betty can adopt a child named Bam-Bam. Predictable storyline provides messages about friendship, honesty, and the shallow rewards of "instant wealth." Some slapstick violence and some sexually suggestive action.

### FLOOD  RATING 2.7
1976　　TVM　　Adventure　　　　　　Age 12+　　98 min.　　　　Color

Steve Brannigan and Paul seem to be the only people in a fishing resort in Brownsville who fully comprehend the implications of a leaking dam. The mayor, John Cutler, and the city council choose to ignore the engineer's report warning of impending danger to the town. A suspenseful drama unfolds as the dam begins to crumble due to the pressure of the rain swollen lake.

### FLOWER DRUM SONG  RATING 2.3
1961　　NR　　Musical　　　　　　　Age 06+　　133 min.　　　　Color

This oriental tale centers around a modern San Francisco kid challenging the old-fashioned views of his rigid Chinese father. It also features some romances, including one in which a nightclub owner sends for a bride from China, then shifts his attention to another. An arranged oriental wedding is featured, complete with its ancient customs. A sweet Rodgers and Hammerstein score and decent choreography.

### FLYING LEATHERNECKS  RATING 2.8
1951　　NR　　Adventure-War　　　　Age 12+　　102 min.　　　　Color

John Wayne plays a merciless Marine commander of an aerial World War II fighting force. He's confronted by a more compassionate officer concerning his obvious cruelty toward his men. Fine dramatic exchanges between the leads and realistic aerial chases make this a very good World War II film. A solid piece of work.

### FLYING TIGERS  RATING 2.8
1942　　NR　　Adventure-War　　　　Age 12+　　100 min.　　　　B&W

World War II melodrama features an air squadron officer (John Wayne) and his rash flying buddy trying to win the love of an attractive nurse while battling the Japanese. Heart-stopping dogfight scenes and pretty fair acting make this a sure-fire winner. The Flying Tigers were American pilots stationed in China who helped fight the invading Japanese prior to the bombing of Pearl Harbor.

### FOLLOW ME, BOYS!  RATING 2.7
1966　　NR　　Drama　　　　　　　Age 06+　　131 min.　　　　Color

This simple, heartfelt tale features Fred MacMurray as the founder of a Boy Scout troop in a 1930's neighborhood. He finds great satisfaction in fulfilling his lifelong dream of leading a troop. Produced with great sincerity of heart, *Follow Me, Boys* is enjoyable Disney fare for the whole family. All-star cast includes MacMurray, Vera Miles and Lillian Gish.

## Secular Movies

**FOOTBALL FEVER** — RATING 3.0(e)
19??    NR    Comedy-Sports    Age 06+    30 min.    Color
Hilarious football special taken from actual NFL game footage. Features bloopers and other comical antics. Good for laughs.

**FOOTBALL FOLLIES** — RATING 3.0(e)
1980    NR    Comedy-Sports    Age 06+    30 min.    Color
Wacky football comedy showing all sorts of crazy bloopers taken from actual NFL football games. "Headcracker Suite" music!

**FOR THE LOVE OF BENJI** — RATING 3.0
1977    G    Adventure    Age 06+    94 min.    Color
An international spy ring pursues our little canine friend through the streets of Athens for the secret formula hidden on his paw. Benji turns the tables on them and discovers a pseudo CIA agent in the bargain. The entire family will enjoy this amusing animal film. Sequel is *Oh Heavenly Dog*.

**FORBIDDEN PLANET** — RATING 3.7
1956    NR    Science Fiction-Adventure    Age 12+    98 min.    Color
*Forbidden Planet* is essentially a 1950's science-fiction rendition of Shakespeare's play, *The Tempest*. Space explorers marooned on Planet Altair come across a madman (Walter Pidgeon) who has built an empire with the aid of his daughter and a robot. The explorers soon find themselves at the mercy of a monster he's created. This intriguing story with ingenious special effects and weird electronic music will appeal to science fiction buffs.

**FOREIGN CORRESPONDENT** — RATING 4.0
1940    NR    Mystery-Drama    Age 12+    120 min.    B&W
In this fascinating Hitchcock spy thriller, an American reporter becomes embroiled in international intrigue - from passionate romance to dealings with villainous Nazi gangs. Reporter Joel McCrae goes to Europe just before World War II to investigate political developments. He observes the assassination of a Dutch diplomat and soon finds himself in danger. One of Hitchcock's best.

**FOREVER YOUNG** — RATING 3.3
1992    PG    Drama    Age 12+    102 min.    Color
A young man (Mel Gibson) volunteers to be "frozen" during a 1939 cryogenics experiment after his girlfriend slips into a coma. He is awakened 50 years later and fills in the gaps with the help of some new friends. Viewers will be captivated by this fascinating drama about friendship, trust, and kindness. Five mild and moderate crude words and one obscenity.

**FOUR FEATHERS** — RATING 3.2
1977    TVM    Adventure-Drama    Age 12+    110 min.    Color
A TV remake of the 1939 classic, this movie tells the story of a young Britisher (Beau Bridges) who has deserted military service during wartime in favor of his wife and family. To prove that he is not a coward, he joins his friends in a fight against Sudanese tribesmen in Africa. His exploits propel him into some suspenseful, dangerous missions. Contains quite a bit of graphic fighting and hand-to-hand battles.

**FOX AND THE HOUND, THE** — RATING 3.2
1981    G    Adventure    Age 06+    83 min.    Color
Heartwarming, feature-length Disney cartoon about a fox orphaned when his mother is killed by hunters. He is befriended by a wise owl, the Widow Tweed and a new hound puppy. When conflict develops between the fox and the hound, they must count on their friendship to get them through. The whole family will enjoy this delightful adventure. An attacking bear may scare very young children.

### FRANK AND OLLIE — RATING 2.5(e)
1995     PG     Documentary     Age 12+     89 min.     Color

A surprisingly entertaining story about two of Walt Disney's most famous animators. The film tracks their lives and their work at Disney in their own words, and shows off their unique sense of humor. Frank and Ollie have known each other since 1931 and have worked on such films as *Snow White, Bambi* and *Pinocchio*. A gentle documentary with fascinating behind-the-scene looks into the world of animation.

### FREAKY FRIDAY — RATING 3.2
1977     G     Comedy     Age 06+     98 min.     Color

A mother and daughter magically swap roles for a day with hilarious results in this insightful Disney comedy-fantasy. Among other things, the 13-year-old girl drives a car recklessly without a license. Some police cars chasing her are destroyed in comical ways. Remarkable performances by Barbara Harris and Jodie Foster. Appropriate for the whole family.

### FREE WILLY — RATING 3.3
1993     PG     Drama     Age 06+     112 min.     Color

Jesse, a troubled 12-year-old boy, makes an unusual friend in Willy, a killer whale at an amusement park. He gains a new sense of self-esteem when he discovers that he can coax more tricks out of Willy than the trainer can. Reluctantly, he realizes that Willy should be set free to enjoy his natural habitat. Somewhat predictable, but an entertaining film for children. Two moderate crude words.

### FREE WILLY 2 — RATING 3.0(e)
1995     PG     Drama     Age 06+     93 min.     Color

Jesse is back in this sequel to the 1993 original *Free Willy*. On a camping trip with his foster family in the Pacific Northwest Jesse spots Willy the whale with his new whale family. When an oil tanker runs aground and causes an oil spill, both Willy's and Jesse's families are in danger. Jesse and his brother learn to work together to save Willy. Some Native American spiritism is included.

### FRIENDLY PERSUASION — RATING 4.0
1956     NR     Drama     Age 12+     140 min.     Color

In southern Indiana, a serene Quaker family struggles to maintain its peaceful existence amid the turmoil of the Civil War. They help two runaway slaves to find freedom. Their pacifist son goes off to war. Tension mounts when two confederate soldiers come to their home. Touching portrayals by Gary Cooper and Dorothy McGuire in this beautiful film. Some battlefield violence.

### FUNNY FACE — RATING 3.7
1957     NR     Musical     Age 12+     103 min.     Color

The ingratiating Fred Astaire plays a sophisticated photographer who turns a naive girl (Audrey Hepburn) into an alluring Paris fashion model. In time he falls in love with the "funny face" of the girl. This elegant musical includes Gershwin hits "S'Wonderful" and "How Long Has This Been Goin' On?" A fairy tale style of plot and colorful French scenery provide a welcome escape.

### FUNNY GIRL — RATING 3.5
1968     G     Musical-Drama     Age 06+     155 min.     Color

Barbara Streisand portrays Ziegfield Follies comedienne Fanny Brice. She sings, dances on roller skates, and cracks jokes, but candidly shows the unhappiness behind the mask of a clown. The first part of the film portrays her rise to stardom and the latter part, her domestic difficulties. The bittersweet musical score includes an unforgettable finale, "Don't Rain On My Parade". Top-notch film. Co-stars Omar Sharif.

### GAMBIT — RATING 3.3
1966     NR     Comedy     Age 12+     109 min.     Color

A slimy villain (Michael Caine) and a Eurasian art thief (Shirley MacLaine) team up to abscond with a priceless piece of sculpture. They aren't all that adept, and things turn out all wrong for them. This all makes for great fun. Suspenseful and thrilling. Crime is glorified somewhat, but Caine turns from his misguided ways to keep the woman he loves.

## GANDHI
**RATING 3.7**
1983    PG    Docudrama    Age 12+    188 min.    Color

This grand, award-winning epic tells the story of the famous Indian leader and his struggle for racial justice and political independence for India. Beginning with his fight for racial justice in South Africa in the 1890's, the story moves to India where he begins his long struggle to win India's independence from the British Empire. Ben Kingsley offers a sensitive and profound portrayal of Gandhi. Several violent scenes.

## GATHERING, THE
**RATING 3.5**
1977    TVM    Drama    Age 12+    104 min.    Color

A dying man (Ed Asner) realizes he has mistakenly alienated his family. With the help of his wife (Maureen Stapleton) the children return home for Christmas, unaware of their father's condition. A powerful message of restoring relationships with one's family comes through clearly. *The Gathering* is a touching Christmas special appropriate for all seasons.

## GENTLE GIANT
**RATING 2.8**
1967    G    Adventure-Drama    Age 06+    93 min.    Color

Six-year-old Mark must learn to deal with the death of his older brother. While visiting the Canadian Rockies with his dad, Mark finds a baby bear and befriends it. This causes tension between Mark, who wants to raise the bear, and his parents, who fear the wild animal will eventually turn wild.

## GETTYSBURG
**RATING 2.8**
1993    PG    Drama    Age 12+    103 min.    Color

An engrossing and poignant retelling of the most famous battle in American history. The Union and Confederacy square off for three days with huge infantry and artillery assaults. During the breaks between the fighting, the soldiers discuss their personal feelings about the war and express deeply held religious views. General Robert E. Lee, the Confederate leader, seeks God's guidance. Many mild crude words and moderately violent scenes, but nothing gory.

## GHOST AND MR. CHICKEN
**RATING 2.3**
1966    NR    Comedy    Age 06+    90 min.    Color

Don Knotts stars in this outlandish comedy about a meek typesetter named Luther who desperately wants to become a reporter. After one mishap that would indicate he is unsuitable, an opportunity comes along for him to spend the night in a "haunted" house and then write a feature story about the experience. He gets more than he bargained for when he gets involved in a murder.

## GIANT
**RATING 3.7**
1956    NR    Drama    Age 12+    201 min.    Color

Rock Hudson and Elizabeth Taylor star in this immortal Western saga that traces a Texas oil baron's family through two generations. Dramatizes the historical transformation of cattle barons to oil millionaires. James Dean plays a ranch hand who turns against Hudson. He dominates the movie when he strikes oil and becomes a contender on the local scene. *Giant* will overwhelm audiences with this grand taste of Texas.

## GIANT OF THUNDER MOUNTAIN, THE
**RATING 2.0(e)**
1994    PG    Adventure    Age 06+    90 min (e)    Color

Adventure tale set in the 1890's about three youngsters who come down with gold rush fever. They encounter a gentle, reclusive giant who befriends them and is later accused of kidnapping them. Great scenery and appealing characters for children, though parents may not be fully entertained. Young viewers will realize the value of truth and trust. A few intense, violent scenes, but generally appropriate for children under 12.

## GIDEON'S TRUMPET
**RATING 3.7**
1980    TVM    Docudrama    Age 12+    105 min.    Color

This serious docudrama deals with an actual Supreme Court case that altered legal history forever. Henry Fonda plays an uneducated, two-bit criminal who studies the law and convinces the court that even the poorest offender should be represented by legal counsel. Convicted of burglary, he wins a retrial from the Supreme Court. Jose Ferrer and John Houseman also star. Interesting drama and good acting. Some mildly crude words.

### GIFT OF LOVE, THE                                                           RATING 2.5
**1978      TVM        Drama                    Age 12+          100 min.           Color**
Nineteen-year-old Beth is an orphan who goes to live with her wealthy aunt and uncle in New York City in 1902. Heart broken over the prospects of an arranged marriage with a man she doesn't love, Beth soon meets and falls in love with a poor Swiss immigrant named Rudy. She is faced with the difficult decision of marrying into wealth or happiness. Lovely costumes of the early 20th century.

### GIGI                                                                        RATING 4.0
**1958      NR         Musical                  Age 12+          116 min.           Color**
This classy turn-of-the-century musical focuses on the training of a young Parisian beauty and her "coming out" into French society. Leslie Caron plays the charming young woman who's being pursued by socialite Louis Jourdan. She's watched over by fatherly Maurice Chevalier. A Lerner and Loewe score includes such unforgettable tunes, as "Thank Heaven for Little Girls" and "I Remember It Well". Great entertainment.

### GIRL CRAZY                                                                  RATING 3.3
**1943      NR         Musical                  Age 12+          99 min.            B&W**
Mickey Rooney plays a young, rich kid who is banished to a boarding school out west by his father because of his incorrigible girl-chasing ways. This tactic fails when he discovers Judy Garland. Giddy Gershwin tunes such as "I Got Rhythm" and "Embraceable You" add to the show's lighthearted appeal.

### GIRL WHO SPELLED FREEDOM                                                    RATING 3.5
**1985      TVM        Drama                    Age 06+          90 min.            Color**
In 1979, teenager Linn Yann (Jode Chinn) and her family escape from war torn Cambodia and are taken in by a caring American family in Chattanooga, TN. In their new environment, they must contend with indoor bathrooms, supermarkets and the prejudices of the local community. Initially Linn Yann speaks very little English but within four years she qualifies to compete in a national spelling bee contest. An inspiring true story.

### GLASS MENAGERIE                                                             RATING 3.3
**1987      PG         Drama                    Age 17+          134 min.           Color**
Joanne Woodward plays a faded southern belle mother in the 1930's who lives with her grown son and daughter in a modest apartment. Her shy daughter, Laura, enjoys playing phonograph records and tending to her collection of glass figurines. After a dinner for Jim, one of her son's single friends, Laura and Jim have a tender conversation in which he shows genuine compassion and concern for Laura. A touching human drama from a play by Tennessee Williams.

### GLORIA                                                                      RATING 3.0
**1980      G          Adventure-Drama          Age 17+          121 min.           Color**
A former mob mistress and the young son of her neighbor try to escape from a mafia gang who is out to kill them. The mob follows them as they run from one hiding place to another. Gloria finally decides she must confront the men and deal the with the problem head-on. Intense, engrossing drama. Few rough words and one profanity.

### GNOME MOBILE, THE                                                           RATING 2.7
**1967      NR         Comedy-Fantasy           Age 06+          84 min.            Color**
In this Disney delight, Walter Brennan plays both a wealthy businessman and a gnome looking for a lost colony of gnomes (small underground beings). Along the way, he encounters an evil side show operator who's capturing gnomes for his show. This exuberant comedy for kids shines with a cute story line and fun special effects. Ed Wynn also stars in this fantasy classic.

### GOING BANANAS                                                               RATING 2.0(e)
**1988      PG         Comedy                   Age 06+          95 min.            Color**
Dom Deluise plays a fussy attendant who accompanies a young boy named Benjamin on a sight-seeing tour of Africa. Deluise doesn't get along with the animals and has numerous comical encounters with them. Along the way, they acquire a monkey named Bonzo. Unfortunately, Bonzo falls into the hands of a circus manager, and the crazy antics get underway again when Deluise and company attempt to recover Bonzo.

## Secular Movies

### GOING MY WAY — RATING 3.7
1944  NR  Drama-Comedy  Age 12+  126 min.  B&W

Bing Crosby plays Father O'Malley, a singing young priest who's assigned to replace a traditional-thinking superior played by Barry Fitzgerald. Their gentle, humorous confrontations are lots of fun. Bing wins him over along with some tough street kids. Bing croons some memorable songs, including "Swinging on a Star" and "Too-ra-loo-ra-loo-ra". This sentimental drama is still a treat for the whole family.

### GOLD DIGGERS: THE SECRET OF BEAR MOUNTAIN — RATING 3.5(e)
1995  PG  Adventure  Age 06+  93min.  Color

Two 13-year-old girls become friends during the summer of 1983. One has just moved to a small country town from the city and the other is the local social outcast. Each learns valuable lessons about friendship as they explore Bear Mountain together in search of a lost gold mine. With enough adventure and suspense to entertain both boys and girls, all ages will enjoy this family-friendly film.

### GOLDEN AGE OF COMEDY, THE (silent) — RATING 4.0
1957  NR  Comedy  Age 06+  78 min.  B&W

This silent film classics collection presents the best from the greatest comedy stars of yesteryear. Among others, it contains Laurel and Hardy's *Two Tars*, Will Rogers' impersonations of silent actors, and rare segments of the follies of Harry Langdon. Robert Youngston compiled this unique series of clips to introduce movie buffs to the silent golden days of movie comedy. An unforgettable treasure.

### GONE ARE THE DAYES — RATING 2.8
1984  NR  Comedy  Age 06+  90 min.  Color

The Dayes family has just witnessed a gangland style murder, and an odd-ball detective (Harvey Korman) is assigned to protect them from the vengeance of a mob. The fun begins when the harried family tries to get away from the criminals and their watchful bodyguard. This zany Disney comedy has some enjoyable acting and colorful photography.

### GONE WITH THE WIND — RATING 4.0
1939  NR  Drama  Age 12+  230 min.  Color

This historical film spectacle, based on Margaret Mitchell's novel, is one of the best. It tells of the melodramatic life of Scarlett O'Hara (Vivien Leigh), a "southern belle" spitfire, during the Civil War. Clark Gable, as the dashing Rhett Butler, shines as Scarlett's lover. The film captures the drama and destruction of the war, especially the scene of the burning of Atlanta. Olivia de Haviland and Leslie Howard also star.

### GOOD EARTH, THE — RATING 4.0
1937  NR  Drama  Age 12+  138 min.  B&W

The rise of a Chinese peasant family to wealth and power is depicted in this careful adaptation of Pearl Buck's immortal novel. It vividly portrays the destructive effects of greed upon the family and the people's struggle for survival against plague and famine. Luise Rainier won an award for her quiet portrayal of the understanding wife. Brilliant direction and breathtaking special effects make this film one of the great ones.

### GOODBYE MR. CHIPS — RATING 3.8
1939  NR  Drama  Age 12+  114 min.  B&W

Oscar-winning Robert Donat masterfully portrays an introverted Latin teacher in an English boys' school in this rendering of the James Hilton novel. The film traces his clumsy beginnings to the days when he's beloved by all of the students. This wonderful tale will pull on everyone's heartstrings.

### GOOFY MOVIE, A — RATING 3.0(e)
1995  G  Comedy  Age 04+  76 min.  Color

A fun cartoon for small children about the adventures of Goofy and his teenage son, Max, as they go camping in order to spend some quality time together. Their trip out West is full of exciting events such as meeting Bigfoot and taking a wild water ride. These goofy antics are sure to keep the children entertained. Some mild cartoon violence.

### GORDY
**RATING 2.0(e)**
1995   G   Comedy   Age 06+   89 min.   Color

The extraordinary story of a common pig, Gordy, who goes in search of his parents and becomes famous. He is befriended by Jinnie Sue, a teenage, country singer who discovers that Gordy is a talking pig. After Gordy saves a millionaire's son from drowning, this clever pig becomes rich and famous. A few scary scenes of the sausage factory may frighten youngsters.

### GRAPES OF WRATH, THE
**RATING 4.0**
1940   NR   Drama   Age 12+   128 min.   B&W

Henry Fonda plays an ex-con in this classic about a group of migratory farmhands from Oklahoma trying to get to California during the Depression. They hope to find work and prosperity there, but only encounter prejudice and hatred. Along with many other desperate people, they end up in crowded, cruel work camps. Based on Steinbeck's novel, this film is a sobering commentary on the misery of the Depression. A gripping, masterful drama.

### GRASS IS ALWAYS GREENER OVER THE SEPTIC TANK, THE
**RATING 2.8**
1978   TVM   Comedy   Age 12+   98 min.   Color

Carol Burnett and Charles Grodin star as a couple fed up with urban life. In an attempt to better their lives, they move to the suburbs only to face a whole new set of problems such as housing repairs, obnoxious insurance salesmen and newfangled sex education in the schools. Based on Erma Bombeck's humorous book, the movie is a treat to watch.

### GREAT DAY IN HARLEM, A
**RATING 3.0(e)**
1995   NR   Documentary   Age 17+   70 min.(e)   Color

A superb documentary worthy of its title, this film is based on a photograph taken in Brooklyn, New York, of about 30 of the all-time great jazz musicians. Jean Bach has taken Art Kane's now-famous photo and captured its nostalgia and excitement with interviews of some of the jazz artists still living. Music lovers will appreciate this tribute, disappointed only because the film is too short.

### GREAT DICTATOR, THE
**RATING 3.8**
1940   NR   Comedy   Age 12+   128 min.   B&W

Charlie Chaplin doubles as a Jewish barber and a dictator of the fictional country of Tomania in this whimsical satire about Adolf Hitler. Jack Oakie plays Benzini Napaloni, the ruler of the enemy country of Bacteria. This is Chaplin's first full-length talkie, and he directs and stars in it with his usual flair.

### GREAT ESCAPE, THE
**RATING 4.0**
1963   NR   Adventure   Age 06+   173 min.   Color

Exquisitely filmed on location in Germany, this powerhouse movie deals with the courageous escape planned by Allied P.O.W.'s from a World War II prison camp. All of the rowdy, uncooperative American prisoners are grouped in one area, so trouble is bound to erupt. A magnificent all-star cast just makes a great script that much better. Suspenseful action scene of a motorcycle chase with Steve McQueen. Great fun! Several hells and damns.

### GREAT EXPECTATIONS
**RATING 4.0**
1946   NR   Drama   Age 06+   118 min.   B&W

A secret benefactor turns a poor orphan lad into a wealthy young gentleman in this Dickens masterpiece. The second of the three adaptations produced from this novel, this one has it all - acting, directing, scripting, and photography. Classic film buffs will appreciate all the work that went into its production. It was filmed again in 1974 as a made-for-TV movie.

### GREAT LOCOMOTIVE CHASE, THE
**RATING 2.8**
1956   NR   Adventure   Age 06+   85 min.   Color

Fess Parker plays a Yankee soldier in the Civil War who's sent behind enemy lines to destroy strategic railroad bridges. In the process, he captures and makes off with a Confederate supply train, and the train conductor follows in hot pursuit. Suspenseful but not too melodramatic. Youngsters as well as adults will enjoy this thrilling tale based on actual historical events.

## GREAT MUPPET CAPER, THE  RATING 3.3
1981  G  Comedy  Age 06+  96 min.  Color

Kermit the frog and Fozzie Bear star in the continuing saga of the muppets. This time, Kermit and Fozzie must travel to England to solve a diamond heist, a la Sherlock Holmes. Along the way, they meet Miss Piggy and the rest of the Muppet Gang. Jim Henson's muppet magic and clever dialogue will delight young and old alike. A wonderful film for the whole family to sit down and enjoy

## GREAT RACE, THE  RATING 2.8
1965  NR  Comedy  Age 06+  150 min.  Color

Set in the early 1900's, this lengthy but funny slapstick comedy describes the first New York to Paris auto race. All the humorous antics along the way are great fun. A cast of thousands includes such notables as Tony Curtis, Natalie Wood, Jack Lemmon, Peter Falk, and Vivian Vance. A hilarious dueling match and slap-bang barroom brawl add to the fun. Good light-hearted amusement.

## GREATEST SHOW ON EARTH, THE  RATING 3.7
1952  NR  Drama  Age 06+  153 min.  Color

This humongous spectacle takes a peek at life under the Big Top, revealing chills and thrills of perilous stunts and the lonely, backstage lives of circus performers. Jimmy Stewart plays a clown with an unknown past. Subplots include a love triangle between the circus owner (Charlton Heston) and two trapeze artists, and conflict between a cruel elephant trainer and his assistant.

## GREEN EYES  RATING 3.7(e)
1976  TVM  Drama  Age 12+  97 min.  Color

A black Vietnam veteran returns to Saigon looking for his son borne by a local barmaid. His search leads to orphanages, tin shacks and dirty streets full of crippled, starving beggars and homeless children. Their plight and a little boy named Trung challenge him to love sacrificially. In a touching reunion scene, the anguished mother tells the American vet about their son's tragic fate. Out-of-wedlock sexual relations treated lightly.

## GREEN PASTURES  RATING 3.8
1936  NR  Musical  Age 12+  93 min.  B&W

An all-black cast vividly narrates the familiar biblical stories of creation, Noah, and Moses from a different perspective in this rousing musical. Rex Ingram does a marvelous job as "de Lawd". A realistic piece of work finely crafted and cleverly directed, *Green Pastures* will capture your heart.

## GREY FOX  RATING 3.6
1982  PG  Western Drama  Age 12+  92 min.  Color

In 1903, Bill Miner, a notorious stagecoach robber, is released from prison in California after serving thirty-three years. Soft spoken Miner, known as the "gentleman bandit", takes to robbing trains in Washington State and British Columbia. He even falls in love and plans to marry a genteel Canadian lady. Eventually the law closes in. He's brought to life by Richard Farnsworth's acting. Intriguing true story.

## GREYFRIARS BOBBY  RATING 2.7
1961  NR  Drama-Comedy  Age 06+  89 min.  Color

A little Skye terrier wins over the residents of the 19th century city of Edinburgh, Scotland, in this British Disney film. The dog is adopted by the entire town after his warm hearted owner (Donald Crisp) dies. This charming story boasts glorious Scottish scenery and glowing performances. Young children will enjoy it.

## GROUNDHOG DAY  RATING 3.5
1993  PG  Comedy  Age 12+  103 min.  Color

A grumpy, arrogant TV weatherman goes to a small Pennsylvania town to cover Groundhog Day festivities. To his horror, he gets stuck in a time warp that replays the last 24 hours over and over. Witty comedy-fantasy with clever twists and turns that is a perfect vehicle for Murray. Some moderate violence and dark humor about suicide may scare younger children.

### GUMBY THE MOVIE
**RATING 2.0(e)**
1995  G  Comedy  Age 04+  90 min.  Color

A cute claymation movie about Gumby and his dog, the famous characters from the 1950's TV show. In this updated version, Gumby's band plays such good music it makes his dog, Lowbelly, cry pearls. Some bullies find out about it and kidnap Lowbelly to get the pearls. Then they go after Gumby himself. Definitely a movie for the kids, *Gumby* contains some violence when dealing with the bad guys.

### GUNGA DIN
**RATING 4.0**
1939  NR  Adventure  Age 06+  117 min.  B&W

Based on Rudyard Kipling's famous poem, this film deals with three British soldiers (Cary Grant, Douglas Fairbanks, Victor McLaglen) in a remote area of 19th century India. A native water boy, Gunga Din, is enamored with bugles and is given one as a reward. When a savage army of Punjab Indians attacks, Gunga Din reacts with a dramatic, sacrificial bugle call. Some intense fighting and a scary snakepit scene. One of the best.

### GUNS OF NAVARONE, THE
**RATING 3.8**
1961  NR  Adventure  Age 12+  157 min.  Color

During World War II, a squad of Allied commandos is assigned to blow up a huge closely guarded German fortress in the Aegean Sea. They are aided by a group of untrained guerilla fighters in this seemingly impossible mission. Solid performances by Gregory Peck, David Niven, and Anthony Quinn enhance the tremendous screenplay. Outstanding special effects. Highly entertaining adventure film.

### GUS
**RATING 2.8**
1976  G  Comedy  Age 04+  96 min.  Color

A poorly performing California football team called the Atoms desperately searches for anything that will improve their team's ability to play. They discover a mule named Gus along with Andy his owner. Fortunately, Gus can kick a football great lengths, which means that they now have a chance to win. All sorts of funny antics take place during the ball games. Tim Conway stars in this fine Disney comedy.

### GUYS AND DOLLS
**RATING 3.0**
1955  NR  Musical  Age 12+  150 min.  Color

Marlon Brando and Frank Sinatra play two small-time New York gamblers in this Hollywood version of a classic Broadway musical. They place a wager about dating an attractive, shy Salvation Army girl (Jean Simmons) they have met. Show-stopping tunes include "Luck Be A Lady Tonight", "If I Were A Bell" and "Adelaide's Lament". Lavishly well done in all respects, this musical is one of the all-time greats.

### HAIL THE CONQUERING HERO
**RATING 4.0**
1944  NR  Comedy  Age 06+  101 min.  B&W

In this boisterous satirical comedy, an undersized young man (Eddie Bracken) in a small town is turned down by the army, but is mistaken for a wartime hero. He makes up a Marine-hero history for himself and gets in on some big time hero worship. William Demarest plays a character who almost steals the show with his humorous portrayal. This funny movie will appeal to every member of the family.

### HAMLET
**RATING 3.5**
1991  PG  Drama  Age 12+  135 min.  Color

Sweeping new version of Shakespeare's famous tale about murder and intrigue, with Mel Gibson magnificently portraying Hamlet. Directed by Franco Zefferelli ("Jesus of Nazareth"), this first-rate work combines exquisite cinematography with the humor and inimitable style of the Renaissance bard. Viewers who appreciate the classics will consider this film a true feast. Adult themes of revenge, murder and suicide.

### HANDFUL OF DUST
**RATING 3.7**
1988  PG  Drama  Age 17+  118 min.  Color

Based on a 1934 novel, *Handful of Dust* tells the rather strange, engrossing story of a young aristocratic British couple whose marriage goes awry. The wife has an adulterous affair which ends in heartache and despair. Heartbroken, her husband goes to South America and is captured by an English jungle emperor. First rate performances and cinematography will appeal to sophisticated moviegoers. Some female native breast nudity.

### HANS BRINKER  RATING 2.7
1979    NR    Musical    Age 06+    103 min.    Color

This enjoyable musical features the familiar tale of a Dutch lad who is primarily responsible for the healing of his bedridden father. Set in 1838 in Holland, *Hans Brinker* features some pleasant, picturesque ice skating scenes. An appealing holiday presentation to delight young and old alike. Stars Richard Basehart and Eleanor Parker.

### HANS CHRISTIAN ANDERSEN  RATING 3.0
1952    NR    Musical-Fantasy    Age 06+    112 min.    Color

Sprightly Danny Kaye plays the traveling story-teller who falls in love with a lovely ballerina in this enchanting musical fantasy. Ballet star Jean Marie gives a superb performance. Tuneful Frank Loesser score includes "Thumbelina" and "Inchworm". Children will love the magical quality of the fairy-tale characters.

### HAPPIEST MILLIONAIRE, THE  RATING 2.7
1967    NR    Musical-Comedy    Age 12+    118 min.    Color

This buoyant Disney romp tells of the wild and wooly lifestyle of Anthony J. Drexel Biddle, an eccentric Philadelphia millionaire. Biddle is definitely not much on conventional ways and lots of wacky things go amiss in his household. Based on a true story, this delightful musical has several toe-tapping melodies. Stars Fred MacMurray and Greer Garson.

### HATARI! (DANGER!)  RATING 3.2
1962    NR    Adventure    Age 12+    159 min.    Color

John Wayne plays the chief of a crew hunting animals for zoos around the world in this lively adventure-comedy. Picturesque action episodes shot in the wilds of Africa highlight this entertaining film. Three hunters chase giraffes, wildebeests and rhinos in a jeep. A magnificent Henry Mancini score offers good background music to heighten the action. Audiences will especially like this.

### HEART IS A LONELY HUNTER, THE  RATING 3.5
1968    G    Drama    Age 12+    125 min.    Color

The story of a compassionate deaf-mute (Alan Arkin) who helps people in a little Southern town and his friendship with a teenage girl (Sandra Locke). This tender, heart-warming film illustrates a striking contrast between the ultimate of human concern and the awful cruelty of men. Arkin received an Academy Award for his role. An inspirational, moving story.

### HEARTLAND  RATING 3.5
1979    PG    Drama-Western    Age 17+    96 min.    Color

A young widow and her daughter from Denver become housekeepers for a dour Scottish rancher on the frontier of Wyoming around 1910. Ultimately, the widow marries the rancher as a matter of convenience. Together they face the hostile winters and other hardships of their existence. Simple well-told and well-acted drama. Well worth watching.

### HEAVEN KNOWS MR. ALLISON  RATING 3.0
1957    NR    Adventure-Drama    Age 12+    105 min.    Color

A tough Marine corporal finds himself stranded along with a quiet Catholic nun on a remote Pacific island completely taken over by the Japanese during World War II. Although the story is rather implausible, the stellar performances by Robert Mitchum and Deborah Kerr make this film work. Audiences will be touched by it.

### HEAVYWEIGHTS  RATING 2.3
1995    PG    Comedy    Age 06+    97 min.    Color

A summer camp for overweight boys goes from bad to worse when the new owner puts the boys on a military style weight-loss program. After some stiff abuse, the boys rebel and as they do, they gain the self-esteem and the confidence that they had been lacking. A funny comedy for children with several moderate crude remarks, as well as some comic violence.

### HEIDI
**RATING 3.3(e)**
1968     TVM     Drama     Age 06+     110 min.     Color

This slick TV rendition of the beloved children's classic features a little Swiss miss taken from her doting grandfather to live with a merciless aunt. Through her love and kindness, Heidi favorably affects those she encounters. Director Blake Edward's daughter, Jennifer, delivers a fetching performance in the title role. Charming story for children of all ages.

### HEIRESS
**RATING 3.8**
1949     NR     Drama     Age 12+     115 min.     B&W

Olivia de Haviland brilliantly plays an extremely wealthy maiden chased by a crafty gold digger (Montgomery Clift) in this super adaptation of Henry James' novel WASHINGTON SQUARE. Ralph Richardson masterfully portrays the heiress' conservative, domineering father. Set in New York City during the early 1900's, this emotion-stirring drama will capture your heart.

### HELLCATS OF THE NAVY
**RATING 2.2**
1957     NR     Adventure-War     Age 12+     82 min.     B&W

Ronald Reagan and the First Lady co-star in this action film about the adventures of a U.S. Navy submarine during World War II. Reagan commands the sub whose mission is to detect Japanese mines for other submarines. When the commander apparently makes a judgment error, it looks like he's in trouble with his crew. This is the only movie the presidential couple appeared in together. Fairly good action sequences. Will appeal to most.

### HELLO DOLLY
**RATING 2.0**
1969     G     Musical     Age 12+     148 min.     Color

This flamboyant screen treatment of the Broadway hit features Barbra Streisand as a conniving widow who plays cupid only to discover that she herself has been matched. Also stars Gene Kelly and Walter Matthau and Louis Armstrong. Streisand's disarming stage presence makes this film a charming diversion.

### HENRY V
**RATING 3.7**
1989     PG     Drama     Age 17+     138 min.     Color

England's young monarch, Henry V, sets forth against France to recapture territory rightfully belonging to England. He's outnumbered five to one, but his faith in Almighty God inspires his men. One graphic battle scene is filled with deadly arrows, swords, battle axes and mace. Rich dialogue, from Shakespeare's pen, will be a special treat for Shakespeare fans. A spectacular adventure with some old English exclamatory profanity.

### HERBIE GOES BANANAS
**RATING 1.8**
1980     G     Comedy     Age 04+     100 min.     Color

The irrepressible Love Bug rides again for the fourth time in this rollicking Disney comedy. Herbie is bound to enter a Brazilian car race, but is hindered by numerous comic obstacles. Audiences will love the scene in which the superbug plays bullfighter. Among others, stars Cloris Leachman and Harvey Korman. Good, clean fun for the entire family.

### HERBIE GOES TO MONTE CARLO
**RATING 2.5**
1977     G     Comedy     Age 04+     104 min.     Color

Herbie the Volkswagen competes in a race from Paris to Monte Carlo and falls in love with a cute car. The plot thickens when some jewel thieves put a diamond in Herbie's gas tank. This third-in-a-series Disney comedy stars Don Knotts, Dean Jones, and Julie Sommars. Perfect entertainment for kids.

### HERBIE RIDES AGAIN
**RATING 3.0**
1974     G     Comedy     Age 04+     90 min.     Color

In this pretty good sequel to THE LOVE BUG, Herbie rescues a little old lady's house that is about to be destroyed by a money-grabbing land developer. Starring Ken Berry, Helen Hayes, Stefanie Powers and Keenan Wynn, this hilarious comedy will mainly appeal to the younger generation. Another Disney favorite in which good defeats evil.

### HIGH AND THE MIGHTY, THE                                             RATING 3.3
1954        NR          Adventure-Drama          Age 12+        147 min.        Color

John Wayne and an all-star cast portray passengers on a disabled airliner enroute from Hawaii to the mainland. Faced with the grim prospect of certain death, they review the value of their individual lives and come to a fresh perspective from the self-examination. An Oscar-winning score gives this suspenseful film an extra boost.

### HIGH NOON                                                            RATING 4.0
1952        NR          Western                  Age 12+         85 min.        B&W

Gary Cooper is a small-town marshall forced to face the leader of an outlaw band alone on his wedding day. As the evil gunman heads for town, Cooper asks for help, but no one comes to his aid. Suspense is heightened by the ominous ticking of the clock in the hotel lobby that signals high noon - the time of the gunfight. Solid moral message about responsibility in this timeless, classic western.

### HIGH SOCIETY                                                         RATING 3.2
1956        NR          Musical-Drama            Age 12+        107 min.        Color

In this enjoyable musical rendition of *The Philadelphia Story*, Bing Crosby plays a wealthy man who tries to stop his ex-wife (Grace Kelly) from remarrying. Frank Sinatra and Celeste Holm play reporters who get involved in Bing's romantic problems. A tranquil Cole Porter score includes the memorable tunes "True Love" and "Did You Evah?"

### HIS GIRL FRIDAY                                                      RATING 4.0
1940        NR          Comedy-Drama             Age 12+         92 min.        B&W

A humorous adaptation of the film *Front Page* tells about a newspaper editor (Cary Grant) and his reporter (Rosalind Russell). She also happens to be his ex-wife. They find themselves wrapped up in an intriguing murder story while fighting a light-hearted battle of the sexes on the side. Director Howard Hawkes employs an "overlapping dialogue" technique to enhance audience interest.

### HOBBIT, THE                                                          RATING 3.3(e)
1977        TVM         Adventure-Fantasy        Age 06+         76 min.        Color

This cartoon is based on J.R.R. Tolkein's wonderful book. It is the tale of a comfortable hobbit, Bilbo, coerced by a wizard to join a dangerous and exciting journey to kill a dragon. The dragon is hoarding a treasure that belongs to a dwarf and his friends. The wizard helps the group out occasionally, but lets them learn a lot on their own. A first-rate children's classic.

### HOLIDAY INN                                                          RATING 3.7
1942        NR          Musical-Drama            Age 12+        101 min.        B&W

Bing Crosby and Fred Astaire perform some of their most beloved numbers in this lightweight Irving Berlin musical. Bing has grown weary of the urban rat race and decides to work at a resort. He and his friend, Fred, compete in a love triangle for Marjorie Reynolds, a fledgling song and dance girl. He croons the Yule favorite "White Christmas" as only Bing can. Audiences will also enjoy Astaire's dancing.

### HOMBRE                                                               RATING 3.5
1967        NR          Western                  Age 12+        111 min.        Color

A white man raised by Indians (Paul Newman) runs into a lot of prejudice in Arizona in the 1880's. He gets to prove himself, though, when he defends a stagecoach filled with panicky passengers from desperadoes. In this unusually thought provoking Western, complex moral issues are raised and sensitively handled by director Martin Ritt. This makes for an intriguing Western.

### HOMECOMING: A CHRISTMAS STORY, THE                                   RATING 3.3
1971        TVM         Drama                    Age 06+         98 min.        Color

In this sentimental pilot for *The Waltons* series, a Depression era mountain family in Virginia gets ready for the Christmas holidays. The father is forced to be away working in a distant town. Meanwhile, the mother (Patricia Neal) encourages the family of seven children to hold on during this difficult time until his return. A beautiful, inspirational film about what it means to be a family.

### HOMEWARD BOUND — RATING 3.3
1993   G   Adventure   Age 06+   84 min.   Color

Excellent remake of Disney's 1963 *Incredible Journey,* seen and told from a pet's view. The two dogs and a cat quickly make friends and learn to protect each other on their incredible journey back to their masters. Each animal represents loyalty, courage, and compassion. Featured voices include Michael J. Fox, Sally Fields, and Don Ameche. An entertaining film with a combination of humor and suspense.

### HONEY, I BLEW UP THE KID — RATING 3.5
1992   PG   Comedy   Age 06+   89 min.   Color

Unorthodox inventor Wayne Szalinski (Rick Moranis) returns to wreak more havoc in this hilarious sequel to *Honey, I Shrunk the Kids.* This time, he accidentally focuses his enlarging ray on his two-year-old son. Instantly, the toddler becomes 50 feet tall, and heads toward the bright lights of Las Vegas. Rollicking family film with some moderate action-type violence.

### HONEY, I SHRUNK THE KIDS — RATING 3.5
1989   PG   Adventure-Comedy   Age 06+   93 min.   Color

One of Disney's best and funniest. Wayne Szalinski (Rick Moranis) develops a machine that can shrink objects, and his children are accidentally reduced to the size of fleas. Then they're mistakenly thrown out with the garbage and must face the jungle-like perils of their back yard. This hilarious, suspenseful film is loaded with terrific special effects. See it!

### HORSE WITHOUT A HEAD — RATING 3.0
1963   NR   Adventure   Age 06+   89 min.   Color

Some inquisitive kids discover a load of stolen loot stashed in a headless toy horse. Of course, the bad guys come after the cash and soon get on the boys' trail. The kids end up foiling the villains, as usual! Pleasant, fun fare for the whole family. British made Disney film.

### HORTON HEARS A WHO — RATING 4.0(e)
1970   NR   Fantasy   Age 04+   26 min.   Color

Meet Dr. Seuss' Horton, an elephant who hears a small voice coming from a speck of dust. The voice tells him that a world called Whoville lives on that small speck. Horton tries to protect Whoville from evil brothers and others in the jungle who don't believe in Whos. A great moral-instilling story about belief and the sanctity of human life, because "a person's a person no matter how small."

### HOT LEAD AND COLD FEET — RATING 2.3
1978   G   Comedy-Western   Age 06+   90 min.   Color

British comedian Jim Dale plays three roles - a father and his twin sons - in this madcap Disney western comedy. The two brothers must run a race to find who will win their father's inheritance of a small town. After a wild obstacle race, they then take on the town's evil mayor. Also starring Don Knotts and Karen Valentine, this slapstick Western chase movie will delight the kids.

### HOUSE ON GARIBALDI STREET, THE — RATING 2.5
1979   TVM   Docudrama-Adventure   Age 17+   98 min.   Color

Fifteen years after World War II, Israeli intelligence agents discover that the Nazi Colonel Adolph Eichman is living in Buenos Aires. The Israeli's resolve to kidnap Eichman and make him stand trial in Israel, but the Nazi fraternal orders pose a threat to their plans. Interesting, well done political melodrama.

### HOUSEKEEPING — RATING 3.0
1987   PG   Drama   Age 12+   116 min.   Color

In this colorful film, a free-spirited aunt (Christine Lahti) moves to the Pacific Northwest to live with her two orphan nieces. Time and convention mean little to Aunt Sylvie, and she allows the girls to do about anything they want to, including skipping school. Her house is a mess too. Sylvie's free spirit and the girls' struggle to deal with her has a unique entertainment appeal.

### HOW THE WEST WAS WON — RATING 3.3
1963     NR     Western Epic     Age 12+     155 min.     Color

Filmed on three-screen cinerama, this sensational Western saga follows an 1830's New England family from youth to old age. They blaze a trail through the wild frontier and encounter hostile Indians. While crossing river and land, they face the hardships of pioneer life. An exceptional all-star cast, including Gregory Peck, Henry Fonda, Jimmy Stewart, and John Wayne, make this an entertaining treat.

### HOWARD'S END — RATING 4.0
1992     PG     Drama     Age 17+     140 min.     Color

Intriguing award-winning adaptation of E.M. Forster's novel about an aristocratic English family whose proper lifestyle crumbles when the recently widowed father marries a down-to-earth, fun loving younger woman. Terrific performances by Vanessa Redgrave, Emma Thompson, and Anthony Hopkins. An exceptional film which will probably appeal to adults only because of its sophisticated dialogue and subject matter. Sex between unmarried couple implied once, but not condoned.

### HUDSUCKER PROXY — RATING 3.5
1994     PG     Comedy     Age 17+     111min     Color

A young mail clerk finds himself promoted to company president after the founder commits suicide. Stock prices drop until the youthful genius invents the hula hoop and becomes famous. This feel-good spoof of the corporate world features slapstick humor and creativity. Several mild crude words, one regular profanity and dark comedic scenes make this film appropriate for older teens and adults only. Co-starring Paul Newman.

### I AM A FUGITIVE FROM A CHAIN GANG — RATING 4.0
1932     NR     Drama     Age 12+     90 min.     B&W

Paul Muni portrays a man convicted of a crime he did not commit. He is sentenced to hard labor in a chain gang and becomes a hardened criminal running from the law. This eye-opening drama paints a bleak picture of the criminal justice system in the Deep South. The viewer follows step by step as Muni reacts to each tragic event. Muni's compelling characterization and a bone-chilling story are worth watching. Some violence.

### I HEARD THE OWL CALL MY NAME — RATING 3.4
1973     TVM     Drama     Age 12+     86 min.     Color

An Anglican priest, Father Mark Brian, is commissioned by the Bishop to a remote Indian fishing village in the Canadian Northwest. In this gentle tale of love and noble courage, the priest eventually wins the respect of the proud, withdrawn Indians because of his deep love for them. All are saddened when they discover he has an incurable disease and hear the "owl call his name." An outstanding, poignant drama.

### I KNOW WHY THE CAGED BIRD SINGS — RATING 3.5
1979     TVM     Drama     Age 12+     96 min.     Color

The story of a gifted young black girl and her brother surrounded by racism. The two children are shuttled between their grandmother in Arkansas and their divorced mother in St. Louis. Set in the Depression era, the film also describes the struggles of their grandmother, a strong Christian who speaks her mind. When young Maya falls victim to rape and sees her father with another woman, her hopes for living in the "white" world fade.

### I REMEMBER MAMA — RATING 3.5
1948     NR     Drama     Age 12+     130 min.     B&W

In this nostalgic drama, a charming Norwegian family adjusts to turn-of-the-century living in San Francisco. Irene Dunne portrays the stern, no-nonsense mama who rears her children with an iron hand. *I Remember Mama* will appeal to all of those with a sentimental nature. Later made into a TV series.

### I WILL FIGHT NO MORE FOREVER — RATING 3.3
1975     TVM     Docudrama-Western     Age 12+     100 min.     Color

A confrontation develops between Chief Joseph and the U.S. Cavalry when he tries to lead his Indian tribe to safety. Based on a true historical account, this film focuses on the bloody battle between the U.S. government and the Nez Perce Indians in 1877. The Indians want to escape the hardships of their reservation by fleeing to Canada, but the U.S. Cavalry is sent to stop them. Much fighting and killing.

### IN SEARCH OF THE CASTAWAYS — RATING 3.2
1962    NR    Adventure    Age 06+    100 min.    Color

Two children searching for their lost sea captain father are helped by a group of intrepid explorers. Amidst landslides, floods, and earthquakes they journey from Victorian England to South America and finally to the South Seas. This Disney adventure features lavish special effects and a spine-tingling plot with strange, exotic animals, hostile savages and frightening isolation. Hayley Mills and Maurice Chevalier star.

### IN THE CUSTODY OF STRANGERS — RATING 2.5
1982    TVM    Drama    Age 12+    95 min.    Color

Danny Caldwell is a rebel who ends up in jail. His father decides that the experience will teach him a lesson, so he lets Danny remain locked-up for the night. Because of further complications, he remains incarcerated for over a month, which makes him psychotic and suicidal. Although the film has some brutal violence, it portrays what can happen to a young man who breaks the law. Good for youth group discussions.

### IN THE HEAT OF THE NIGHT — RATING 4.0
1967    NR    Mystery-Drama    Age 17+    109 min.    Color

Rod Steiger portrays a Southern sheriff who unwillingly joins up with a big-city black detective (Sidney Poitier) to solve a complex murder mystery. This Oscar-winning film skillfully portrays the mounting tension between the two men. Racial tension in the small southern town abounds. As the plot thickens, mutual respect gradually develops between the hostile lawmen. Masterful performances.

### INCREDIBLE JOURNEY, THE — RATING 3.3
1963    NR    Adventure    Age 06+    80 min.    Color

Lost in the forest, two dogs and a cat encounter life-threatening situations as they struggle through 250 miles of Canadian wilderness to find their human family. They tangle with a ferocious lynx, a hostile farm dog and a savage bear, but somehow prevail over them all. They use their wits, teamwork and just plain luck to finally get home. This endearing Disney film will appeal to all audiences, young and old.

### INCREDIBLE JOURNEY OF DOCTOR MEG LAUREL, THE — RATING 2.8
1978    TVM    Drama    Age 12+    150 min.    Color

Lindsay Wagner plays a physician during the depression who returns to her Appalachian home to administer the latest medical technology. The backward mountain folk, however, resist her scary new-fangled notions. Led by the superstitious Granny Arrowroot, the local medicine woman, they challenge the good doctor's modern knowledge and intentions. This captivating TV drama offers a look at Appalachian folk ways.

### INDIAN IN THE CUPBOARD — RATING 3.5(e)
1995    PG    Fantasy    Age 06+    95min.    Color

A whimsical tale about a magic cupboard. Nine-year-old Omri discovers its powers and puts a small Indian figurine into it, thus bringing to life Little Bear. When Omri's friend also puts a cowboy figurine into the cupboard, the trouble begins. However, Little Bear and the cowboy soon learn to get along. A wonderful tale for the whole family. Several mild crudities and one regular profanity.

### INDISCREET — RATING 3.5
1958    NR    Comedy    Age 12+    100 min.    Color

Cary Grant plays a wealthy American politician and playboy who courts an alluring European actress (Ingrid Bergman) in an off and on manner. He tells everyone he is married to avoid getting involved, but he just can't get her off his mind. Things start popping when she discovers his secret. This British urbane comedy sparkles with the witty exchanges between the lovers. Elegant sophisticated comedy.

### INN OF SIXTH HAPPINESS — RATING 3.5
1958    NR    Drama    Age 12+    158 min.    Color

This inspirational biographical film tells the noble story of Gladys Aylward, a British missionary. A poor servant girl, Gladys saves her pennies to become a missionary and is sent to war-torn China. Ingrid Bergman masterfully portrays the brave woman who overcomes her own insecurity and awkward social adjustment in a foreign land. Eventually she leads a group of orphan children across enemy lines to safety. Well-acted.

## INSPECTOR GENERAL                                    RATING 3.5
**1949          NR          Musical-Comedy          Age 12+          102 min.          Color**
Danny Kaye whimsically portrays a village fool traveling as a medicine man in this hilarious musical comedy. He's mistaken for a high-ranking official in Napoleon's cabinet by some frightened Russian peasants. Chaos reigns when Kaye is presented to the local potentates. He gets mixed up in matters of the court and doesn't understand what's happening. Kaye displays the full range of his talent.

## INTERNATIONAL VELVET                                 RATING 2.5
**1978          PG          Drama          Age 06+          126 min.          Color**
Sarah Brown comes to live with her aunt Velvet Brown upon the death of her parents. Sarah finds warmth in the home of Velvet, the winner of an olympic medal years before. Sarah decides to become a horsewoman and is trained by the world's best teacher, Captain Johnson. Training for the Olympics, she develops her sense of self worth and matures.

## INVADERS FROM MARS                                   RATING 3.3
**1953          NR          Science-Fiction          Age 06+          78 min.          Color**
Filmed in 3-D, this fast-paced sci-fi adventure features a young boy sighting a Martian invasion and takeover of a small town. None of the residents believe him, so he attempts to prove that it's not a figment of his imagination. The Martians hypnotize Earthlings to use them as saboteurs. Entertaining Saturday afternoon fare for kids. Space monsters may be too scary for small children.

## I.Q.                                                  RATING 3.7
**1995          PG          Comedy          Age 12+          95 min.          Color**
Ed, a young auto mechanic falls madly in love from a distance with Catherine, the niece of Albert Einstein. Einstein and his old cronies, who are also scientists, introduce Ed to Catherine (Meg Ryan). She is told the handsome young man is highly educated. In fact, Ed does have a few smarts which surprise even Einstein himself. A fun, romantic comedy with a few crude words and a few mildly suggestive remarks.

## IRON AND SILK                                         RATING 3.0
**1990          PG          Drama          Age 12+          92 min.          Color**
Moving autobiographical account of an English teacher's adventures in modern day China. The youthful American struggles to bridge the culture gap by learning karate and trying to befriend his new students. Meanwhile, he falls in love with a beautiful medical student. A powerful film for the whole family that has beautiful scenery, perceptive insight into a foreign culture, and a romantic story. Some martial arts violence.

## IRON WILL                                             RATING 2.3(e)
**1993          PG          Adventure          Age 12+          109 min.          Color**
A courageous teenager enters a challenging dog sled race to earn money for college in this exciting Disney film. Competing with hardened racing veterans, he must overcome insurmountable odds. His surprising performance earns him the nickname "Iron Will". Based on a true story, this uplifting film applauds determination and hope. Some moderately violent scenes and sometimes scary villains probably are too intense for young children.

## ISLAND AT THE TOP OF THE WORLD, THE                   RATING 2.9
**1974          G          Science Fiction-Adventure          Age 06+          89 min.          Color**
At the turn of the century an Englishman rents a balloon to look for his lost son in the Arctic. He finds the boy in a lost Viking civilization, a mythical Shangri-la in a deep valley heated by a volcano. The Vikings are descendants of Grif the Red. Untouched by the modern world, these Vikings have not changed their primitive ways. Good adventure story.

## IT HAPPENED AT THE WORLD's FAIR                       RATING 2.5
**1963          NR          Musical-Romance          Age 06+          105 min.          Color**
Two crop duster pilots find romance and fun in this bouncy musical. A cute little Chinese girl matches a young couple together at the Seattle's World Fair. The couple is played by Elvis Presley and Joan O'Brien. Singable tunes include "A World of Our Own" and "Happy Ending." Elvis fans will enjoy this earlier film effort. All the excitement of the rides and special events are captured in this musical romance.

### IT HAPPENED ONE NIGHT
**RATING 4.0**
1934    NR    Comedy    Age 12+    105 min.    B&W

With his usual roguish charm, Clark Gable plays a jaded news reporter who wins over a runaway society heiress (Claudette Colbert) on a cross-country bus ride. Gable has every intention of turning her in to reap the cash reward, but has a change of heart. There are some hilarious scenes as the reporter and the spoiled rich girl clash. In one comedy sequence, they are forced to share a room in a motor court. Delightful.

### IT SHOULD HAPPEN TO YOU
**RATING 3.0**
1954    NR    Comedy    Age 12+    81 min.    B&W

Tired of obscurity, an ambitious fashion model (Judy Holiday), rents a Columbus Circle billboard space in New York City to promote her career in this amusing comedy. She attracts the attention of a slick soapsuds heir (Peter Lawford). Her quiet boyfriend (Jack Lemmon) becomes very upset with her sudden "fame". Lemmon, in his film debut, is the perfect foil for boisterous, starry-eyed Holiday. Thoroughly entertaining film.

### IT TAKES TWO
**RATING 3.0(e)**
1995    PG    Comedy-Drama    Age 06+    101 min.    Color

Twins Mary-Kate and Ashley Olsen play two unrelated 9-year-olds who accidentally meet at a summer camp for underprivileged children. One of the girls is the daughter of the camp's benefactor and the other a feisty street-wise orphan. They become friends, then change places as they plot to match the rich girl's widowed father with the poor girl's pretty social worker. Both touching and funny, it's good family entertainment.

### IT'S A MAD, MAD, MAD WORLD
**RATING 3.0**
1963    G    Comedy    Age 12+    162 min.    Color

This all-star comedy includes the likes of Milton Berle, Ethel Merman, Sid Caesar, Buddy Hackett, and Jonathan Winters as part of a greedy group frantically racing to find a buried treasure. The fun never stops in this truly funny comedy classic. Spencer Tracy plays the worldly-wise detective who tracks their progress. Contains much slapstick and comical property destruction.

### IT'S A WONDERFUL LIFE
**RATING 4.0**
1946    NR    Drama    Age 06+    129 min.    B&W

Jimmy Stewart portrays George Bailey, a small-town savings and loan president. He's devoted to serving the people, but a greedy wealthy townsman attempts to drive George to ruin. George's life of sorrow and sacrifice tempts him to end it all. When God sends a guardian angel to show him how bad off the town would be without him, George realizes he has a lot to live for and more friends than he imagined. Heartwarming.

### IVANHOE
**RATING 3.3**
1952    NR    Adventure    Age 12+    106 min.    Color

This swashbuckling adaptation of the Sir Walter Scott novel features Robert Taylor as Ivanhoe, a medieval knight endeavoring to rescue King Richard the Lionhearted imprisoned in Austria. He is also called upon to protect two fair damsels (Elizabeth Taylor and Joan Fontaine) from a villain. Ivanhoe and Robin Hood fight the evil Prince John. Fancy sword fights and high adventure. Remade as a TV movie in 1982.

### IZZY AND MOE
**RATING 2.9**
1985    TVM    Comedy    Age 12+    100 min.    Color

Jackie Gleason and Art Carney star as two vaudeville has-beens in this made-for-TV comedy. They come to New York and sign up as federal agents during the Prohibition days of the 20's. They get into sticky comical situations trying to clean up the alcohol industry. This story is based on the true life adventures of Isadore Ginstein and Morris Smith. Fans of *The Honeymooners* will delight in this hilarious reunion.

### JANE DOE
**RATING 3.2**
1983    TVM    Drama    Age 17+    96 min.    Color

A suspenseful thriller about a woman (Jane Doe) victimized by a brutal attack. She miraculously survives, but has a severe case of amnesia. She's the only one who can provide clues to the man who tried to murder her. The killer continues to stalk her, hoping to finish the job before she regains her memory. Her husband, a police detective and a psychiatrist join forces to solve the case. Suspenseful drama. One subdued profanity.

## Secular Movies

### JASON AND THE ARGONAUTS                                           RATING 3.2
1963        NR          Adventure-Fantasy          Age 06+          104 min.          Color

Spectacular movie version of *The Voyage of Argo* written by Greek historian Apollonius of Rhodes. Jason is sent on a journey in search of the Golden Fleece in his effort to rescue his land from an evil tyrant. He encounters numerous problems before he can complete his journey. Special effects are outstanding and will appeal to young viewers. Good introduction to the world of Greek mythology.

### JERICHO MILE, THE                                                 RATING 3.3
1979        TVM         Drama                      Age 12+          97 min.           Color

Larry Murphy (Peter Strauss) runs daily at the Folsom State Prison where he's incarcerated for life. When the warden discovers his talent, a coach comes in to prepare him for the Olympic trials. Drug dealing inmates try to keep him from competing, but a black inmate (Roger Mosley) comes to his aid. Then, the prison walls come tumbling down in a unique way. Some fighting and stabbing. Excellent.

### JESSE OWENS STORY, THE                                            RATING 3.0
1984        TVM         Docudrama                  Age 12+          175 min.          Color

This film documents the life of American olympic runner Jesse Owens and his outstanding performance during the Berlin Olympics in 1936. The performance of the black man shattered the Nazi notion of Aryan racial superiority. Hitler was so incensed that he left the games. This is a wonderful film depicting intense personal achievement in the face of strong prejudice.

### JETSONS: THE MOVIE                                                RATING 2.3
1990        G           Drama-Fantasy              Age 04+          82 min.           Color

The Jetsons, the TV cartoon family, make their movie debut in this colorful, imaginative animated film. George Jetson and his family are living happily in a futuristic city on earth, but must move to an orbiting asteroid on the edge of the galaxy. His new factory is being sabotaged by some furry creatures and he must find out why. Youngsters will enjoy this gentle, non-violent space age cartoon filled with humor and music.

### JOHNNY TREMAIN                                                    RATING 3.2
1957        NR          Drama                      Age 06+          80 min.           Color

A young apprentice to a silversmith joins the Sons of Liberty in Boston. He gets involved in the blood, sweat, and tears of the Revolutionary War in this historical Disney feature. In 1773, Johnny learns the value of the colonist's struggle for freedom. Patriotic pictures of the Boston Tea Party, skirmishes at Concord, Paul Revere's ride and patriotic songs are sprinkled throughout the film. A nice treat.

### JOLSON STORY, THE                                                 RATING 3.7
1946        NR          Musical                    Age 12+          128 min.          Color

This biographical film traces the career of the famous vaudeville and Broadway star. The son of a cantor becomes a show biz hit in 1920's, but his marriage hits the rocks. Jolson dubbed his voice into the memorable sound tract, and Larry Parks does a remarkable job of lip-syncing to the songs. A toe-tapping score includes "April Showers" and "You Made Me Love You", "My Mammy" and "Swanee". A sequel with other Jolson songs was made in 1949.

### JOURNEY OF AUGUST KING, THE                                       RATING 3.0(e)
1995        PG-13       Drama                      Age 17+          91 min.           Color

Set in North Carolina in 1810, this unusual story is about a widower, August King, who protects a young runaway female slave. Although they are attracted to each other, no sexual relationship develops. Some intense scenes include a dog killed by a bear, and a male runaway slave hung and cleaved in two viewed from a distance. It's basically a story of hope and friendship during a very dark period in our country's history.

### JUAREZ                                                            RATING 3.3
1939        NR          Drama                      Age 12+          132 min.          B&W

In this glimpse of turbulent Mexican history, Paul Muni plays the famed Mexican peasant Benito Juarez. He leads the revolt against Emperor Maximilian in 1863. In the violent struggle Mexico ultimately regains its independence. While the Emperor is losing an empire, Empress Carlotta (Bette Davis) is losing her mind. Fine acting performances by Claude Rains and Bette Davis, plus a lavishly staged production.

### JUDGE PRIEST                                                                           RATING 3.5
**1934        NR        Drama-Comedy              Age 12+        80 min.            B&W**
Cliches and humor abound as a practical-minded small town judge, played by beloved humorist Will Rogers, wins the adoration of the local yokels. His policies are controversial as he campaigns for re-election. This nostalgic slice of Americana fairly drips with an Old South flavor, including Uncle Tom played by Stepin Fetchit. Amusing character sketches.

### JUDGMENT AT NUREMBERG                                                                  RATING 4.0
**1961        NR        Drama                     Age 17+        178 min.           B&W**
This provocative drama asks the question, "My country: right or wrong?" An American judge (Spencer Tracy) must deal with this issue in deciding the fates of Nazi war criminals who were only following government orders in World War II. Each of the former Nazi leaders is on trial in this courtroom drama. Brilliant portrayals by an all-star cast and a riveting story about the final judgment of World War II.

### JULIA                                                                                  RATING 3.7
**1977        PG        Drama-Adventure           Age 17+        118 min.           Color**
Two young girls in England, Lily and Julia, become life-long friends. Julia goes to Vienna to study medicine, but gets involved in protests against Nazis. Lily travels to Germany in order to locate her friend. At Julia's request, Lily embarks on a risky, tense train trip to secretly deliver some money to Berlin. Contains two profanities and one vulgarity. Intriguing, well done dramatic adventure.

### JUMANJI                                                                                RATING 4.0(e)
**1995        PG        Adventure-Fantasy         Age 06+        104 min            Color**
This wildly imaginative adventure centers around an ancient game found by a young boy. While examining it, he is violently drawn into the game's eye and whisked away, returning years later as a grown man. He and two young people must play the game to conquer it and are subjected to violent natural catastrophes and wild animal attacks. Too intense for younger children. Magic fantasy game portrayed as evil.

### JUNGLE BOOK, THE                                                                       RATING 3.0
**1942        NR        Fantasy-Adventure         Age 04+        109 min.           Color**
Rudyard Kipling's incredible tropical yarn springs to life in this vivid film. Mowgli, a young boy adopted and raised by wolves, learns their language and ways of the jungles in India. He also learns that each animal has distinctive character traits. Mowgli discovers men have flaws as he foils three jewel thieves. Many suspenseful twists in the plot. Disney grabbed hold of this fun story and turned it into a 1967 cartoon.

### JUSTIN MORGAN HAD A HORSE                                                              RATING 2.5
**1972        G         Drama                     Age 12+        91 min.            Color**
Charming Walt Disney tale of the man who founded the Morgan horse breed, the first truly American horse. Set in Vermont in the 1790's, Justin Morgan sees potential in a young colt he inherits and dreams of making the horse into something great. After years of careful training, Justin nearly sees all his hopes dashed by a harsh twist of fate.

### KARATE KID, PART II                                                                    RATING 2.8
**1986        PG        Adventure-Drama           Age 12+        127 min.           Color**
In this action-packed sequel, young Daniel's karate mentor, Miyagi, finds out his father is dying back in Okinawa. He quickly rushes to his side with his student in tow. While there, the karate master meets up with an old enemy, and Daniel tangles with some rough village hoods. Contains violent, sometimes bloody, karate fights. Miyagi insists that karate be used only in self defense and he and Daniel only resort to fighting when forced to.

### KATHERINE                                                                              RATING 3.2
**1975        TVM       Drama                     Age 17+        98 min.            Color**
Young girl in a wealthy family graduates from college and becomes a social reformer during the turbulent sixties and early seventies. She travels to Peru to teach the poor, then returns to the United States to join a revolutionary group opposing capitalism and racism. She lives with one of the revolutionaries during her involvement with them, and struggles through difficult, traumatic events. Well done.

## KEY LARGO                                                                                       RATING 3.5
1948      NR      Drama-Suspense           Age 12+           101 min.           B&W

Back from the war, Bogey wants to settle down in a peaceful business. But he gets caught up in a dangerous situation in an old hotel in the Florida Keys. He, an attractive widow (Lauren Bacall) and others end up hostages held by a tough gangster (Edward G. Robinson). At first, war-weary Bogart refuses to fight back, but Robinson pushes him over the brink. A howling hurricane interrupts their encounter. Great classic.

## KID FROM LEFT FIELD, THE                                                                        RATING 2.8
1979      TVM     Drama                    Age 06+           100 min.           Color

A former baseball star (Ed McMahon) is relegated to the stands as a hot dog vendor. But he uses his bat boy son (Gary Coleman) to relay a winning strategy to the San Diego Padres, who are in the doldrums. He takes his beloved Padres from the basement to the World Series. Will delight diehard fans, young and old.

## KID IN KING ARTHUR'S COURT, A                                                                   RATING 2.5(e)
1995      PG      Fantasy-Adventure        Age 06+           90 min.            Color

A teen-age baseball player is magically transported by Merlin back in time to help King Arthur save his failing kingdom. He must defeat the villainous Lord Belasco and his henchmen. Based on Mark Twain's enchanting tale, this film's comical antics will delight the young at heart. A few moderate crude words and subdued regular profanity, and some occult magic.

## KID WITH THE 200 I.Q., THE                                                                      RATING 2.2
1983      G       Comedy                   Age 06+           96 min.            Color

The leading actors in this campus caper are Gary Coleman as the thirteen-year-old genius and his idol, a professor of astronomy, Robert Guillaume. Coleman goes to Brighton University as a scholarship student because he is so brilliant. However, he is very young and short and the students make fun of him. Even his favorite professor makes life difficult for him. Eventually, though, things change for the better.

## KING AND I, THE                                                                                 RATING 3.8
1956      NR      Musical                  Age 12+           133 min.           Color

In this exotic Rogers and Hammerstein musical, the mysterious King of Siam (Yul Brynner) falls in love with a plucky British governess (Deborah Kerr) hired to teach the royal children. A magnificent musical score includes such enchanting melodies as "Shall We Dance," "Hello, Young Lovers" and "Getting To Know You." Cultures clash, temperaments flair, East meets West and the result is romance under the stars.

## KING KONG                                                                                       RATING 4.0
1933      NR      Adventure                Age 12+           100 min.           B&W

In a search for prehistoric animals on a remote island, the giant ape King Kong is discovered. He's transported to America, where he gets in big trouble. This ultimate in monster films features Kong tearing apart New York City to find a honeymoon nest for Faye Wray. The result is mass hysteria. It takes modern technology — World War I biplanes — to stop King Kong. Classic battle episode featuring King Kong on the Empire State Building.

## KING'S ROW                                                                                      RATING 3.8
1941      NR      Drama                    Age 12+           127 min.           B&W

Ronald Reagan gives his best performance as a man bewildered by the pervasive evil that besets his hometown in the midwest. A victim of a minor accident, Reagan awakes from surgery to find both his legs amputated. Robert Cummings plays his friend, a psychiatrist fresh from Vienna, who helps him cope with his tragedy. Vivid cinematic art and realistic character portrayals help dramatize the decay within his town.

## KISMET                                                                                          RATING 2.3
1955      NR      Musical                  Age 12+           113 min.           Color

A prince turns pauper and falls for a peasant girl while a beggar pretends to be a prince and goes for a dancing girl. No one seems to stay in place in this movie rendition of the glamorous Arabian folk tale. It features a beggar poet, his lovely daughter, and the ancient ways of Baghdad. The plot thickens when the lovers must return to their real lives. A "Stranger in Paradise" theme provides haunting background music.

### KITTY: RETURN TO AUSCHWITZ
**RATING 3.0**
1979     TVM     Docudrama     Age 12+     90 min.     Color

An intense docudrama about a middle-aged woman who survived the horrendous tortures of a Nazi concentration camp. She is compelled to return to Auschwitz with her son many years later. She shows him what she experienced and how she coped with the unreal situation. Emotionally charged action as she relives the horror. A shocking account of man's inhumanity to man, as well as the triumph of the human spirit.

### KNUTE ROCKNE - ALL AMERICAN
**RATING 3.0**
1940     NR     Drama-Sports     Age 06+     98 min.     Color

Ronald Reagan portrays George Gipp, Knute Rockne's star player in this biography of the famed Notre Dame football coach. Overflowing with sentiment, this is one of the best football films ever produced which extols the old college try. Pat O'Brien's enthusiastic portrayal of the legendary coach, Knute Rockne, is a memorable movie experience. "Go in there and win it for the Gipper" may not be in the video version.

### LADY AND THE TRAMP
**RATING 3.8**
1955     NR     Drama     Age 04+     75 min.     Color

This animated Disney classic features a beautiful pedigreed cocker spaniel that runs away from home to escape neglect. She meets up with Tramp, a ragamuffin mongrel, who teaches her the fine art of surviving on the run. Touching scenes of romance come to life in the doggy world. They share death-defying adventures together. The directors carefully combine an action-packed script with a bright musical score.

### LADY TAKES A CHANCE, A
**RATING 3.0**
1943     NR     Comedy-Western     Age 12+     86 min.     B&W

During a tour of the old West, a naive New York City office girl takes a trip to Oregon to escape the big city. She falls in love with a rugged broncobuster (John Wayne) who doesn't want to get hitched. So she manages to get herself stranded and stays around the rodeo circuit for a while. This hayseed comedy has its own special appeal. Wayne falls off his horse into her lap and she falls head over heels for him. Fun.

### LAND OF FARAWAY, THE
**RATING 2.9**
1988     PG     Adventure-Fantasy     Age 12     95 min.     Color

An orphan boy's life changes when he is magically swept off to The Land of Faraway. He meets his long-lost father, now the king of the country. To gain his fabulous inheritance, he must defeat the wicked Kato. With a friend he embarks on an adventuresome journey to confront Kato, encountering a mystic forest, mountain caves, a whispering well and a genie. Some violent fighting and stabbing and some magical powers and weapons.

### LANTERN HILL
**RATING 3.3**
1990     TVM     Drama     Age 12+     110 min.     Color

Based on the book by Lucy Maud Montgomery, author of *Anne of Green Gables*, this delightful film portrays the struggles of a family torn apart when the parents separate. Jane, the shy daughter, discovers the truth behind the separation of her parents during a visit to her father and attempts to reunite her parents with the help of a wise elderly lady.

### LASSIE
**RATING 3.5**
1994     PG     Drama     Age 06+     95 min.     Color

A troubled boy experiences depression when his beloved mother dies. En route to his new home in the country, he adopts a stray collie who becomes his steadfast companion. This well-done film emphasizes that even the toughest kid can become a productive family member. Children will love this poignant story of a boy and his dog. One moderate crude and two moderate obscenities, along with some moderate violence.

### LAST COMMAND, THE
**RATING 2.8**
1955     NR     Docudrama-War     Age 12+     110 min.     Color

Movie action fans will be thrilled by this realistic historical tale. It recounts a group of heroic Texas soldiers defending the Alamo from the crushing onslaught of the Mexican army in 1836. The good guys lose, but win the respect of the world and become legendary heroes. Action-packed battle scenes and fine acting makes this film worth watching. Stars Ernest Borgnine and Sterling Hayden.

# Secular Movies

### LAST FLIGHT OF NOAH'S ARK — RATING 2.7
1980　　G　　Adventure　　Age 06+　　97 min.　　Color

An out-of-work pilot flies farm animals to a Pacific island to help out a woman missionary. A forced landing finds him stranded on a desert island with the animals and the kids. This latter day Robinson Crusoe faces rough times and learns to love his menagerie of animals. Together with some post-war Japanese soldiers, they construct an ark to transport the animals to their destination. Good Disney entertainment.

### LAST HURRAH, THE — RATING 3.8
1958　　NR　　Drama　　Age 12+　　110 min.　　Color

The days of honest politicians seem to be numbered as Spencer Tracy plays an Irish mayoral incumbent who runs for office one last time. He steadfastly refuses to go with the flow of dishonest politics and is cruelly shoved aside. Although full of good Irish wit, viewers will be moved by its bittersweet pathos.

### LAURA — RATING 4.0
1944　　NR　　Mystery-Drama　　Age 12+　　88 min.　　B&W

When an attractive socialite is apparently murdered, the straight-laced detective assigned to the case falls in love with the missing socialite's portrait. She later turns up alive. The tough detective has difficulties with the sophistication of Park Avenue society. Effective as a love story and as a mystery, this poignant film contains an unforgettable musical score. One of the most unique mysteries to come out of Hollywood.

### LAWRENCE OF ARABIA — RATING 3.5
1962　　PG　　Adventure-Docudrama　　Age 17+　　222 min.　　Color

This seven-time Oscar winner explores the turbulent life of T.E. Lawrence, the British leader who instigated an Arab revolt against Turkey during World War I. Peter O'Toole (Lawrence) organizes a guerilla Arab army to antagonize the oppressive Turks with camel attacks, desert raids and train wrecks. Re-released in 1989. It contains some brutal, bloody battle scenes but no vulgar language. Not appropriate for children.

### LEFT HAND OF GOD — RATING 3.0
1955　　NR　　Adventure　　Age 12+　　87 min.　　Color

Humphrey Bogart plays an American World War II pilot disguised as a priest in order to escape from a treacherous Oriental warlord (Lee Cobb). Trouble comes when he gets involved in the personal wars of the outlaw Chinese warlord. But he works a minor miracle. Gene Tierney adds appeal as the heroine. The convincing performances of the lead actors sustain interest. Modern viewers will enjoy this great wartime movie.

### LIFE AND ASSASSINATION OF THE KINGFISH — RATING 3.2
1977　　TVM　　Docudrama　　Age 17+　　98 min.　　Color

Political docudrama tracing the life and career of flamboyant Louisiana politician Huey P. Long, beginning with his assassination. Flashbacks tell of his dramatic rise from a small town attorney to governor of Louisiana, then Senator. Describes how this notorious polticial boss dominated Louisiana politics for a generation. Ed Asner plays the Kingfish. Well done, intriguing drama. Many hells and damns.

### LIFE AND TIMES OF GRIZZLY ADAMS — RATING 1.5
1976　　G　　Adventure　　Age 06+　　93 min.　　Color

Scenic film about a burly fur trapper (Dan Haggerty) leaving civilization and his young daughter when he is accused of a crime he did not commit. Out in the wilderness, he befriends an enormous grizzly bear. He cannot return to civilization even when he is found innocent. His daughter grows up and tries to bring him back home. Young children will like this story and the beauty of the mountain wilderness. Later made into TV series.

### LIFE WITH FATHER — RATING 3.7
1947　　NR　　Comedy　　Age 12+　　118 min.　　Color

This autobiographical work about author Clarence Day's eccentric father glows with heartfelt warmth and good humor. Also follows Clarence in his growing up years. It's a nostalgic peek at turn-of-the-century living in New York City. Viewers will chuckle when father refuses to be baptized, creating a big ruckus while loving every minute of it. This delightful piece will be remembered by viewers for years to come.

### LIFE WITH MIKEY
**RATING 3.5**
1993　　PG　　Comedy　　Age 12+　　91 min.　　Color

Two brothers (Michael J. Fox and Nathan Jones) operate a struggling talent agency for children. They try to turn a 10-year-old pickpocket into a star of a cookie commercial, but the plan backfires when the little girl proves to be more than they bargained for. Fox is perfect as a former child star now grown up, trying to run the business. A funny family film with one obscenity.

### LILI
**RATING 3.8**
1953　　NR　　Musical-Drama　　Age 12+　　81 min.　　Color

A French orphan girl (Leslie Caron) joins a carnival and is dazzled by the suave charm of a magician-puppeteer. He fancies himself a ladies' man even though he's married. The sixteen-year-old girl is infatuated in this romantic whimsy. This light, springy musical includes many peppy tunes, as well as a dream sequence with dancing puppets. Also starring Zsa Zsa Gabor, *Lili* is an enchanting experience.

### LILIES OF THE FIELD
**RATING 3.5**
1963　　NR　　Drama-Comedy　　Age 12+　　92 min.　　B&W

Homer Smith (Sidney Poitier) a traveling black handyman, meets up with some German nuns in New Mexico. He keeps to himself to avoid conflict, but they persuade him to build a chapel and soon the nearby town gets involved. This leads to many charming, comical incidents. Homer teaches them English and sings gospel songs with them. Poitier's performance and those of the quaint, determined nuns are delightful.

### LIMELIGHT
**RATING 3.3**
1952　　NR　　Comedy-Drama　　Age 12+　　145 min.　　B&W

In this famous Charlie Chaplin special, a has-been music hall comic rescues a depressed ballerina from suicide and makes her feel good about herself again. Although he is too old for her and reduced to begging himself, he ends up building his own self-confidence in the process. He confronts the problem of suffering and handles it well. *Limelight* showcases the scintillating comedy talent of Chaplin and Buster Keaton.

### LION KING, THE
**RATING 3.7**
1994　　G　　Adventure-Musical　　Age 06+　　88 min.　　Color

Mesmerizing Disney cartoon about Simba, a young lion who must battle his evil Uncle Scar for his right to the throne. Simba joins forces with a young female lion, a warthog and a meercat to rid the country of the evildoers. Messages about responsibility and repaying evil with kindness stand out. One moderate crude word and some contact with dead spirits can be interpreted as occultic. A frightening, graphic stampede may upset young children.

### LIONHEART
**RATING 3.2**
1987　　PG　　Adventure-Drama　　Age 12+　　104 min.　　Color

Richard III, King of England, is organizing a crusade to free Jerusalem of Moslem influence. A young French nobleman plans to participate in the Crusade, but ends up protecting a group of children from slave traders and escorting them to the French coast. Along the way they are again attacked by slave traders, led by the evil Black Knight. Christianity is respected in the story. Technically and artistically excellent film.

### LITTLE HOUSE ON THE PRAIRIE, THE
**RATING 3.0**
1974　　TVM　　Drama　　Age 06+　　100 min.　　Color

Laura Ingalls Wilder's personal account of family life on the wild frontier comes to life in this TV pilot for the long-running TV series. Following the Civil War, a family makes a long trek from Wisconsin to the Kansas prairie to establish their home. They face the hardships of the frontier as a close knit, loving family. Director Michael Landon also stars as the compassionate father who provides protection for his family.

### LITTLE LORD FAUNTLEROY
**RATING 3.5**
1980　　TVM　　Drama　　Age 06+　　120 min.　　Color

A destitute New York urchin (Ricky Schroeder) is adopted by his wealthy British grandfather (Alec Guiness). The cheerful, lovable boy goes to England to live with his rather stern grandfather and wins him over. He becomes heir to his estate. The little lord is a champion of damsels in distress and proves his virtue. Guiness portrays the elderly lord with effortless grandeur. Close attention given to historical detail.

## LITTLE NEMO: ADVENTURES IN SLUMBERLAND　　　　　　　　　　RATING 3.0
1992　　　G　　　　Fantasy-Advemture　　　Age 04+　　　85 min.　　　Color

In this Disney animated feature, a small boy dreams he is invited to Slumberland to become the sole heir to the throne. He disobeys the King by opening the Forbidden Door, and later must rescue the king from some nightmare creatures. Children under ten will enjoy the fast-paced action and the imaginative fantasy lands. Some magical phenomena, but not as scary as some of the standard Saturday morning fare

## LITTLE PRINCESS, THE　　　　　　　　　　　　　　　　　　　RATING 3.3
1939　　　NR　　　Drama　　　　　　　　　Age 06+　　　91 min.　　　Color

Shirley Temple plays a pampered Victorian tyke who loses her wealthy father in the Boer War. In her quest to find her dad, she faces many obstacles. First she is shuttled off to boarding school, where she is mistreated by her classmates. Cruel adults try to block her efforts, but her pluck and charm win out. Viewers will empathize with the mistreated little girl. Shirley Temple fans will love it.

## LITTLE RASCALS　　　　　　　　　　　　　　　　　　　　　　RATING 2.1
1994　　　PG　　　Comedy　　　　　　　　Age 06+　　　83 min.　　　Color

The lovable "Our Gang" characters are back in this remake featuring Spanky, Alfalfa, Darla and Buckwheat. The gang is having trouble deciding whether to let Alfalfa, who is "in love" with Darla, drive their go-cart in an upcoming race. Alfalfa also must deal with a rich kid vying for Darla's attentions. The usual practical jokes abound, along with some rather modern suggestive references and two moderate crude words.

## LITTLE WOMEN　　　　　　　　　　　　　　　　　　　　　　　RATING 4.0
1994　　　PG　　　Drama　　　　　　　　　Age 12+　　　118min.　　　Color

An all-star cast brings Louisa May Alcott's beloved book back to the screen. It follows the exploits of the March sisters and their mother as they struggle in Massachusetts during the Civil War. Tragedy looms close as the sisters must make choices about love, pursuing careers and staying together. A great movie which shows the power of a close-knit family with loving relationships.

## LITTLE WOMEN　　　　　　　　　　　　　　　　　　　　　　　RATING 4.0
1933　　　NR　　　Drama　　　　　　　　　Age 06+　　　115 min.　　　B&W

This marvelous adaptation of Louisa May Alcott's classic novel deals with four sisters growing up in New England during the Civil War. They learn how to deal with life and encounter a variety of experiences along the way. Katharine Hepburn brilliantly portrays Jo, the incurable tomboy. A fine piece of Americana.

## LITTLEST HORSE THIEVES, THE　　　　　　　　　　　　　　　RATING 3.0
1976　　　G　　　　Adventure　　　　　　　Age 06+　　　104 min.　　　Color

Set in turn-of-the-century England, this effective Disney film focuses on the horrible plight of some mining pit ponies which are to be slaughtered because they have outlived their usefulness. When three children find out about the ponies' fate, they develop a plan to steal the ponies and rescue them from danger. Exciting adventure film for the kids.

## LONE RANGER, THE　　　　　　　　　　　　　　　　　　　　　RATING 2.7
1956　　　NR　　　Western　　　　　　　　Age 06+　　　86 min.　　　Color

The masked man rides again in his search for justice. This premiere presentation of TV series features the Lone Ranger and his faithful sidekick Tonto. Sensing the turbulent times, they struggle to avert range wars. They try to make peace with hostile Indians while fighting a group of unfriendly white settlers. The masked hero saves the day. Adventure of yesteryear when the silver bullet found its target and good won out.

## LONELIEST RUNNER, THE　　　　　　　　　　　　　　　　　　RATING 2.5
1976　　　TVM　　Drama　　　　　　　　　Age 06+　　　78 min.　　　Color

A thirteen-year-old boy with bed-wetting problems experiences the emotional shame that accompanies such trauma. He runs a lot to hide his problem from his parents and friends. In time, he overcomes his psychological pain and later becomes an Olympic gold medalist runner. The child's dream of being "somebody" comes true. Director Michael Landon makes a brief appearance as the adult Olympic runner. Viewers will be inspired by this courageous story.

### LONELY ARE THE BRAVE
**RATING 3.3**
1962   NR   Adventure-Western   Age 12+   107 min.   B&W

Kirk Douglas plays a displaced cowboy in a modern world who goes to jail to help his friend. He escapes, but is chased by helicopters, jeeps and other modern vehicles with electronic, computerized communication technology. A semi-truck finally catches up with the cowboy and his horse "Whiskey". Cast includes Walter Matthau and Gina Rowlands in this thinking man's Western. A tribute to the last cowboy.

### LONG, LONG TRAILER, THE
**RATING 2.8**
1954   NR   Comedy   Age 12+   103 min.   Color

If you like Lucille Ball and Desi Arnaz, you'll love this movie about a newlywed couple who buy a very large trailer instead of a home. Their misadventures as they try to pull the trailer over mountains, through the woods and through towns will delight the whole family. Lucille Ball is up to her old slapstick tricks as she tries to cook dinner in a moving vehicle.

### LONG VOYAGE HOME, THE
**RATING 3.8**
1940   NR   Adventure   Age 12+   105 min.   B&W

A gripping tale of merchant seamen carrying a load of dangerous explosives on a tramper steamer. They share a longing for the sea as well as similar thoughts and ambitions. Adapted from four one-act plays by Eugene O'Neill. John Wayne stars.

### LONG WAY HOME, A
**RATING 3.3**
1981   TVM   Drama   Age 12+   98 min.   Color

This moving film deals with a young man's deep craving to be reunited with his brother and sister after being deserted by his migrant worker parents. The three children are put in separate foster homes and years later the young man tries to reunite them. Timothy Hutton sensitively portrays the bewildered young man. Brenda Vaccaro does a fine job as a caring social worker who reluctantly decides to help him find his family.

### LOOKING FOR MIRACLES
**RATING 3.5(e)**
1990   TVM   Drama   Age 12+   103 min.   Color

During the Depression, Ryan Delaney graduates with honors from his Toronto high school, but has a hard time finding a job. He finally lands a job at a summer camp, but he lies about his qualifications. Completely unqualified, he has to comically bumble through camp. To make matters worse, his younger brother is attending the camp and following his every move. One regular profanity and one scene of boys smoking.

### LORENZO'S OIL
**RATING 3.8**
1992   PG-13   Drama   Age 17+   135 min.   Color

Parents of a young boy afflicted with a rare disease fight to get the latest medical treatment. They become obsessed with finding a cure, but are constantly thwarted by the inflexible medical community. Stellar performances by Nick Nolte and Susan Sarandon as the beleaguered parents, and Peter Ustinov as the only doctor willing to help them. One obscenity. Subject matter is too intense for young children.

### LOVE BUG, THE
**RATING 3.3**
1969   G   Comedy-Fantasy   Age 06+   107 min.   Color

This charming Disney comedy features Herbie, a feisty little Volkswagen with a mind of its own and magic talents to match. An unhappy race car driver (Buddy Hackett) finds out he can win the big one with a crazy little Volkswagen. Dean Jones and Michele Lee come along for the ride. They wow the race car fans and leave everyone laughing. Amazing stunts and hilarious slapstick chases will delight all ages. Followed by three sequels.

### LOVE LAUGHS AT ANDY HARDY
**RATING 2.0**
1946   NR   Comedy-Drama   Age 12+   93 min.   B&W

In this segment of the *Andy Hardy* series, lovable Andy returns home from World War II army service to once again struggle with the anguish of romantic love. Much to his despair, Andy finds his fiancee about to marry her guardian, and he is asked to be best man. Mickey Rooney hams it up as the lively, lovable Andy who was America's favorite teenager in the 1940's. A fine slice of Americana.

## LOVE LEADS THE WAY — RATING 3.1
**1984　　TVM　　Drama　　　　　　　　Age 12+　　99 min.　　Color**
When Morris Frank goes blind after a freak boxing accident, he does not know what to do. Finally, he trains a dog to help him get around and becomes the first man in the United States with a seeing-eye dog. He overcomes the heartache of lost love, and the prejudice of a seeing world. This is an inspiring story that may evoke a few tears.

## MAGIC OF LASSIE, THE — RATING 2.5
**1978　　G　　Drama　　　　　　　　　Age 06+　　90 min.　　Color**
The country's beloved collie stars in this heartwarming version of *Lassie Come Home*. Grandfather (Jimmy Stewart) refuses to sell his money-making vineyard to a wealthy bad guy. Vengefully, the villain forces the gentle land owner to give him his family pet. There are tears a plenty as Lassie tries to reunite with the family. The nip and tuck action keeps the audience on the edge of their seats. Kids will love it.

## MAGNIFICENT OBSESSION — RATING 3.0
**1954　　NR　　Drama　　　　　　　　　Age 12+　　108 min.　　Color**
Rock Hudson portrays a playboy whose drunk driving causes an accident that blinds a young woman. Shattered with grief, he completely changes his lifestyle. The handsome, irresponsible "swinger" becomes a renowned surgeon so that he can personally restore the accident victim's eyesight. Although heavy on melodrama, this film will touch the hearts of viewers.

## MALTESE FALCON, THE — RATING 4.0
**1941　　NR　　Mystery-Drama　　　　　Age 12+　　101 min.　　B&W**
This priceless cinematic treasure features Humphrey Bogart as Sam Spade, a tough-minded detective, tracing down a statue of a black bird embedded with precious gems. When his partner is killed, Spade makes an all-out effort to square things. He's joined by a group of bad guys so there's plenty of double-crossing and foul play. A great cast, a fast-paced script, and brilliant direction.

## MAN FOR ALL SEASONS, A — RATING 3.6
**1966　　NR　　Docudrama　　　　　　　Age 12+　　120 min.　　B&W**
In this Oscar-winning effort, Sir Thomas Moore refuses to help King Henry VIII break away from the Catholic church to form the Church of England. Opposing Henry's divorce, Sir Thomas literally loses his head. The power struggle that results makes for fascinating drama. Many good speeches . A magnificent supporting cast includes Orson Welles and Vanessa Redgrave. Remade as a TV movie in 1988.

## MAN FOR ALL SEASONS, A — RATING 3.5
**1988　　TVM　　Docudrama　　　　　　Age 12+　　158 min.　　Color**
Charlton Heston plays Sir Thomas More, who rises to the position of Lord Chancellor during the reign of Henry VIII. When the Catholic Church refuses to grant King Henry a divorce, the King establishes the Church of England, with himself as its head. More refuses to agree to Henry's divorce or new title and is eventually beheaded as a traitor. A moving story about courage.

## MAN FROM ATLANTIS — RATING 2.7
**1977　　TVM　　Science-Ficton　　　　　Age 06+　　100 min.　　Color**
The last survivor of an underwater kingdom joins forces with an attractive marine biologist to thwart the efforts of an evil madman trying to destroy the earth. The submarine superman with gills instead of lungs defies the dangers of the deep to retrieve a top secret submarine for the Navy. Our undersea hero (Patrick Duffy) can even outswim the dolphins! A TV series spun off from this movie. Fun and exciting.

## MAN FROM CLOVER GROVE, THE — RATING 1.3(e)
**1974　　G　　Comedy-Drama　　　　　Age 06+　　97 min.　　Color**
Claude is a benevolent toy maker who donates his creations to a local orphanage. A major toy manufacturer comes to town and offers Claude a job making toys for the company. He uses his income to establish trust funds for other orphanages. The story is humorous and has a romantic interest as well. Fun film depicting people with charitable attitudes.

### MAN FROM SNOWY RIVER    RATING 3.3
1982     PG     Adventure-Drama     Age 06+     105 min.     Color

This fascinating Australian western tale features a teenage boy who becomes a man when he goes to work on a large ranch. Kirk Douglas plays the tough rancher who hires him to round up unbroken horses. A romance develops between the ambitious young man and the rancher's daughter. The lad is determined to prove his worth to the girl's skeptical, hostile father. Spectacular scenery and glorious horse chases. One profanity.

### MAN IN THE IRON MASK, THE    RATING 3.0
1977     TVM     Drama     Age 12+     100 min.     Color

Richard Chamberlin plays dual roles as identical twins, Louis and Felipe. In this Alexander Dumas tale about twin brothers separated at birth, one becomes a peasant swordsman who joins the three musketeers. The other becomes the evil king of France. Felipe tries to capture the throne which rightfully belongs to him. Fact and fiction are intermingled. Louis has a mistress and there are references to his infidelity.

### MAN IN THE SANTA CLAUS SUIT, THE    RATING 2.7
1978     TVM     Comedy-Fantasy     Age 06+     104 min.     Color

Three men (Gary Burghoff, Bert Convy, and John Byner) each lease an enchanted Santa Claus suit that radically changes their lives for the better. Fred Astaire, the magical shopkeeper, endows the suit with magical qualities which solve problems. Fred Astaire also plays six other roles. Each character has a special need that only Santa can fill. This lighthearted holiday special portrays the meaning of Christmas.

### MAN IN THE WHITE SUIT, THE    RATING 3.8
1952     NR     Comedy     Age 12+     84 min.     B&W

In this gentle satire about big business, Sir Alec Guiness plays a modest scientist who invents a super fabric that won't stain or wear out. Panicked, the trade union members and the textile manufacturers seek to kill the formula before it's patented. The escapades of the naive inventor drive him from pillar to post as everyone is outraged by the quality of his invention. Filmed in England, this comedy is a real delight.

### MAN WHO SHOT LIBERTY VALANCE, THE    RATING 3.8
1962     NR     Western     Age 12+     122 min.     B&W

Lawyer (Jimmy Stewart) attempts to clean up an unruly Western town with intelligence instead of violence. Forced into a shootout with the villain (Lee Marvin), the lawyer is credited with shooting his enemy. John Wayne plays the mysterious cowboy who actually fired the shot. How the lawyer and the cowboy clash in handling everything from outlaws to women makes for great entertainment. John Ford directs.

### MAN'S FAVORITE SPORT?    RATING 2.7
1964     NR     Comedy     Age 06+     120 min.     Color

A sports columnist (Rock Hudson) who's never fished discovers that he's been entered in an angling contest by a pretty but mischievous woman. Hilarious havoc results when he must go fishing to preseve his reputation. He gets all tangled up, stepping all over his lines and looking like a buffoon in a boat. His slapstick antics will keep you laughing. A few mild comical sexual innuendoes.

### MANCHURIAN CANDIDATE, THE    RATING 3.5
1962     NR     Drama     Age 17+     126 min.     B&W

In this complex thriller, Frank Sinatra portrays a Korean War veteran. He thinks that the Communists have brainwashed a fellow soldier (Laurence Harvey) and programmed him to kill key political figures so they can put their man in the White House. Sinatra races against time to stop the evil plot. One of the shootings in the film is jolting as is a strangulation. But the story has some romantic interludes which soften it.

### MANDELA    RATING 3.1
1987     TVM     Docudrama     Age 12+     100 min.     Color

An outstanding biography of South African leader Nelson Mandela beginning in early 1950 when he was a young laborer. He begins organizing the blacks to protest against the treatment they are receiving from the white minority. The film also recounts the 23 years that Mandela spent in prison. Though this film may not be completely accurate in every detail, it is a moving testimony to the courage of one man.

### MARK TWAIN AND ME  RATING 3.5(e)
1991    TVM    Drama    Age 12+    100 min.    Color

Mark Twain, during his famous trip to England, goes to London on his way to speak at Oxford. Twain is depressed, having just lost his wife. While in London, Twain meets eleven-year-old Dorothy. They become close friends and stay that way until Twain's death four years later. A delightful story about the wonderful possibilities of friendship between adults and children. Colorfully told with no objectionable elements.

### MARTY  RATING 3.7
1955    NR    Drama    Age 12+    91 min.    B&W

Oscar-winning Ernest Borgnine sensitively portrays a middle aged New York butcher who has given up on finding love. Marty feels he is too unattractive to appeal to anyone. Love finds him, however, when he meets a plain school teacher at a dance who's as lonely as he. They both overcome their fears and pressure from friends and fall in love. A tender love story about likable down-to-earth people.

### MARY POPPINS  RATING 4.0
1964    NR    Musical-Fantasy    Age 06+    139 min.    Color

Julie Andrews charmingly sings, Dick Van Dyke nimbly dances and two kids are completely enchanted in this award-winning family film. It's about a magical governess changing the lifestyle of a proper British family from rigid and strict to warm and loving. Tunes like "Chim-Chim-Cher-Ee" and "A Spoonful of Sugar" plus animated sequences all have a wonderful glow. Mary sings, flies and magically introduces the kids into a chalk drawing.

### MASADA  RATING 3.0
1984    TVM    Drama-War    Age 12+    131 min.    Color

A group of renegade Jews led by Eleazar (Peter Strauss) flee Jersualem during the Roman destruction in 70 A.D. They head for the mountain fortress of Masada where they hold the Roman army in check though outnumbered five to one. Peter O'Toole is brilliant as the Roman leader, Flavius Silva. Impressive historical epic of courage. Sword fighting, stabbing and killing. Few sexually oriented lines and near nudity.

### MASS APPEAL  RATING 3.0
1984    PG    Drama    Age 17+    99 min.    Color

Father Tim Farley (Jack Lemmon) is an apathetic, worldly priest challenged by a young, fiery seminary student he has befriended. He must make a serious choice: Should he remain content to win favor with his well-do-do congregation, or should he challenge them to greater commitment? Some of Father Farley's decisions conflict with his superior. The seminary student defends homosexuality, but Lemmon stands firmly against it. Timely.

### MEET ME IN ST. LOUIS  RATING 4.0
1944    NR    Musical    Age 12+    113 min.    Color

An all-American family in St. Louis may have to move to New York and miss the 1903 World's Fair in St. Louis. Tension abounds within the family at this prospect. Judy Garland sings all-time favorite tunes like "The Trolley Song" and "Have Yourself a Merry Little Christmas." Warm and richly sentimental, this musical leaves viewers with good feelings. Perfect for holiday viewing.

### MEMORIAL DAY  RATING 3.2
1988    TVM    Drama    Age 17+    95 min.    Color

Matt Walker, a Vietnam vet, is a successful attorney defending a construction contractor guilty of approving faulty work. When Matt's best friend appears after twelve years and then commits suicide, all this changes. Suddenly, the emotions of the past begin to surface, and Matt has to face the terrible reality of the war. Contains two vulgarities and several hells and damns.

### METEOR MAN  RATING 2.6
1993    PG    Comedy    Age 12+    100 min.    Color

A mild-mannered inner city schoolteacher is struck by a mysterious flaming meteor from outer space. This endows him with superhuman strength and the ability to fly which he uses to fight a neighborhood gang. Comical performances by James Earl Jones and Bill Cosby. Scenes depicting young boys with weapons may be unsuitable for younger audiences. A few moderate crude words, along with two moderate slang obscenities.

### MICKEY'S CHRISTMAS CAROL — RATING 4.0
**1984   G   Drama-Animated   Age 04+   26 min.   Color**

Disney's animated version of Dickens' timeless work features Mickey Mouse as Bob Cratchit. Other familiar cartoon characters play the roles of Scrooge and the ghosts of Christmas Past, Present, and Future. Scrooge, the miser, discovers there's more happiness in giving than in receiving. Good for the kids during the holidays.

### MIGHTY DUCKS, THE — RATING 2.8
**1992   PG   Comedy   Age 06+   100 min.   Color**

A reluctant coach takes an adolescent, rag-tag hockey team under his wing and transforms the players into champions. During practices, all sorts of comical mishaps and bloopers occur, but the coach refuses to give up on them. The team learns sportsmanship and earn self-esteem. Exciting and suspenseful plot. Several mild and moderate crude words, two moderate obscenities, and hockey game violence.

### MILLION DOLLAR DUCK — RATING 2.3
**1971   G   Comedy   Age 06+   92 min.   Color**

While Professor Albert is using a duck for an experiment, it accidentally wanders into a radiation chamber and gets a good dose. When the professor's experiments fail, he takes the duck home as a pet. To his delight, he discovers that it now lays golden eggs. The new source of wealth is a bonanza for the professor but also brings much grief as he gets into money troubles. Entertaining Disney comedy.

### MIRACLE DOWN UNDER — RATING 3.5
**1987   NR   Drama   Age 06+   106 min.   Color**

Christmas 1891 in Australia is approaching but the O'Day family will not have much of a celebration. The drought has caused new hardships and the family lacks money to buy gifts. But little Ned thinks he sees Father Christmas, who in actuality is an outlaw. The boy experiences new hope for a joyous celebration as he tenderly demonstrates how to give. A touching holiday film about a loving family.

### MIRACLE ON 34TH STREET — RATING 3.8
**1947   NR   Drama   Age 06+   96 min.   B&W**

This Yuletide classic features a charming Macy's department store Santa. He claims he's actually the real Santa and calls himself Kris Kringle. To prove his claims to a skeptical child (Natalie Wood), he agrees to go on trial. The lawyers debate Kringle's sanity, but what's really on trial is the existence of Santa Claus. The little girl learns the importance of believing in the midst of a jaded, pessimistic world. A beautiful message.

### MIRACLE ON 34TH STREET — RATING 3.5
**1994   PG   Drama   Age 06+   110 min.   Color**

In this remake of the 1947 classic, a skeptical young girl has been told that there is no Santa Claus. When she meets an eccentric old man who claims that he is Santa Claus, she begins to believe. The true spirit of Christmas comes through in this delightful movie. Richard Attenborough gives a fine performance as the jolly old man. One moderate crudity.

### MIRACLE WORKER — RATING 3.3
**1979   TVM   Docudrama   Age 06+   98 min.   Color**

This color adaptation of the 1962 *Miracle Worker* film features Patty Duke as Anne Sullivan, Helen Keller's iron-willed teacher and guide. Melissa Gilbert intelligently portrays Helen, the defiant blind and deaf mute. Student and teacher struggle for power over each other. Sullivan finally triumphs, and Helen receives the priceless gift of understanding. Though not as powerful as the original, this version has same poignant quality.

### MISS ROSE WHITE — RATING 3.5
**1992   TVM   Drama   Age 12+   100 min.   Color**

A touching story about a Jewish family from Poland immigrating to the U.S. Rose, the daughter of the family, changes her last name to White and distances herself from her family to better fit into mainstream America. When her older sister, persecuted for many years in Poland, finally arrives in the U.S., Rose and her older sister learn about compassion, tolerance and the importance of family.

## Secular Movies

### MISSILES OF OCTOBER, THE                                    RATING 3.5
1974        TVM         Docudrama              Age 17+         155 min.         Color

This riveting drama recounts the true story of President Kennedy's actions to prevent Russians from building up their offensive missile command in Cuba during 1962. President Kennedy and his staff make decisions that could plunge the world into a nuclear war. William DeVane as President Kennedy, Ralph Bellamy as Adlai Stevenson and Martin Sheen as Attorney General Bobby Kennedy. Some mild rough words.

### MISSION, THE                                                RATING 3.0
1986        PG          Drama-Historical       Age 17+         125 min.         Color

A Jesuit priest (Jeremy Irons) resumes his missionary work among South American Indians in the 1500's despite political factions in the Church. Robert DeNiro plays a former slave trader who undergoes conversion and becomes a priest. He fights to prevent the closing of the mission when Portugal takes over the colony. Thought-provoking Biblical issues. Culminates in an intense battle. Much native breast nudity.

### MISTER ROBERTS                                              RATING 4.0
1955        NR          Comedy-Drama           Age 12+         123 min.         Color

Henry Fonda plays Navy Lieutenant Roberts, an officer anxious to be in the thick of World War II sea battles. His ship, however, is assigned to stay outside of the war zone. In fact, his biggest conflict is with his cantankerous captain (James Cagney). William Powell plays the ship's doctor, and Jack Lemmon won an Oscar for his role as the con-artist, Ensign Pulver. An entertaining well played comedy-drama.

### MOGAMBO                                                     RATING 3.2
1953        NR          Adventure-Drama        Age 12+         115 min.         Color

Rakish Clark Gable portrays a big game hunter who finds himself caught in a love triangle with two gorgeous women. This zesty remake of *Red Dust* has it all - a great cast, romance and adventure. Gable plays a tough, savvy jungle guide for an anthropologist and his wife (Grace Kelly). Ava Gardner plays the woman who is after Gable. Viewers will enjoy another memorable film from the golden days.

### MONKEY BUSINESS                                             RATING 3.5
1931        NR          Comedy                 Age 12+         77 min.          B&W

Viva the Marx Brothers! In this outrageous comedy, Groucho, Chico, Zeppo, and Harpo stow away in a cruise ship and wreak their usual havoc while aboard. Each impersonates Maurice Chevalier to escape the ship. Later on they become a gangster's bodyguards. Hilarious slapstick gags are still funny today. After all, who can resist this wonderful comedy team with their timeless appeal.

### MONKEY TROUBLE                                              RATING 3.1
1994        PG          Comedy                 Age 06+         95 min.          Color

An organ grinder's delightful capuchin monkey steals the show in this amusing, lighthearted film. Professional gangsters spy him picking pockets and decide they want to use him and his master as partners in crime. A madcap chase ensues that will leave you laughing. Refreshing film that teaches the importance of telling the truth and respecting another's property. Some moderate violence.

### MONKEY'S UNCLE, THE                                         RATING 1.8
1965        NR          Comedy                 Age 06+         90 min.          Color

Martin is the smartest guy on campus and develops a method to teach a chimp to think on a higher level. Meanwhile, two members of the football team need help to pass their exams. Martin tries his teaching method on the football jocks, enabling them to get "A's" in the course. Unfortunately, this is just the beginning of their problems. Exciting, humorous Disney film.

### MONTH BY THE LAKE, A                                        RATING 3.0(e)
1995        PG          Drama-Comedy           Age 17+         99 min.          Color

Set in Italy right before WWII, this story features a middle-aged school teacher, Miss Bentley, vacationing at beautiful Lake Como. She becomes attracted to Major Wilshaw, another guest, but he seems more interested in a flirtatious American governess. In the meantime, a young, rich Italian begins pursuing Miss Bentley. It's fun to watch these four nice people interact in this nostalgic setting. Good adult entertainment.

### MOONCUSSERS
**RATING 2.2**
1962     NR     Adventure     Age 06+     85 min.     Color

Pirates attack passing ships and loot all the cargo. Dan Hallit comes into town to stop their activities. The townspeople join Hallit in their search for the crooks and the possibility of recovering the stolen property. A huge action sequence takes place at the end and the mooncussers feel the hand of justice. Continual fighting in this Disney film where good wins over evil.

### MOONSPINNERS
**RATING 2.8**
1964     NR     Adventure     Age 06+     118 min.     Color

Adorable Hayley Mills plays a young, naive vacationer in Crete, off the coast of Greece. She gets mixed up in a jewelry smuggling ring in this Hitchcock-style Disney thriller. One young man who is falsely accused of theft works with her to demonstrate his innocence. Kids and adults will enjoy this fun, light-hearted expedition filmed on location.

### MOUNTAIN FAMILY ROBINSON
**RATING 2.3**
1979     G     Adventure     Age 06+     100 min.     Color

This colorful nature film deals with a family who retreats from their fast-paced urban world to a more peaceful environment. Trouble arises when a forest ranger tells them to leave. Beautiful scenery and wild life are featured in their adventures. Similar to the *Wilderness Family* adventure, this film champions family togetherness and tolerance.

### MOUSE THAT ROARED, THE
**RATING 3.7**
1958     NR     Comedy     Age 12+     85 min.     B&W

Peter Sellers plays three different roles in this rollicking comedy about a tiny country that declares war on America to restore its treasury. They plan to lose the war early so they can then receive American foreign aid. Imagine their surprise when they win the war! Viewers will appreciate the keen, political satire that runs throughout the film.

### MR. HOLLAND'S OPUS
**RATING 3.5(e)**
1996     PG     Drama     Age 12+     144 min.     Color

This uplifting story about a high school music teacher stars Richard Dreyfuss as Mr. Holland. A frustrated composer and reluctant teacher, Mr. Holland becomes engrossed in his school work and a hero to his students. When his only child is born deaf, it's devastating to the passionate music lover. Strong family values and magnitude of teachers' influence on students emphasized. Some crude language, one obscenity and one regular profanity mar the dialogue.

### MR. JOHNSON
**RATING 3.2**
1991     PG-13     Drama     Age 17+     102 min.     Color

Poignant drama about cultural conflicts during 1923 British colonial rule in west Africa. A charming, resourceful black clerk endears himself to his English employers, but his character flaws soon get him in trouble. This fascinating story is reminiscent of the more genteel movies of yesteryear. Male rear nudity a few times, along with some mild and moderate crude words and a few sexually suggestive remarks.

### MR. MAGOO IN SHERWOOD FOREST
**RATING 3.5(e)**
1964     NR     Adventure-Animated     Age 04+     85 min.     Color

Excellent animated version of the Robin Hood story featuring the loveable Mr. Magoo as Friar Tuck. Magoo's voice is by Jim Backus who played Mr. Howell on *Gilligan's Island*. Magoo joins Robin Hood and the gang as they seek to thwart the evil activities of King John, sheriff of Nottingham.

### MR. MAGOO, MAN OF MYSTERY
**RATING 3.2(e)**
1965     NR     Adventure-Animated     Age 04+     96 min.     Color

Mr. Magoo takes on numerous identities in this entertaining collection of stories. As Dr. Watson, he aids Sherlock Holmes in a baffling case. Next he assumes the identity of Dr. Frankenstein and ends up in trouble. As the Count of Monte Cristo, Magoo takes revenge on enemies. Finally, as Dick Tracy he encounters a batch of sinister characters.

## MR. MAGOO'S CHRISTMAS CAROL — RATING 3.6(e)
**1962 NR Drama-Animated Age 04+ 53 min. Color**
This is a superb animated version of *A Christmas Carol*. Mr. Magoo is Ebenezer Scrooge, the miser who hates people. This makes his intolerance of Christmas even more intense. Fortunately, he is visited by three spirits who seek to show him the error of his ways and the awful consequences if his life remains unchanged. This is great entertainment for children and adults.

## MR. MAGOO'S STORYBOOK — RATING 3.6(e)
**1964 NR Drama-Animated Age 04+ 117 min. Color**
Mr. Magoo assumes the identities of numerous characters from classic stories. He is all seven dwarfs in "Snow White". Next Magoo takes on windmills as disoriented knight Don Quixote of La Mancha. He concludes as Puck in Shakespeare's *A Midsummer Night's Dream*. As with the other Magoo productions, this is good, wholesome entertainment for children.

## MR. NORTH — RATING 3.0
**1988 PG Comedy Age 17+ 97 min. Color**
Story of Yale graduate Theophilus North who wants to do something different with his life. He decides to tutor children and work with the elderly. Theophilus discovers he is full of static electricity, which enables him to heal various ailments. He's sincere and genuinely cares for others. *Mr. North* is a pleasant, entertaining story. Contains one suggestive scene.

## MR. SMITH GOES TO WASHINGTON — RATING 4.0
**1939 NR Drama-Comedy Age 12+ 129 min. B&W**
Jimmy Stewart portrays an idealistic, young boy scout leader who becomes a senator. He is devastated by the political corruption on Capitol Hill, but refuses to participate. He runs into trouble with his backers, who expect him to be easily manipulated. Instead, he exposes illegal activities in a persuasive filibuster scene that ranks as one of the best in American films. A movie that espouses Christian values.

## MR. SUPERINVISIBLE — RATING 2.5
**1973 G Adventure-Comedy Age 06+ 90 min. Color**
Peter is a bio-chemist who discovers a cure for the common cold. At the same time, one of Peter's friends has also discovered a way to make people invisible and wants Peter to make them visible again. Now, enter the Russians who attempt to steal the cold cure so that the Soviet Union can get credit for the cure. A comedy battle erupts as the Russians and Peter contend for the cold cure.

## MRS. MINIVER — RATING 3.5
**1942 NR Drama Age 12+ 134 min. B&W**
This seven-time Oscar winner features irrepressible Greer Garson as the mother of an English family during World War II. She must face the agonizing heartbreak and traumatic changes wrought by World War II. With quiet strength and grace, she helps her family cope with these difficulties. She also has a run-in with a downed Nazi pilot.

## MUPPET CHRISTMAS CAROL, THE — RATING 3.3
**1992 G Fantasy Age 06+ 85min. Color**
Creative adaptation of Dickens' holiday classic, featuring the indomitable muppets, Kermit the Frog as Bob Cratchit and Miss Piggy as his wife. Michael Caine plays the crotchety miser who experiences a dramatic change of heart. This film celebrates the true spirit of Christmas with messages of compassion and hope. Kids will love the Muppets' humorous antics and catchy tunes. The ghosts in Scrooge's dreams may disturb very young children.

## MUPPET MOVIE, THE — RATING 3.2
**1979 G Adventure Age 04+ 94 min. Color**
Kermit the Frog, tired of life in a Georgia swamp, travels to Hollywood in pursuit of fame and fortune. On the way, he picks up a varied assortment of fellow Muppets. Kermit prefers a major contract with a name studio instead of making TV commercials for fried froggie legs. He ends up with a contract with Orson Welles. An all-star cast includes Mel Brooks, Bob Hope, and Steve Martin. Will appeal to kids of all ages.

## MUPPETS TAKE MANHATTAN, THE    RATING 3.0
1984    G    Adventure-Musical    Age 04+    93 min.    Color

Jim Henson's adorable characters try to get a break on the Broadway stage with a musical written by Kermit the Frog. They find out, however, that it's not as easy as it looks. New muppet "Rizzo the Rat" is introduced and Kermit and Miss Piggy get married. Cheery songs and a fairly good story will brighten up any child's day. An amusing piece of fun.

## MURDER ON THE ORIENT EXPRESS    RATING 3.5
1974    PG    Mystery    Age 12+    128 min.    Color

Albert Finney portrays Hercule Poirot, the impeccable Belgian detective, in this entertaining Agatha Christie suspense thriller. When a murder is committed on a luxury train bound for Turkey, everyone on the train, of course is a suspect. Each suspect is questioned thoroughly by Detective Poirot. Surprise ending. A veteran cast includes Lauren Bacall, Richard Widmark, and Ingrid Bergman. Complex plot may be over children's heads.

## MUSIC MAN, THE    RATING 3.7
1962    NR    Musical    Age 06+    150 min.    Color

There's trouble in River City when slick-talking Harold Hill (Robert Preston) arrives to organize a marching band. The charming con-artist talks the parents into buying band uniforms and instruments. He even persuades skeptical Marian, the librarian (Shirley Jones), to believe in him. A rousing musical score features jubilant songs like "Trouble", "Seventy-Six Trombones" and "Wells Fargo Wagon."

## MY BRILLIANT CAREER    RATING 3.7
1979    G    Docudrama    Age 12+    101 min.    Color

In this autobiographical film, an independent-thinking Australian farm woman chooses to forego her gentleman farmer suitor. She is determined to remain single to pursue a career in writing. Since the setting is the turn of the century, however, she encounters fierce opposition from her family. Striking performances and a realistic script makes this film an enjoyable treasure.

## MY FAIR LADY    RATING 3.7
1964    NR    Musical    Age 12+    170 min.    Color

Professor Henry Higgins (Rex Harrison) is determined to turn a poor Cockney flower-girl (Audrey Hepburn) into a society lady to win a bet with a colleague. He manages to rid her of her cockney accent, but can't change her irrepressible personality. To his dismay, he ends up "growing accustomed to her face". Musical score includes "The Rain in Spain" and "On the Street Where You Live". Bright, brilliant.

## MY FATHER'S GLORY    RATING 3.7
1991    G    Drama    Age 12+    110 min.    Color

Sentimental French film with English subtitles based on the childhood remembrances of Maurice Pagnol, a famous French author. It focuses on a summer vacation, including his encounter with a mountain boy. This humorous chronicle of life explores the follies of parents from a child's eye. Because of the film's intellectual subject matter, young children may not understand its themes. Two moderate obscenities, one moderate crudity and some child nudity.

## MY FAVORITE BRUNETTE    RATING 3.3
1947    NR    Comedy    Age 06+    87 min.    B&W

Bob Hope is a professional photographer who masquerades as a private eye to rescue a fair damsel in distress, Dorothy Lamour. He tries to help Dorothy out of a tight fix. But a gang of mobsters (Peter Lorre, Lon Chaney, etc.) are determined to rub both of them out of the picture. Hope fans will love this hilarious comedy.

## MY SWEET CHARLIE    RATING 3.5
1970    TVM    Drama    Age 12+    97 min.    Color

Patty Duke portrays a young, pregnant, unmarried woman kicked out of the house by her parents. She ends up taking refuge in a vacant cottage on a Gulf Coast seashore. A black New York lawyer on the run from the police does the same. They eventually get along so well that they help each other out as the police are tracking them down. A moving social drama with racial overtones. Patty Duke received the first Emmy for a TV movie for her role.

### MYSTERIOUS ISLAND                                                                RATING 3.5
1961        NR          Science Fiction Adventure        Age 12+        101 min.        Color

Adapted from the Jules Verne tale, two Yankee captives escape from a Confederate jail in a hot-air balloon. Unfortunately, they are blown off-course and land on a nightmarish island inhabited by oversized roosters, bees and crabs. The island turns out to be Captain Nemo's experimental lab. When a volcano erupts, they scramble to escape. Scary special effects and a chilling, fast-moving plot.

### MYSTERY OF FIRE ISLAND                                                            RATING 3.0(e)
1981        G           Mystery                          Age 06+        45 min.         Color

A young girl named Darla and her youthful cousin Jess attempt to explain some very suspicious activities in a small seaside village. One of the local fishermen has disappeared and a surfer with scuba gear goes out to sea every night. When Darla and Jess pursue their investigation, they find the fisherman and trouble. Young people will be intrigued by this mystery adventure.

### NADIA                                                                              RATING 3.0(e)
1984        TVM         Docudrama-Sports                 Age 06+        99 min.         Color

Engaging story about gymnast Nadia and her struggle to achieve olympic quality. It appears that her coach, Bela, has guarded her so closely that she has lost the ability to be disciplined on her own. Though Bela has his own problems, his wife helps him so that he can train not only Nadia, but other aspiring gymnasts as well. Filmed on location in Yugoslavia, *Nadia* is well done, fine entertainment.

### NANCY DREW MYSTERIES: GHOSTWRITER'S CRUISE                                        RATING 2.0(e)
1977        TVM         Mystery                          Age 12+        50 min.         Color

One of Nancy Drew's more exciting adventures has her aboard a cruise ship, vacationing with some friends. Suddenly, a mystery writer on board begins to receive death threats and Nancy is the only one who can track the suspect down before he carries out his threat. One of a series taken from the popular television show of the 1970's, Nancy's exploits will keep viewers on the edge of their seats.

### NAPOLEON AND SAMANTHA                                                              RATING 2.9
1972        G           Adventure                        Age 06+        91 min.         Color

An orphan boy named Napoleon (Michael Douglas) wants to keep his deceased grandfather's pet lion. He and his friend Samantha (Jodie Foster) run away with the animal across the rugged Oregon wilderness to meet up with a sheepherder. On the way, they experience life-threatening adventures. Good family viewing.

### NATIONAL VELVET                                                                    RATING 3.7
1944        NR          Drama                            Age 06+        125 min.        Color

Two youngsters set their sights on training their beloved horse to win the Grand National Race. Starring a very young Elizabeth Taylor and boyish Mickey Rooney, this magnificent family film will delight horse lovers. In the final race scene, Velvet disguises herself as a boy jockey and rides her horse in the race. Both Rooney's and Taylor's best youthful performances. Magnificent family film will particularly appeal to young girls.

### NATIVITY, THE                                                                      RATING 2.3
1978        TVM         Docudrama-Biblical               Age 06+        97 min.         Color

Well done story about Christ's birth and the parents of Christ. It is actually a love story about Mary and Joseph with a good supporting cast such as British star Leo McKern as Herod. The wise men and kings are beautifully portrayed. The emotions and relationships surrounding the birth of Christ are brought out in this tender, inspiring video.

### NEVER CRY WOLF                                                                     RATING 3.5
1983        PG          Adventure                        Age 12+        105 min.        Color

A biologist-author braves the Arctic wilderness to determine if the wolves have been killing the caribou. Befriended by an old Eskimo man, he experiences many adventures. He must contend with mice encroaching on his campsite and a herd of wild caribou. When he learns the wolves only attack sick animals, he concludes that man is more dangerous than other animals. Fleeting, obscured view of male nudity and a scene of the biologist eating roasted mice.

### NEVER ENDING STORY PART II      RATING 2.3
1991     PG     Fantasy-Adventure     Age 06+     89 min.     Color

Colorful sequel about a young boy who escapes from his humdrum life into the storybook world of Fantasia. There, he battles a wicked queen whose sole desire is to destroy earthlings' ability to discern. This clever fantasy poignantly portrays the priceless treasure of parent-child relationships. Children will enjoy this delightful excursion into magical lands. Some frightening monsters and a sensuous queen may offend some viewers.

### NEW ADVENTURES OF PIPPI LONGSTOCKING      RATING 1.5
1988     G     Adventure     Age 06+     100 min.     Color

When eleven year old Pippi is separated from her pirate father in a shipwreck, she finds her way back to her old homestead. Living alone, she makes friends with two children. Eventually she's forced into an orphanage where she learns to love the orphans. This amusing, light hearted film will appeal particularly to children.

### NEWSIES      RATING 2.2
1992     PG     Musical     Age 12+     125 min.     Color

This charming musical features ragged street children who sell newspapers in New York City at the turn of the century. They go on strike against a powerful publisher who attempts to run them out of business. Exuberant songs and eye-catching, foot-stomping choreography makes this film a real crowd-pleaser. A delightful blend of "West Side Story" and "Oliver." One regular profanity along with one moderate crude word.

### NIGHT CROSSING      RATING 2.7
1981     PG     Adventure     Age 06+     107 min.     Color

Based on a true story, this suspenseful Disney film recalls the 1979 escape of two East German families via hot-air balloons to the other side of the Wall. Their escape follows the unsuccessful attempt of a fleeing teenage boy who is riddled with bullets. Some very tense moments as they are chased by vicious border guards. A dramatic, entertaining story starring John Hurt and Jane Alexander.

### NIGHT THEY SAVED CHRISTMAS, THE      RATING 3.2
1984     TVM     Adventure-Fantasy     Age 06+     100 min.     Color

In this delightful children's movie, three children work with Santa Claus (Art Carney) in an effort to protect his toy factory. It's in danger of being destroyed by an oil company exploring the North Pole. This leads to some exciting adventures. Clever, colorful and imaginative fantasy.

### NIGHT TRAIN TO KATHMANDU, THE      RATING 2.5(e)
1988     NR     Adventure-Fantasy     Age 06+     102 min.     Color

A husband and wife team, both archeologists, travel to Kathmandu, Nepal, with their teenage daughter, Lily, and young son. On the train, Lily meets a handsome young Indian man, Johar, who joins them as a servant. Two local archeologists tell them of a mysterious "lost city" which appears briefly every forty years in Nepal. The archeologists discover that Johar is the prince of the lost city and must return to it. Intriguing, colorful film.

### NINETEEN EIGHTEEN (1918)      RATING 2.7
1984     PG     Drama     Age 12+     94 min.     Color

A dangerous influenza epidemic grips a small Texas town during World War I. By the creator of "Tender Mercies," this movie shows the different ways people react to the tragic epidemic, including one woman who loses both her infant and her husband. Matthew Broderick gives a fine performance as a young man unable to decide what to do in the midst of the crisis. Movie contains several mild crude words.

### NO TIME FOR SERGEANTS      RATING 3.5
1958     NR     Comedy     Age 12+     111 min.     B&W

In this wonderfully funny comedy, homespun humorist Andy Griffith delightfully portrays a Georgia country boy drafted into the Air Force. Through plain ignorance, he creates crisis situations and almost makes nervous wrecks out of his superiors. Andy also manages to create chaos for his buddies. This hilarious film version of a Broadway play will tickle every viewer's funnybone.

### NORTH AVENUE IRREGULARS, THE — RATING 2.3
1979   G   Comedy-Drama   Age 06+   100 min.   Color

A righteously indignant young priest forms a vigilante committee made up of equally outraged church women to fight a local gambling operation. Lots of action including fighting, shooting and car crashes. Karen Valentine and Cloris Leachman star in this easy going Disney film based on a true story. The major theme is crime doesn't pay! Fun for the whole family.

### NORTH BY NORTHWEST — RATING 4.0
1959   PG   Adventure-Suspense   Age 12+   136 min.   Color

This spine-tingling Hitchcock classic features Cary Grant as an advertising agent mistakenly identified by the police as an assassin. Some spies are after him too, because they think he's an enemy espionage agent. Eva Marie Saint stars as Grant's romantic interest, and James Mason plays a very convincing villain. Remarkable action-chase scenes, including the ones involving a crop duster and Mount Rushmore.

### NORTH TO ALASKA — RATING 3.3
1960   NR   Adventure-Comedy   Age 12+   122 min.   Color

John Wayne, Stewart Granger and Fabian play rough and ready prospectors in this comical adventure. Their struggles include dealing with a sleazy con man, a headstrong kid brother, and a troublesome woman. Wayne travels back to Seattle to fetch his buddy's fiancee, but she's already married to someone else. A beautiful woman he meets on the boat agrees to meet his friend. Unfortunately, all three prospectors fall in love with her.

### NOT MY KID — RATING 3.1
1985   TVM   Drama   Age 12+   100 min.   Color

This perceptive TV drama shows the mindless destruction that drug abuse causes in a respectable doctor's family. A fifteen-year-old girl, Susan, almost succeeds in hiding her habit, but her parents finally realize what's happening. In a show of tough love, they put her in a drug treatment center. A moving, graphic film that deals with a couple's denial of a serious problem. Contains three moderate vulgarities and many hells and damns.

### NOT WITHOUT MY DAUGHTER — RATING 2.8
1991   PG13   Drama   Age 17+   114 min.   Color

Compelling, tension-filled drama of an American woman (Sally Field) and her young daughter held hostage in Teheran by her Iranian-born husband. When she attempts to escape, he becomes harsh and dictatorial. This film vividly portrays life in oppressive Teheran and the practices of Islam. Several moderate and severe violent scenes of the husband beating his wife. One regular profanity and one moderate crude word.

### NOW YOU SEE HIM, NOW YOU DON'T — RATING 2.2
1972   G   Comedy   Age 06+   88 min.   Color

Dean Higgins runs a college in financial straights. If the school defaults, it will be converted into a gambling establishment. Higgins enters a golf tournament to win the necessary funds, but this turns into a comical disaster. The only alternative to make money is a student's (Dexter) science project which makes people invisible. From here on, it's one madcap comical happening after another.

### NUTCRACKER — RATING 3.0
1993   G   Musical-Fantasy   Age 04+   92 min.   Color

Enchanting ballet rendition of Tchaikovsky's timeless masterpiece, featuring Macaulay Culkin as the handsome Nutcracker Prince. Wide-eyed, 11-year-old Marie falls in love with him and becomes his princess. The beautifully choreographed performances are set among spectacular backdrops, including a snowy forest and multi-colored, patterned interiors. Children of all ages will love this colorful ballet story.

### NUTTY PROFESSOR, THE — RATING 3.3
1963   NR   Comedy   Age 06+   107 min.   Color

Jerry Lewis stars in probably one of his funniest films ever. This one features a nerdy college professor in love with a coed. He turns himself into a smooth-talking man about town after drinking a magic formula he cooked up in his lab. A humorous satire on *Dr. Jekyll and Mr. Hyde* and on social attitudes regarding physical attractiveness. Lewis fans will love their hero's fun slapstick gags.

### OF MICE AND MEN                                                        RATING 3.0
**1981        TVM        Drama              Age 12+        125 min.        Color**

Robert Blake's adaptation of John Steinbeck's unforgettable story about two friends, Lenny and George. Lenny (Randy Quaid) is a huge man, but mentally slow and looks to George for guidance as they work on the farms of California. George (Robert Blake) tries to protect Lenny's innocence, but something goes terribly wrong when the farm owner's wife enters the picture. A well-acted thought-provoking movie, with one sexually suggestive scene.

### OKLAHOMA!                                                              RATING 3.2
**1955        NR         Musical            Age 06+        145 min.        Color**

This grand Rodgers and Hammerstein musical sparkles with an old-fashioned romance that develops between an Oklahoma cowboy (Gordon MacRae) and a country girl (Shirley Jones). Bouncy tunes like "A Surrey with the Fringe on Top" and "I'm Just a Girl Who Can't Say No" are included. Many enjoyable dance scenes in this all-time favorite musical. Entertaining look at the land with the waving wheat.

### OLD YELLER                                                             RATING 3.3
**1957        NR         Drama-Adventure    Age 06+        83 min.         Color**

A stray golden retriever captures the heart of a young boy who adopts him as a pet. Yeller earns his way by keeping the boy out of trouble and protecting them from a bear, a wolf and a wild boar. Beautiful portrayal of farm life in 1859 Texas. This Disney film has a sad ending, but children and adults will love it.

### OLIVER TWIST                                                           RATING 3.8(e)
**1982        TVM        Drama              Age 06+        100 min.        Color**

This classic tale features an abandoned street urchin "adopted" by a scruffy gang of pickpockets until a wealthy benefactor offers him more pleasant surroundings. George C. Scott delivers an admirable performance as Fagin, the ringleader of the gang. Viewers will delight in this marvelous adaptation of a timeless treasure. Good period piece.

### OLIVER!                                                                RATING 4.0
**1968        G          Musical            Age 12+        153 min.        Color**

Musical based on *Oliver Twist* features Dickens' sparkling tale about an orphan boy who falls in with a mob of pickpockets. Dickens' tale has never looked better. An exhilarating musical score including such well-known songs as "Consider Yourself," "As Long As He Needs Me" and "Who Will Buy?" will delight viewers of all ages. Dazzling choreography and elaborate sets just add flavor to a zesty presentation.

### ON THE TOWN                                                            RATING 4.0
**1949        NR         Musical-Comedy     Age 12+        98 min.         Color**

In this exuberant musical treat, Gene Kelly and Frank Sinatra play sailors on a twenty-four hour leave in New York City. They manage to fall in love and lose their love all in the same day. Kelly, of course, puts on his dancing shoes. "Old Blue Eyes" even joins the fun singing "New York, New York". Classic entertainment filmed on location.

### ON THE WATERFRONT                                                      RATING 4.0
**1954        NR         Drama              Age 12+        108 min.        B&W**

This shocking drama exposes the horrible corruption in the harbor unions of New Jersey. Marlon Brando remarkably portrays an honest longshoreman who doesn't fit in with the system. His goal is to expose the mobsters who control the system. He runs into foul play but triumphs over it. Rod Steiger plays a scheming brother and Lee J. Cobb plays Brando's boss. Intense, award-winning film for serious viewers.

### ON VALENTINE'S DAY                                                     RATING 2.5
**1986        PG         Drama              Age 17+        106 min.        Color**

In a small Texas town in 1917, newlyweds Horace and Elizabeth share the heartaches and joys of different people who come to stay in their rooming house. These include Elizabeth's father, who is not happy with his son-in-law; Bessie, a talkative teenager; tormented alcoholic Mr. Bobby; and mentally disturbed George Tyler. Delightful story and good performances. Few moderately crude words and two profanities.

### ONCE UPON A FOREST                                                RATING 2.5
1993        G          Fantasy                Age 04+        80 min.         Color

A group of small forest animals learn how to survive under the tutelage of a wise old owl. Their mischievous, fun-loving ways constantly test the teacher's patience. Soon, however, the animals are faced with real danger when a gasoline truck overturns and spills gasoline in the forest. A clever, animated story for children featuring the voice of Ben Vereen, but with some misleading messages about environmental issues and land developers.

### ONE AGAINST THE WIND                                              RATING 3.3
1991        TVM        Drama                  Age 12+        100 min.        Color

Mary Lindell is an Englishwoman living in France during the start of World War II. When France is invaded by Germany, Mary and her son and daughter become caught up in helping the English soldiers escape. The first Englishman she saves also happens to fall in love with her and so the romance begins. An exciting war-time movie with only a little war-time violence that is not excessive.

### ONE HUNDRED AND ONE DALMATIONS                                    RATING 3.5
1961        NR         Adventure-Drama        Age 04+        80 min.         Color

Perhaps one of Disney's finest animated projects, this film features two dogs trying to save their enormous brood from being destroyed by some ruthless villains. The lines between good and evil are sharply drawn. Parents and children will enjoy the thrilling story and charming characters. Wonderful, clean fun.

### ONE MAGIC CHRISTMAS                                               RATING 2.8
1985        PG         Drama                  Age 06+        95 min.         Color

Mary Steenburgen plays a woman who has such a negative attitude towards Christmas that she is considered a Mother Scrooge by everyone. When death strikes the father of the family, a guardian angel is assigned to the family to bring back their Christmas cheer. Santa exercises supernatural powers when he restores the father to life and helps find the kidnapped children. Even the mother comes to believe in Santa Claus and angels.

### ONLY YOU                                                          RATING 3.2
1994        PG         Comedy-Romance         Age 12+        102 min.        Color

A romantic adventure about a young woman engaged to a doctor in Pittsburgh. When she briefly sees whom she believes to be the man of her childhood dreams, however, she leaves her fiance and chases after him. It takes her all the way to Italy. Some beautiful scenery and surprising plot twists make this a delightful romantic comedy. Several mild crude words, one regular profanity, and mild sexual innuendoes only slightly mar this fine film.

### OPERATION DUMBO DROP                                              RATING 3.0(e)
1995        PG         Comedy                 Age 06+        102 min.        Color

Based on the true story of five American soldiers transporting an elephant to a remote tribe during the Viet Nam war. The elephant is offered to the tribe in exchange for help in the war against the Viet Cong. Though none of the soldiers want to be assigned to this job, the hardships and humor bring them together. Some fighting and several mild crude words, but basically a family film.

### OPERATION PETTICOAT                                               RATING 3.7
1959        NR         Comedy                 Age 12+        124 min.        Color

Cary Grant plays a submarine captain intent upon mending his disabled ship in this rip-roaring comedy. Tony Curtis comes to his rescue as a slick wheeler-dealer. To add to their troubles, a bevy of Navy nurses must join their crew. More mayhem occurs when the captain gets orders to carry a group of Filipino families and a goat through the islands. Set in the South Pacific during World War II, this movie will keep viewers laughing.

### ORDEAL OF DR. MUDD, THE                                           RATING 3.3
1980        TVM        Drama                  Age 17+        158 min.        Color

A true story about a man falsely accused of aiding John Wilkes Booth in Booth's successful assassination of President Lincoln. The man serves three years of a life sentence before the ruling is overturned. In prison, he is savagely mistreated but his honesty and integrity bring him through. The severe abuse of the prisoners may be too intense for younger viewers, but this is a compelling film for adults.

## ORPHAN TRAIN
**RATING 3.3**
1979　　　TVM　　　Drama　　　　　　　　Age 06+　　　150 min.　　　Color

A compassionate social worker in the mid-1800s starts a soup kitchen for New York City's street children. She soon realizes they need homes. She takes them to the Midwest frontier by train, hoping that some of the farming families will adopt them. This fictionalized story is based on the first of hundreds of orphan trains funded by what became the Children's Aid Society of New York. A touching, soul-stirring film.

## OTHER SIDE OF THE MOUNTAIN
**RATING 2.5**
1975　　　PG　　　Docudrama-Romance　　　Age 06+　　　103 min.　　　Color

This true story is about Jill Kinmont, an Olympic-bound skier who is paralyzed from the neck down in an accident. The drama depicts her accident and her courageous attempts at an uphill recovery. Some difficulties develop with her boyfriend, however. Believable and well done, it is an excellent tribute to one woman's determination and hope. Contains nine mild and moderate crude words and one profanity.

## OUR TOWN
**RATING 3.5**
1940　　　NR　　　Drama　　　　　　　　Age 12+　　　90 min.　　　B&W

Movie adaptation of Thornton Wilder's Pulitzer Prize winning play starring William Holden. Fine story that deals with the problems and trials that beset the inhabitants of a small New Hampshire town. Portrays the day-to-day happenings and characters in Grover's Corners, including two young lovers (Holden and Martha Scott) and the families of each. Those from small communities will particularly appreciate the unique problems and joys that came with such an environment.

## PACK OF LIES
**RATING 3.2(e)**
1987　　　TVM　　　Drama-Suspense　　　Age 12+　　　100 min.　　　Color

In a quiet London neighborhood, the Jenkins family are the best of friends with their seemingly ordinary next-door neighbors. One day, however, a top secret police agent asks the Jenkins to spy on their neighbors. The Jenkins family is drawn into an ever-increasing web of intrigue and suspense as they must lie to their neighbors to cover up the investigation. A first class nail-biter.

## PAGEMASTER, THE
**RATING 2.3**
1994　　　G　　　Fantasy-Adventure　　　Age 06+　　　76 min.　　　Color

Rich Tyler (Macaulay Culkin) is about to take a wondrous journey to the land of books. In cartoon form, he discovers the great tales of adventure and fantasy such as *Moby Dick* and *Alice in Wonderland*. Through these books, Rich learns how to deal with his own life better, and overcome the feelings of fear which he has. A fine film with a few scary scenes too intense for young children.

## PAINTED HILLS, THE
**RATING 3.2**
1951　　　NR　　　Adventure　　　　　　Age 06+　　　90 min.　　　Color

Lassie tale set in the west in the 1870's. An old miner, Jonathan, strikes a rich vein of gold in the mountains with the help of his trusty dog Shep (Lassie). But he's double-crossed by his greedy partner who wants all the gold. With Lassie's help, the villain is outsmarted and his deception exposed. Fast moving adventure story with impressive outdoor scenery.

## PALEFACE
**RATING 3.3**
1948　　　NR　　　Comedy-Western　　　Age 06+　　　91 min.　　　Color

Outlandish comedy featuring Bob Hope as a cowardly, timid dentist who manages to get himself into numerous problems, namely gunfights. He manages to overcome the obstacles with the aid of sharpshooter Jane Russell (Calamity Jane) backing him up. Good western entertainment for everyone.

## PARENT TRAP, THE
**RATING 3.3**
1961　　　NR　　　Comedy　　　　　　　Age 06+　　　124 min.　　　Color

Twin girls meet for the first time when their divorced parents unknowingly send them to the same summer camp. Once they discover who each other is, they devise a plan to reunite their parents into a happy family. This is the original Walt Disney production starring Hayley Mills, David Swift and Brian Keith. The comedy is clever and suitable for all ages.

## PASSAGE TO INDIA                                                  RATING 3.4
**1984        PG        Drama              Age 17+        163 min.        Color**

A young British woman (Judy Davis) visits India during the time of British colonial rule. She goes on an outing with an Indian doctor and upon their return accuses him of rape. The case is tried in a British court and has a rather surprising outcome. Has no crude language, nudity or violence, but not appropriate for children. Captures both the grandeur and racial discrimination of British rule in India.

## PASTIME                                                            RATING 3.5
**1991        PG        Drama              Age 12+        94min.         Color**

Character study about a 41-year-old minor league baseball player whose dream is to beat the record for the longest professional career. Unfortunately, the team owner wants to retire him. When a mean-spirited teammate breaks the news, his life comes to a tragic end. This somber film shows the folly of one man valuing athletic achievement rather than personal responsibility. Some drinking, many mild crude words, and one severe obscenity.

## PEBBLE AND THE PENGUIN, THE                                        RATING 2.2(e)
**1995        G         Fantasy            Age 04+        76 min.         Color**

The animated tale of Hubie the penguin and his quest to marry the beautiful penguin Marina. To marry her, he must find the perfect pebble with which to woo her. Unfortunately, the evil penguin Drake has other ideas and throws Hubie to the vicious leopard seals. Hubie must make a long journey back to regain his love. Some scary scenes may be too intense for very young children.

## PENNY SERENADE                                                     RATING 3.5
**1941        NR        Drama              Age 12+        120 min.        B&W**

Emotionally charged story of a couple who adopt a child following the death of their own unborn baby. Unfortunately, the second child has difficulties, leaving the couple questioning their own relationship. An intense but wonderful drama. Excellent performance by Cary Grant and Irene Dunne.

## PERSUASION                                                         RATING 2.5(e)
**1995        PG        Drama              Age 17+        103 min.        Color**

Jane Austen's classic romantic novel is set in England in the early 1800's. An English nobleman's daughter turns down a very handsome suitor on the advice of a friend who thinks he is not socially acceptable. Later he returns as a very prominent captain in the British Navy, but will the two ever get together? This gentle love story will appeal particularly to teenage girls and young women.

## PETE'S DRAGON                                                      RATING 2.5
**1977        G         Fantasy-Musical    Age 04+        105 min.        Color**

Children will enjoy this music filled fantasy about Elliot, an animated dragon. He can appear and disappear at will and comes to the aid of a mistreated nine-year-old boy who's the only one who can see him. He helps the boy learn the lessons of life as he grows up. Features star studded cast, including Helen Reddy, Mickey Rooney, Red Buttons and Shelly Winters.

## PETER PAN                                                          RATING 3.5
**1953        G         Adventure-Fantasy  Age 06+        77 min.         Color**

Walt Disney film about three children who encounter Peter Pan and magically fly with him to Never-Never Land. Here they encounter mermaids, Indians, and Captain Hook, Peter Pan's arch enemy. The conflict between Peter Pan and Captain Hook leads to many suspenseful chases and threatening encounters. Humorous, tender and poignant film. One violent killing and some drunkenness.

## PHILADELPHIA STORY                                                 RATING 3.8
**1940        NR        Comedy-Drama       Age 12+        112 min.        B&W**

Katherine Hepburn stars as a spoiled, stuffy, rich girl who is consumed with the desire to have a sincere, normal romance. Cary Grant plays her ex-husband whom she still loves. James Stewart is a reporter who falls in love with her and manages to get her committed to a marriage proposal. But the outcome of all these relationships remains in doubt. This is a top rate film.

### PIANO FOR MRS. CIMINO, A                                                                RATING 3.5
1982          TVM          Drama                    Age 12+          96 min.          Color

Esther Cimino is battling senility and her sons have her declared incompetent. They take control of her assets, which they greedily divide between themselves. Karen, Esther's granddaughter, works to help her regain her dignity. Esther petitions the court to grant her the right to manage her own affairs. Fine sensitive movie depicting the problems faced by the elderly.

### PICTURE BRIDE, THE                                                                        RATING 3.2
1995          PG-13        Drama                    Age 17+          98 min.          Color

In 1918, Matsuji, a Japanese farmer living in Hawaii, sends for a young bride from Japan. To the bride's horror, Matsuji is older and poorer than his letters indicated. Matsuji must win her love quickly in this old-fashioned romantic tale with only a few suggestive elements, some rear female nudity and an incident of communicating with the spirit of a dead person. A great period piece with English subtitles.

### PIED PIPER OF HAMELIN, THE                                                              RATING 4.0(e)
1985          TVM          Drama-Fantasy            Age 04+          63 min.          Color

A classic story based on the Robert Browning poem about a small town that is invaded by rats after a flood. The people are greeted by a piper who claims he can rid them of the problem for a price. The agree to let him handle the problem, which he does successfully. The real problems begin when the town refuses to pay the piper for his services.

### PIED PIPER OF HAMELIN                                                                   RATING 2.5(e)
1957          TVM          Musical-Fantasy          Age 06+          92 min.          Color

The mayor of a town near Hamelin pleads for help for its children because of a recent flood. Unfortunately, the council and mayor turn a deaf ear to his plea. But soon rats come to Hamelin because of the flooding. A piper comes to town claiming he can drive the rats away. The work is done, but the town refuses to pay. Something dreadful is in store for Hamelin. A delightful musical version of this famous fairy tale.

### PINOCCHIO                                                                                 RATING 4.0
1940          G            Fantasy                  Age 04+          88 min.          Color

Re-release of Disney's animated classic magical story of a little puppet who becomes a real boy. Jiminy Cricket acts as his conscience, and finds out that it's no easy job! How Pinocchio becomes a real boy and a hero will delight young children. Colorful scenery and imaginative characters add to the entertainment quality of this film. Many moderately violent scenes may frighten very young children.

### PIONEER WOMAN                                                                             RATING 2.8
1973          TVM          Drama-Western            Age 12+          78 min.          Color

William Shatner (Captain Kirk of *Star Trek* fame) stars in this true to life drama about the experiences faced by families who uproot themselves and head to homestead farmland in 1867 Wyoming. The joys and difficulties are particularly insightful, especially when they are presented from the perspective of the women who must endure the difficulties with their husbands.

### PIRATES OF PENZANCE                                                                       RATING 3.0
1983          PG           Musical-Adventure        Age 06+          112 min.         Color

Delightful Gilbert & Sullivan musical about a young man who leaves a band of pirates for a better life. He falls in love with one of several lovely sisters who live on a beautiful cove near the sea. When the old gang tries to get the young man to rejoin them, they all get involved in an enormous brawl with the local police. Enhanced by a variety of lively song and dance numbers. Angela Lansbury, Linda Ronstadt and Kevin Kline star. Great fun!

### PISTOL: BIRTH OF A LEGEND                                                                 RATING 3.3
1991          G            Docudrama                Age 06+          104 min.         Color

Moving childhood biography of Pete Maravich, renowned basketball star who played for the Atlanta Hawks. "Pistol's" father, a coach for Clemson University, gives direction and vision to him. He and his son convince the high school team to play the segregated black team for the unofficial state championship. A wonderful family movie about a strong father-son relationship.

### PLACE FOR ANNIE, A                                                                        RATING 4.0
1994         TVM        Drama                    Age 12+         98 min.          Color

Moving story about a divorced pediatric nurse (Sissy Spacek) who seeks to adopt an HIV-positive baby as a foster parent. Trouble ensues when the birth mother, a former drug addict dying of AIDS, wants the child back. Because of her love for the child, the nurse invites the mother to live in her home. Viewers will need a box of tissues for this heartwrenching tearjerker. Several mild crude words.

### POINT, THE                                                                                RATING 3.8
1971         TVM        Musical-Fantasy          Age 06+         73 min.          Color

This is a very unusual story about a boy named Oblio who must leave his homeland because he is born with a round head. In his kingdom everything and everyone has a pointed top. This interesting animated tale has a fine musical score and demonstrates the foolishness of determining the worth of someone because they are different.

### POLLYANNA                                                                                 RATING 3.5
1960         NR         Drama                    Age 06+         134 min.         Color

This fine story features the popular Hayley Mills as an exceptional thirteen-year-old who has the ability to encourage all those she comes into contact with. With her magnetic personality she imparts a positive outlook on life. She is especially successful in helping the older people feel good about themselves and life. All-star cast including Jane Wyman, Agnes Moorehead and Donald Crisp.

### POPE JOHN PAUL II                                                                         RATING 3.8(e)
1984         TVM        Docudrama                Age 12+         147 min.         Color

Excellent historical overview of the life and times of Pope John Paul II. Covers the Pontiff's adult life from his opposition to Nazism and Communism to his inauguration as Pope in 1978. Presents revealing insights to his personality, ambitions and convictions. Albert Finney gives a magnificent portrayal of one of the most influential leaders in the world.

### PRANCER                                                                                   RATING 3.2
1989         G          Drama-Fantasy            Age 06+         103 min.         Color

As Christmas approaches, nine-year-old Jessica Riggs discovers a wounded reindeer in the snow-covered woods near her house. She's convinced it belongs to Santa and nurses it back to health in an old barn. Amidst all the curiosity and discussion this generates in the community, Jessica softens crusty hearts and creates a renewed Christmas spirit in her town. In this very delightful Christmas story, Christ is exalted through traditional hymns and Christmas carols.

### PRIDE AND PREJUDICE                                                                       RATING 4.0
1940         NR         Drama                    Age 12+         118 min.         B&W

Jane Austen's novel comes to life in this story about five women who are eagerly searching for the right man. One woman in particular is attracted to the man she despised at first because of his arrogant spirit. The setting is 19th century England. Laurence Olivier, Greer Garson and Maureen O'Sullivan enhance the quality of this excellent classic film.

### PRIDE OF THE YANKEES                                                                      RATING 3.8
1942         NR         Docudrama                Age 06+         127 min.         B&W

Magnificent biographical presentation about the life of baseball star Lou Gehrig, who died of ametropic lateral sclerosis, commonly known as Lou Gehrig's disease. It follows Gehrig's career from his childhood days to the time he is struck by the fatal disease. Gary Cooper gives an expert performance, supported by such stars as Walter Brennan and Sam Wood. This is a moving story that will be appreciated by all.

### PRINCE AND THE PAUPER, THE                                                                RATING 2.7
1978         PG         Drama-Adventure          Age 06+         113 min.         Color

The Prince of Wales in 16th century England and a pauper boy discover that they look very much alike. They seize the opportunity to switch places and experience the other's lifestyle. The adventure, however, becomes a test of endurance, as the young prince valiantly struggles to return to the palace and regain his throne. Courage, perseverance and integrity determine the outcome.

### PRINCE OF CENTRAL PARK, THE                                                  RATING 3.0
**1977        TVM        Adventure                    Age 06+        76 min.        Color**
When a young brother and his sister find the environment of a foster home too unpleasant to endure, they decide to leave in search of a better life and independence. They find refuge in a tree house located in Central Park. While trying to survive, a kindly old lady befriends them and contributes to their needs. Starring roles for Ruth Gordon, Harvey Hart and Brooke Shields.

### PRINCESS AND THE PIRATE, THE                                                  RATING 3.0
**1944        NR         Comedy                       Age 06+        94 min.        Color**
Bob Hope is at it again as a man on the run with a beautiful woman (Virginia Mayo) on his arm. This time he is trying to escape the clutches of an evil pirate expertly played by Walter Brennan, but lands up the prisoner of another evildoer, Slezak. This typical Bob Hope fare provides good fun and an enjoyable cast. Ends with great gag.

### PRINCESS BRIDE, THE                                                            RATING 3.2
**1987        PG         Adventure-Fantasy            Age 12+        98 min.        Color**
A uniquely humorous adventure about a fair maiden who reluctantly agrees to marry the Prince of her country. Before the marriage takes place, she's kidnapped by three comical villains, but the Prince and masked pirates try to rescue her. This leads to a series of adventuresome, amusing escapades. Contains battles and a torture scene which could disturb children. One profanity. Some of the best humor seen in recent films.

### PRINCESS CARABOO                                                              RATING 3.3
**1994        PG         Drama-Adventure              Age 12+        94 min.        Color**
A mysterious, young woman appears in a small British village, dressed like a gypsy, wearing a turban. The townsfolk are convinced that she is a princess from a South Sea island. Is she or isn't she? The plot twists will keep viewers guessing. Based on a true story, and set in the early 1800's. One moderate crude word in an otherwise enchanting movie with great acting.

### PRINCESS WHO HAD NEVER LAUGHED, THE                                           RATING 3.5
**1985        NR         Drama-Comedy                 Age 04+        52 min.        Color**
Delightful tale about a Princess who lives in a kingdom where seriousness is the only acceptable form of human expression. Unhappy with such an arrangement, she dares to laugh and express those forbidden emotions. Excellent entertainment for both children and adults.

### PRIVATE LIFE OF SHERLOCK HOLMES, THE                                          RATING 3.5
**1970        PG         Mystery-Drama                Age 12+        125 min.       Color**
Sherlock Holmes (Ronald Stephens) and Dr. Watson get involved with midgets, the Loch Ness monster, and Queen Victoria. Our detectives go dashing here and there with a lovely spy in a madcap romp through 19th century England and Scotland. All ends with some adventure and surprise, but also more laughs and crazy schemes. Holmes is accurately portrayed as using cocaine.

### PROTOTYPE                                                                     RATING 2.2(e)
**1983        TVM        Science-Fiction-Drama        Age 12+        97 min.        Color**
Absorbing drama about the problems resulting from man-made humans. Scientists and government officials clash over ownership of a very human robot. In a sense this is a modern version of Frankenstein. Inventor of the robot steals it from the Pentagon because he thinks they will reprogram it to accomplish a destructive mission. Mild crude language used several times.

### PROUD REBEL, THE                                                              RATING 3.2
**1958        NR         Drama                        Age 12+        103 min.       Color**
Alan Ladd stars as a rowdy southern Civil War veteran who decides to take a long journey throughout the Yankee states. He is desperately searching for a doctor who can give his mute son the treatment he needs. His travels are interrupted when he meets and falls in love with a lonely woman (Olivia deHaviland) who is attempting to keep her farm going.

### PURPLE PEOPLE EATER                                        RATING 2.0
1988        G        Adventure-Fantasy        Age 06+        91 min.        Color

Billy Johnson and his grandfather Sam get to be good friends when Sam moves in to take care of Billy and his younger sister for a while. Things really pick up when a furry, one-eyed purple creature lands in Billy's yard. The creature is very musical, which leads Billy and some friends to form a band and put on some lively concerts. Clever, fun musical adventure for young people.

### PURSUIT                                        RATING 2.2(e)
1972        TVM        Drama        Age 17+        74 min.        Color

Government agent is responsible for arresting a right-wing politician gone mad. The suspect has nerve gas in his possession and is threatening the president of the United States and the city of San Diego. Federal agent must beat the madman at his own game. The film contains a slight attack on nuclear development and the military establishments.

### PUSS IN BOOTS                                        RATING 3.5
1984        TVM        Drama-Fantasy        Age 04+        51 min.        Color

Shelly Duvall narrates this classic tale about a cat who's out to find the easy life by making his master rich. He plans to do this by winning a castle owned by an evil ogre for his master. He also arranges for his master to marry the king's daughter. Delightful children's show from the *Faerie Tale Theatre*.

### QUIET MAN, THE                                        RATING 4.0
1952        NR        Comedy-Drama        Age 12+        129 min.        Color

Story of a boisterous boxer (John Wayne) who returns to his native Ireland in hopes of finding a wife and settling down to family life. He acquires the respect and admiration of the townspeople, and seeks to win the affections of a young woman (Maureen O'Hara). Beautiful scenery and cinematography.

### QUO VADIS                                        RATING 3.2
1951        NR        Drama-Historical        Age 12+        171 min.        Color

A fine cast of stars and superb story make this film exceptional viewing. Robert Taylor plays a Roman soldier during the reign of madman Nero and his persecution of Christians. Deborah Kerr is the Christian girl who captures his affections. Her faith and his involvement with her could result in their deaths. Nero fiddles while Rome burns. Spectacular drama.

### RACE FOR YOUR LIFE, CHARLIE BROWN                        RATING 2.5
1977        G        Adventure        Age 04+        75 min.        Color

Usual Peanuts cartoon featuring Charlie Brown as the underdog who seems to fail at virtually everything he attempts. This time, Charlie Brown must participate in a camp raft race, which provides quite a challenge for the not-so-brave Brown. Unlike many cartoons, this Peanuts show will be fun viewing for adults.

### RAID ON ENTEBBE                                     RATING 3.3
1977        TVM        Docudrama        Age 12+        150 min.        Color

In July 1976 terrorists hijack a jetliner loaded with Jewish passengers and force it to land in Uganda. Israel puts together a commando team to rescue them. They storm the airport with guns blazing. The raid is a sensational success, and most of the Jewish captives are rescued alive. Many intense battles result in some deaths and the virtual destruction of the airport. Strong cast of characters including Charles Bronson, Martin Balsam, John Saxon and James Woods.

### RAISIN IN THE SUN, A                                     RATING 3.8
1961        NR        Drama        Age 12+        128 min.        B&W

In the 1950's, a black family seeks to escape their crowded Chicago apartment life by moving into an all-white neighborhood. To say the least, their problems are just beginning. This film reveals the difficulties that minorities face when they seek to improve themselves. Sidney Poitier and Lou Gossett, Jr. give outstanding performances.

### RARE BREED, THE                                         RATING 2.5
**1966        NR        Western            Age 12+        108 min.        Color**
Fine western about the introduction of the Hereford to the American cattle scene. Texas cattleman Jimmy Stewart grudgingly assists an English woman (Maureen O'Hara) who has brought her Hereford bull to St. Louis to be used in crossbreeding with longhorns. Stewart and Brian Keith play rivals seeking O'Hara's affection.

### REAR WINDOW                                              RATING 4.0
**1954        NR        Mystery-Drama      Age 12+        112 min.        Color**
Jimmy Stewart and Grace Kelly give a superb performance in this classic Hitchcock mystery. Stewart lives in a low-income apartment complex with interesting neighbors. While recovering from a broken leg, he becomes obsessed with spying on a particular neighbor (Raymond Burr) who is acting suspiciously. Stewart is sure that this neighbor has murdered his wife. How he convinces his girlfriend (Kelly) of the murder will entertain mystery-suspense fans.

### REBEL WITHOUT A CAUSE                                    RATING 3.8
**1955        NR        Drama              Age 12+        111 min.        Color**
Powerful story dealing with the problems of youth and how they cause divisions between parents and teens. Self-esteem, communication problems with adults, and the importance of friendships play heavily in this excellent film. This was the picture that put James Dean on the Hollywood map. Also strong performances by Natalie Wood, Jim Backus and Dennis Hopper.

### RED ALERT                                                RATING 3.0
**1977        TVM       Adventure-Drama    Age 12+        95 min.         Color**
Scientific suspense drama involving a nuclear power plant accident in Minnesota. Fourteen men are caught in the containment center as the poisonous gases escape. The computer responsible for the alert system has been tampered with and bombs have been planted in five locations. Human ingenuity must outwit the computer. Great suspense and mystery make this an exciting movie.

### RED RIVER                                                RATING 4.0
**1948        NR        Western            Age 12+        125 min.        B&W**
One of the finest American westerns made featuring John Wayne as a strong cattle drive foreman. He must contend with his rebellious son (Montgomery Clift), who has been placed in his charge. This film highlights the development of the Chisholm Trail into a major cattle drive route. High action and beautifully made film.

### REHEARSAL FOR MURDER                                     RATING 3.3
**1982        TVM       Drama-Mystery      Age 17+        100 min.        Color**
Following the death of a famous actress on the night of her Broadway debut, a playwright leads a group of actors through one of his productions. It was written specifically to reveal who murdered the actress. The actors are reluctant to go through it, but feel obligated. An engrossing murder story with many twists and surprises. Viewers are kept guessing right down to the end.

### REMAINS OF THE DAY                                       RATING 3.8
**1993        PG        Drama              Age 17+        135 min.        Color**
Aristocratic, pre-World War II drama about a stuffy, English butler (Anthony Hopkins) whose devotion to his work blocks out all emotion. A high-spirited housekeeper (Emma Thompson) teases him in an attempt to bring out his human side. Meanwhile, his master holds secret meetings with Nazi officials, but as butler, he must keep silent. A fascinating, but sad love story for adults. Unforgettable performances.

### RETURN OF THE KING                                       RATING 4.0(e)
**1980        TVM       Fantasy-Adventure  Age 12+        80 min.         Color**
The final installment in J.R.R. Tolkien's Christian-based trilogy The Lord of the Rings. In this animated conclusion, the two hobbits Sam and Frodo hold the entire destiny of Middle Earth in their hands, in the form of the One ring. If they can destroy it, they can break the evil Sauron's hold over Middle Earth. Unfortunately, Sam and Frodo have to pass right through Sauron's back door to get to the Mountain of Doom, the only place that can destroy the ring.

### Secular Movies

**RETURN TO MAYBERRY** — **RATING 3.0**
1986   TVM   Comedy   Age 06+   104 min.   Color
Fun, entertaining movie uniting many of the old *Andy Griffith Show* stars. Andy and Helen return to Mayberry to be with Opie and his family. While visiting, the election for sheriff is coming and Andy decides to run against Barney, who is involved in an investigation concerning the sighting of a "monster" in the local lake. Lots of laughs and nostalgic reflection. Very popular TV movie.

**RIDE THE HIGH COUNTRY** — **RATING 4.0**
1962   NR   Western   Age 12+   94 min.   Color
Excellent western featuring Randolph Scott and Joel McCrea in what is considered their finest performances. Two aging gunfighters agree to oversee the safe delivery of a gold shipment. During their tour they reflect on the different directions their lives have taken. McCrea wants to do well so he can retire, but the action heats up when Scott tries to steal the gold. A superb script, exceptional acting, and inspiring scenery.

**RIKKI TIKKI TAVI** — **RATING 4.0(e)**
1975   TVM   Adventure   Age 04+   30 min.   Color
Orson Wells narrates the animated story of Rikki Tikki Tavi, a mongoose adopted by a British family living in India. Based on Kipling's story, Rikki bravely defends the family against two evil and cunning cobras. Kids and adults alike will enjoy this delightful story which teaches the power of love and sacrifice. No questionable elements in this well-done cartoon, drawn by Chuck Jones of Bugs Bunny fame.

**RIO BRAVO** — **RATING 3.7**
1959   NR   Western   Age 12+   141 min.   Color
John Russell attempts to free his kill-crazy brother from jail. This poses a challenge for the town sheriff (John Wayne), whose only assistance comes from a drunk (Dean Martin), a woman (Angie Dickinson), a cantankerous old man (Walter Brennan), and a punk kid (Ricky Nelson). Excellent western action coupled with fine cast make this worthy viewing.

**RIO LOBO** — **RATING 2.7**
1970   G   Western   Age 12+   114 min.   Color
John Wayne stars in this lighthearted western in the style of *Rio Bravo*. Wayne is an ex-Union colonel who's out to get even for some past injustices. Movie has great dialogue and lots of action. Other notable performances are given by Jack Elam, Jorge Rivero and Sherry Lansing.

**ROCK-A-DOODLE** — **RATING 3.0**
1992   G   Musical   Age 04+   77 min.   Color
Chanticleer, a singing rooster whose crowing makes the sun rise, becomes a rock and roll singer in the city under the influence of the evil Grand Duke of Owl. This musical delight has great animation, bouncy tunes, and cute animal personalities with the voices of Glen Campbell and Christopher Plummer. Magical incantations, some cartoon violence and a sensual bird character mar this otherwise fun film.

**ROMAN HOLIDAY** — **RATING 3.8**
1953   NR   Drama   Age 12+   119 min.   B&W
An American newspaperman (Gregory Peck) is given a news scoop about a princess (Audrey Hepburn) who has slipped away from her stifling royal lifestyle. Hepburn tries to disguise herself as one of Rome's common people. When she encounters Peck, the romance begins. The question then becomes, how will it end?

**ROMERO** — **RATING 3.5**
1989   PG-13   Docudrama   Age 17+   105 min.   Color
Story of Archbishop Oscar Romero of El Salvador who was assassinated in 1980 as he held mass in San Salvador. Romero abandoned his pacifist instincts to be a champion for the poor and oppressed. This film portrays one man's efforts to practice a social gospel in his impoverished country. It is worth seeing, but Romero stood for liberation theology. Because of the nature of this picture, graphic killings are shown.

### ROOKIE OF THE YEAR                                                                RATING 3.5
1993        PG          Comedy                      Age 12+         103 min.            Color

A young boy realizes his dream of pitching in the big leagues when his arm heals unusually well after an accident. While the world gasps in amazement, 12-year-old Henry is catapulted into the World Series, creating as many problems as solutions. The likable boy finds a way to win the hearts of his teammates. An enjoyable tale filled with humor and imagination. Several moderate crude words.

### ROOSTER COGBURN                                                                    RATING 2.7
1975        PG          Western-Adventure           Age 06+         107 min.            Color

John Wayne plays Rooster Cogburn, an over-the-hill U.S. Marshal in the west in the late 1800's. While tracking down a gang of bank robbers, Rooster is joined by Ule Goodnight (Katherine Hepburn), a Christian missionary whose father has been killed by the gang. A humorous conflict develops between the two as their different viewpoints clash. Ends with an exciting river raft episode. Very entertaining. Violent shooting and fighting.

### ROSENCRANTZ AND GUILDENSTERN ARE DEAD                                              RATING 2.8
1990        PG          Drama-Comedy                Age 17+         118 min.            Color

Intellectual comedy, for those so inclined, about two minor characters in *Hamlet* highlighted from the play who try to understand their true identities. As the duo are swept into the play, they attempt to unravel the mystery of why they're in the action at all. Sophisticated farce requiring a prior knowledge of "Hamlet" as well as some grasp of modern scientific discoveries. Some rear nudity.

### RUDYARD KIPLING'S JUNGLE BOOK                                                      RATING 3.5
1994        PG          Adventure                   Age 12+         111 min.            Color

The latest film based on Kipling's classic tale. The story concerns Mowgli, a man raised by wolves, who falls in love with a beautiful Englishwoman and comes out of the jungle to be with her. Along the way, he must fight the prejudices of British soldiers and protect the animals of the forest. Some violent fighting may be too intense for yourng children. Also, several mild crude words.

### RUMPELSTILTSKIN                                                                    RATING 2.5
1987        G           Fantasy-Musical             Age 04+         84 min.             Color

In this classic fairy tale, the father of a poor girl boasts that his daughter (Amy Irving) can spin straw into gold. The local greedy king summons her to his palace to perform this impossible task. A mischievous magical little gnome played by Billy Barty offers to rescue her, but demands her first born child in return. Children, as well as parents, will enjoy this famous fairy tale filled with music, mirth and story telling enchantment.

### RUN SILENT, RUN DEEP                                                               RATING 3.3
1958        NR          Adventure-Drama             Age 12+         93 min.             B&W

Commander Clark Gable and his Lieutenant, Burt Lancaster, are officers on a World War II submarine who experience a bitter conflict. Gable has replaced Lancaster as captain, which heightens the tension. They set out from Pearl Harbor to destroy a Japanese cruiser. This war movie focuses more on the human side of war rather than the battle action. It is considered one of the finest World War II submarine movies.

### RUNAWAY BARGE, THE                                                                 RATING 2.5(e)
1975        TVM         Adventure                   Age 12+         78 min.             Color

Interesting action movie about three men who try to make a living operating a modern day Mississippi riverboat. Trouble begins when they come across a riverboat hi-jacking operation. At one point, a barge filled with explosive gases gets out of control and a daring rescue attempt gets underway.

### RUNNING WILD                                                                       RATING 2.9
1973        G           Drama-Western               Age 12+         102 min.            Color

While doing a story on the state of Colorado, a photographer discovers that wild mustangs are receiving hostile treatment from a cattle baron. With the aid of a rodeo stock supplier and an Indian chief, the photographer sets out to put an end to the baron's activities. Animal lovers will be moved by the efforts of numerous people to save the horses. Excellent performances by Lloyd Bridges and Dina Merrill.

### RUSSIANS ARE COMING, THE — RATING 3.0
1966  NR  Comedy  Age 12+  120 min.  Color

Hilarious comedy about a Russian sub that runs aground off Nantucket Island near the New England coast. It causes a tremendous uproar among the inhabitants because they don't know whether to be afraid or not. Jonathan Winters and Alan Arkin perform some wacky comic antics that will greatly amuse everyone.

### SABRINA — RATING 3.5(e)
1995  PG  Comedy  Age 12+  127 min.  Color

This remake of the 1954 Audrey Hepburn and Humphrey Bogart film is just as much fun with Julia Ormond and Harrison Ford. Updated to the present, this version includes witty dialogue, gorgeous scenery and beautiful musical score. The young Sabrina is still a lovesick girl pining after the younger son of the family who employs her father as their chauffeur. High marks for wholesome treatment of love in the nineties.

### SABRINA — RATING 3.5
1954  NR  Comedy  Age 12+  113 min.  B&W

Rich playboy William Holden falls in love with the chauffeur's daughter (Audrey Hepburn). His older brother (Humphrey Bogart) tries to win her away from his brother because he considers Holden to be a less than desirable choice for the naive girl. A fun film with a good cast makes this exceptional entertainment.

### SACRED GROUND — RATING 2.7
1983  PG  Western  Age 12+  100 min.  Color

During pioneer days, a burly white man and his pregnant Indian wife unknowingly build a cabin on an Indian burial ground. The Indians are angered and attack. The Indian woman survives only long enough to give birth to her baby. The remainder of the film depicts the struggle between the Indians and the white man to obtain possession of the baby. Contains some moderately crude language and some graphic killings.

### SAKHAROV — RATING 3.5
1984  TVM  Docudrama  Age 17+  118 min.  Color

Powerful true story about Russian nuclear scientist Andrei Sakharov who challenges the Soviet system by taking a stand for free speech. The result is house arrest and hospitalization as well as harassment for Sakharov and his family. An engrossing film depicting the struggle of this courageous fighter who stood up to communist oppression. Strong cast includes Jason Robards, Jr., Glenda Jackson and Michael Bryant. One vulgarity.

### SAN FRANCISCO — RATING 3.7
1936  NR  Drama-Adventure  Age 12+  115 min.  B&W

Intriguing story of love and adventure on the Barbary Coast. This is a movie where the poor and rich fall in love, resulting in many problems caused by the radically different economic and social strata. The famous earthquake provides an exciting climax. Clark Gable and Spencer Tracy give fine performances along with Jeanette MacDonald.

### SANDS OF IWO JIMA — RATING 3.5
1949  NR  Drama-War  Age 12+  110 min.  B&W

John Wayne stars as a tough Marine top sergeant in this fine depiction of the World War II invasion of Iwo Jima island. This fierce battle cost both the United States and Japan thousands of lives. The story shows the need to take this important island airfield from Japan so that B-29 bombers and their fighter escorts will have access to targets in Japan. War enthusiasts will enjoy the actual war footage.

### SANTA CLAUS: THE MOVIE — RATING 2.7
1985  PG  Fantasy-Drama  Age 06+  112 min.  Color

This is an entertaining tale about the origin of Santa Claus. As the story is told, we get a good glimpse of his toy shop and the reindeer. When the 20th century arrives, Santa befriends an orphan boy and a little rich girl. One of Santa's elves ends up in New York where he's deceived by a selfish toy villain. But Santa saves the day. Starring cast includes Dudley Moore, John Lithgow, Burgess Meredith and Judy Cornwell.

### SANTA CLAUSE, THE                                                                RATING 3.7
1994         PG          Comedy                    Age 06+         97 min.          Color

Comedian Tim Allen stars as Scott Calvin, a skeptical no-nonsense businessman who is miraculously transformed into Santa Claus after the previous Santa accidentally dies. Calvin must make a reluctant trip to the North Pole to understand that he is indeed Santa Claus. Allen's slow transformation into Santa is a delight. A few suggestive remarks are the only detractors to this fine film.

### SARAH, PLAIN AND TALL                                                            RATING 3.3
1991         TVM         Drama                     Age 12+         98 min.          Color

A recently widowed farmer in the Midwest advertises for a wife in an Eastern paper. Soon, Sarah (Glenn Close), an "old maid" from Maine, arrives for a month's visit. Sarah immediately discovers that the farmer and his daughter and son are still grieving for his dead wife. Sarah must quietly win them over in this touching Hallmark production. A movie the whole family can enjoy.

### SAVANNAH SMILES                                                                  RATING 2.8
1982         PG          Adventure-Drama           Age 06+         107 min.         Color

Rich child, tired of the neglect she finds in the land of the wealthy, decides to run away in search of a better life. Unfortunately, she falls into the hands of two bungling criminals who hold her for ransom. But she shows no fear of them and they are won over by her love. Theft is portrayed in light-hearted manner and there is some mild violence. Refreshing, heartwarming story.

### SAVING GRACE                                                                     RATING 3.0
1986         PG          Drama                     Age 06+         112 min.         Color

A young Pope (Tom Conti) comes to the point where he cannot tolerate the mundane activities associated with his position. Desiring work that has purpose, he sneaks out of the Vatican and relocates in a poor Italian village. Realizing the people have lost there sense of worth, he seeks to rekindle it. At the same time, he renews his own. The Pope gets involved in some suspenseful conflicts in the village. Good drama.

### SCARLET PIMPERNEL                                                                RATING 3.3
1982         TVM         Adventure                 Age 12+         98 min.          Color

During the French revolution, none of the French royalty was safe from death by the mob. An Englishman known as the Scarlet Pimpernel helps them escape safely to England. The Pimpernel's wife, however, may be aiding the new French government's takeover. This well-acted remake of the 1934 movie is a fast-paced adventure for the whole family. Several mild crude words.

### SCARLET AND THE BLACK, THE                                                       RATING 3.5
1983         TVM         Adventure                 Age 12+         143 min.         Color

In this thrilling adventure, Gregory Peck stars as a Vatican official who ignores the precepts of neutrality during World War II and aids prisoners of war. Throughout this ordeal, Peck is dogged by a shrewd Nazi officer (Christopher Plummer) who tries to put an end to this "Good Samaritan". Set in German occupied Rome, their suspenseful cat-and-mouse game is highlighted by the fine acting.

### SCENT OF GREEN PAPAYA                                                            RATING 3.3
1994         NR          Drama                     Age 17+         103 min.         Color

This engrossing foreign film centers around the life of Mui, a Vietnamese girl who grows up as a servant to wealthy families in Vietnam before the war. From her perspective, life is filled with peace, even in the midst of the war and family upheavals. While her several employers go through stressful times, Mui remains calm. In Vietnamese with English subtitles. A first-rate movie, rich in character development.

### SCROOGE                                                                          RATING 2.8
1974         G           Musical                   Age 06+         157 min.         Color

This is a musical version of Charles Dicken's classic *A Christmas Carol*. The good people in a Christian land are preparing to celebrate the birth of the Savior, but Mr. Ebenezer Scrooge has no time for Christmas or those who share in it. He is busy counting his money and collecting debts. He is visited by three ghosts who seek to show him the tragic outcome of his life if things don't change. Well done, appealing musical.

### SEA HAWK, THE                                                                    RATING 3.7
1940      NR      Adventure            Age 12+      127 min.         B&W

Errol Flynn is an adventurous seaman who takes to the high seas with a devoted band of men to lead England against the Spanish. Piracy, romance, swordplay, and other dramatic elements make this an exciting adventure set on the high seas.

### SEARCHERS, THE                                                                    RATING 4.0
1956      NR      Western              Age 12+      119 min.         Color

John Ford directed this masterpiece, setting the standard for westerns. John Wayne plays a frontiersman, ex-Confederate soldier and Indian hater who has lost his family in an Indian raid. His niece (Natalie Wood) has been captured and forced to become a squaw. Wayne begins a search to seek revenge and he also plans to kill his niece, whom he considers defiled. Other frontiersmen want to rescue the girl, and a clash develops.

### SEARCHING FOR BOBBY FISCHER                                                        RATING 3.8
1993      PG      Drama                Age 12+      110 min.         Color

A 7-year-old chess prodigy becomes famous after winning matches against some of the greatest chess masters of the world. Pressure begins to build when his father expects him to win at any cost. This absorbing film explores how the stamp of genius may affect the life of an otherwise normal little boy. Solid acting performances by Ben Kingsley as his expert teacher. Two regular profanities.

### SECOND BEST                                                                       RATING 3.5
1994      PG-13   Drama                Age 17+      105 min.         Color

Inspiring story about a troubled boy adopted by a man who has just lost his father. The boy, belying his normally tough exterior, comforts him and their relationship deepens. This is an extraordinary film of two people dealing with memories of the past to understand the present. Some violent scenes and one moderate obscenity make this film inappropriate for younger children.

### SECRET GARDEN, THE                                                                RATING 3.5
1987      TVM     Drama                Age 12+      100 min.         Color

Not the 1993 feature movie, but a *Hallmark Hall of Fame* adaptation of Frances Burnett's classic children's story. A young English girl, orphaned in India, returns to England to her wealthy uncle's estate. Exploring the grounds, she finds a hidden garden overgrown from years of neglect. With the aid of an ailing cousin and a friend, she restores the garden to its original beauty. An enchanting story with magnificent scenery.

### SECRET LIFE OF WALTER MITTY, THE                                                  RATING 3.0
1947      NR      Comedy-Musical       Age 12+      105 min.         Color

Danny Kaye stars in this outstanding musical comedy. It is about a timid man who has the unique talent of living in two worlds—one real and one fantasy where he longs to be a brave hero. Viewers will enjoy Kaye's interaction with his two worlds, as well as his performance of "Anatole of Paris."

### SECRET OF NIMH, THE                                                               RATING 3.3
1982      G       Fantasy-Drama        Age 06+      83 min.          Color

A young widowed mouse must seek help when her child becomes gravely ill and her home is threatened. She stumbles into a laboratory and discovers a pack of super intelligent rats who willingly provide the aid she desperately needs. This is a fine animated story suitable for children. Adults will likely enjoy it too.

### SECRET OF ROAN INISH                                                              RATING 3.7
1995      PG      Drama-Fantasy        Age 12+      103 min.         Color

A young Irish girl hears rumors that her brother, who she thought was dead, may still be alive, wandering the island of Roan Inish. As she goes in search of him, the beautiful Irish countryside provides the perfect setting for a strange discovery based on Irish folklore and dealt with as fantasy. One violent scene may be too intense for young children, but this is a family treasure.

### SEND ME NO FLOWERS — RATING 3.0
**1964  NR  Comedy  Age 06+  100 min.  Color**

Rock Hudson, fearing he is on the verge of death, wants to insure his wife's (Doris Day) continued stability and happiness. He asks his best friend (Tony Randall) to locate a suitable man for her to date. Unfortunately, she is unaware of his motives and plan. Paul Lynde also appears in a hilarious role as a cemetery plot salesman.

### SENSE AND SENSIBILITY — RATING 3.5(e)
**1995  PG  Drama  Age 12+  136 min.  Color**

This Jane Austen novel has become an award-winning film starring Emma Thompson. Three sisters and their mother are left destitute when their father dies, leaving the entire estate to a half-brother. The girls' search for love and marriage takes them on a puzzling but merry chase in an 1800s English setting. Strong messages about family loyalty and hope in the face of adversity make this a winner for all.

### SEPARATE BUT EQUAL — RATING 3.5
**1991  TVM  Docudrama  Age 12+  200 min.  Color**

Sidney Poitier plays the part of Thurgood Marshall, an NAACP lawyer in the 1950's and later Supreme Court Justice who fights to end separate but equal segregation practices. The film loosely chronicles the unequal treatment of black students and the lack of good teaching materials and facilities. Though not supposed to be a documentary, it does express feelings and emotions of many Black Americans during that time. One moderate crudity.

### SEPTEMBER GUN — RATING 2.5(e)
**1983  TVM  Western  Age 12+  94 min.  Color**

In this light-hearted western, Robert Preston plays an aging gunfighter who assists a nun and some Apache Indian orphans. They travel to a town in Colorado, where the nun plans to set up a home for the children. But a corrupt mayor doesn't like the idea. Clever comedy.

### SERGEANT YORK — RATING 3.5
**1941  NR  Drama-War  Age 12+  134 min.  B&W**

Gary Cooper plays a pacifist Tennessee hillbilly who is unfortunately drafted into World War I. Once there, he comes to realize that the war effort is legitimate. He goes on to capture over one-hundred Germans, making him one of America's greatest military heros. Excellent supporting cast and rural atmosphere. Contains some realistic battle scenes.

### SESAME STREET-FOLLOW THAT BIRD — RATING 2.8
**1985  G  Musical Adventure  Age 04+  88 min.  Color**

As a result of an unsuccessful family relationship with a Dodo family, Big Bird sets out across the great Midwest in search of his friends on Sesame Street. Numerous appearances by notable celebrities make this movie entertaining for adults who like a simple comedy. Children will especially enjoy this film.

### SEVEN ALONE — RATING 2.5
**1975  G  Adventure-Western  Age 06+  96 min.  Color**

Set in the 1840s, this film focuses on the plight of seven children who must continue their trip West following the death of their parents. Fortunately, a thirteen-year-old boy is willing to assume the responsibility of guiding them on their 2,000 mile trek. They are confronted with difficult situations and crises along the way.

### SEVEN BRIDES FOR SEVEN BROTHERS — RATING 4.0
**1954  NR  Musical-Western  Age 12+  103 min.  Color**

Spectacular song and dance film. Howard Keel stars as a mountain man who decides to find himself a bride. His boisterous brothers, not wanting to be left out, also decide to marry immediately. Numerous scenes such as the barn-raising and dance numbers enhance the quality of this classic musical.

### SEVEN DAYS IN MAY  RATING 3.5
1964   NR   Suspense-Drama   Age 12+   120 min.   B&W

In this suspense-filled screenplay, numerous high-level military and political officials are involved in a plot to overthrow the U.S. government. Frederick March plays the U.S. president under pressure. The threat of nuclear war looms over the heads of all and tension mounts toward a dramatic conclusion. Burt Lancaster, Kirk Douglas, Ava Gardner, and Edmund O'Brien also star.

### SEVEN LITTLE FOYS, THE  RATING 3.0
1955   NR   Comedy-Musical   Age 06+   95 min.   Color

Bob Hope stars in one of his more dramatic roles depicting the life and times of the vaudeville family known as the Singing and Dancing Foys. The father's neglect of his family comes back to haunt him as he faces some severe family problems. This is a very moving but humorous film with some great moments. James Cagney makes a dancing appearance as George Cohan.

### SHADOWLANDS  RATING 3.8
1993   PG   Drama   Age 17+   130 min.   Color

Anthony Hopkins brilliantly portrays famed British author and professor C.S. Lewis in this heart-rending drama. For years, Lewis has closed himself off to romantic relationships. Then, a Jewish American divorcee' (Debra Winger) awakens him to love and caring. A cathartic, emotional film that expresses the value of commitment and transforming power of love. Also portrays the crisis of faith which Lewis experiences.

### SHADOW RIDERS  RATING 2.8
1982   TVM   Western   Age 12+   96 min.   Color

At the end of the Civil War, two brothers who fought on opposite sides of the war, return to their home in Texas. When they arrive, they discover that their sisters and all the townswomen have been kidnapped by rebel guerrillas. The two brothers must work together, with another brother and their uncle, to save the women. A heart-pounding Louis L'Amour western with some fighting violence

### SHAGGY D.A., THE  RATING 2.2
1976   NR   Comedy   Age 06+   90 min.   Color

Willey Daniels' house has been robbed and others have met the same fate. To fight the problem, he decides to run for district attorney. Prior to the campaign, an Egyptian ring is stolen from the local museum. When the words inscribed on the ring are spoken, Daniels turns into a shaggy dog. Daniels frantically tries to find the ring, conceal his problem and keep his campaign going all at the same time.

### SHAKIEST GUN IN THE WEST  RATING 2.0
1967   NR   Comedy   Age 06+   101 min.   Color

Jesse Hayward (Don Knotts) is a bumbling dentist who travels west to establish his practice. He is tricked into marrying Penny Cushings, an outlaw turned spy who is searching for the men who are selling guns to the Indians. Poor Jesse finds himself involved with crooks and hostile Indians and his sharpshooter wife rescues him from many a danger. Great comedy for the entire family.

### SHALL WE DANCE  RATING 3.5
1937   NR   Musical-Comedy   Age 12+   116 min.   B&W

Fred Astaire and Ginger Rogers play a dance team that must pretend to be married in order to achieve success in the entertainment field. Astaire and Rogers perform many tuneful dancing routines. Features a memorable Gershwin musical score including "Let's Call the Whole Thing Off," "They All Laughed," and "They Can't Take That Away from Me."

### SHANE  RATING 4.0
1953   NR   Western   Age 12+   118 min.   Color

Flawless western about an ex-gunfighter Shane (Alan Ladd) who returns to his profession to protect homesteaders from ruthless villains. Shane finds himself idolized by one of the couple's sons. Movie builds to a climax in the showdown between the homesteaders and cattlemen. This is considered to be one of the finest westerns ever made. Breathtaking scenic background.

### SHELL SEEKERS, THE                                                                    RATING 3.3(e)
**1994        TVM        Drama                        Age 12+        98 min.        Color**
Angela Landsbury brilliantly portrays an aging British mother who regrets the lack of positive influence she has had on her children. Disturbed by this reality, she attempts to make amends, but is rejected. Sparks fly when she refuses to sell her artistic father's masterpieces for her children's financial well-being. An outstanding Hallmark Hall of Fame presentation teaching responsibility for one's choices and the importance of honoring parents.

### SHENANDOAH                                                                            RATING 3.2
**1965        NR        Drama                         Age 12+        105 min.       Color**
James Stewart gives one of his finest performances in this story about a Virginia widower who has a passive interest in the Civil War, until the conflict begins to disrupt his family. Eventually he must get involved to protect his children. Impressive scenery. Later made into a Broadway musical. All-star cast.

### SHIPWRECKED                                                                           RATING 3.3
**1991        PG        Adventure                     Age 12+        91 min.        Color**
A young Norwegian goes to sea in his ailing father's place to pay the family debts. Thus begins a series of adventures that includes pirates, a stowaway, and hidden treasure. An exciting film in the tradition of "Treasure Island" that has beautiful cinematography and background music. This wonderful family outing gives us the bigger-than-life world of a boy on the high seas of old.

### SHOWBOAT                                                                              RATING 3.0
**1951        NR        Musical                       Age 06+        107 min.       Color**
Fine musical about life and love on a Mississippi showboat. Good cast (Agnes Moorehead, Howard Keel, Ava Gardner) helps the story along. Jerome Kern score is the zestful heart of this musical drama. Noted for the song, "Old Man River" and others.

### SINGIN' IN THE RAIN                                                                   RATING 4.0
**1952        NR        Musical                       Age 12+        103 min.       Color**
One of the all-time great musicals with outstanding song and dance routines by Gene Kelly. It's the delightful story of a two-man comic dance team who get into the movies at the time they're changing from silent to talkies. Fine song and dance performances by Debbie Reynolds and Donald O'Connor add zest to the show. It's one of the most enjoyable musicals ever made in Hollywood. Features Kelly's memorable "Singin' in the Rain" number.

### SISTER ACT 2: BACK IN THE HABIT                                                       RATING 3.0
**1993        PG        Comedy-Musical                Age 12+        106 min.       Color**
Whoopi Goldberg once more poses as a nun, this time at a Catholic high school. As a "hip" music teacher, she tames a class of rebellious teenagers and earns their respect. Because of their talent, she enters them in a music competition. Positive messages, lots of jazzy gospel music and dancing. Immensely enjoyable show that leaves a good feeling. A few moderate crude words along with one regular profanity and one obscenity.

### SISTER KENNY                                                                          RATING 3.0
**1946        NR        Docudrama                     Age 12+        116 min.       B&W**
Rosalind Russell stars as an Australian nurse who fought for and won the need to provide a vaccine for polio. Her perseverance and determination prevail over a medical community that is both skeptical and jealous of her findings. Fine acting and suspense.

### SIXTEEN DAYS OF GLORY                                                                 Rating 3.0(e)
**1986        G         Documentary                   Age 06+        145 min.       Color**
Exciting and inspiring story of the 23rd Olympic games held in Los Angeles. Filled with pagentry and pathos, it relives the sixteen glorious days in the summer of 1984 when Olympic team athletes competed in every imaginable sport. Focuses on the behind-the-scenes drama in the lives of several athletes who participated in the events. The music score and singing are inspiring and the cheering crowd exhilerating.

### SKEEZER  RATING 3.0
**1982    TVM    Drama           Age 06+    100 min.    Color**

*Skeezer* is the engrossing story of Casey, a lonely young woman and her long haired sheepdog called Skeezer. Casey works in a home for emotionally disturbed children and eventually convinces the supervising doctor that Skeezer would be good for the children. Casey works hard to prove that the dog can help provide the love and care that the children so desperately need. Surprisingly enjoyable and touching story.

### SKYLARK  RATING 3.2
**1993    TVM    Drama           Age 12+    96 min.    Color**

Sequel to the popular and romantic *Sarah, Plain and Tall* features Sarah (Glenn Close) and her family facing a prolonged drought. As the drought makes it increasingly hard for families to stay on their farms, Sarah reluctantly decides to take the children to her family home in Maine. The beautiful sea contrasts with the stark prairie of the Midwest, but Sarah's love for her husband drives her back to her real home.

### SNATCHED  RATING 2.5
**1972    TVM    Adventure-Suspense    Age 12+    90 min.    Color**

The young, beautiful wives of three wealthy businessmen are kidnapped and held for three million dollars ransom. Their husbands are plunged into an agonizing nightmare. Further tension develops when one of the men refuses to pay the ransom, thus jeopardizing the lives of the others. This is a suspenseful movie with an unexpected twist.

### SNOOPY COME HOME  RATING 3.3
**1972    G    Drama           Age 04+    70 min.    Color**

In this delightful *Peanuts* cartoon, Snoopy goes to visit his former owner in the hospital. He's seriously considering moving back to his old home, but finally acknowledges that his life with Charlie Brown was far better than he realized. This is fun viewing for children, and adults as well.

### SNOW WHITE AND THE SEVEN DWARFS  RATING 4.0
**1983    TVM    Fantasy-Drama    Age 04+    53 min.    Color**

First class production of the classic Grimm story about a beautiful woman who comes under the spell of the evil witch. With the aid of the comical dwarfs, Snow White is rescued by the handsome prince. Vincent Price gives an excellent performance as the witch's advising mirror.

### SNOW WHITE AND THE SEVEN DWARFS  RATING 4.0
**1937    G    Fantasy           Age 06+    83 min.    Color**

Re-released version of Disney's timeless animated classic about the raven-haired beauty and her lovable, eccentric friends. The lovely Snow White and the amusing dwarfs develop a deep friendship filled with warmth & humor. Then, the wicked witch appears to spoil the fun. This delightful feature continues to enchant viewers of all ages. The very young may find the witch scenes frightening, but no really offensive elements.

### SNOWBALL EXPRESS  RATING 2.0
**1972    G    Comedy           Age 06+    99 min.    Color**

In this really fun movie, Johnny Baxter and his family inherit a rundown hotel in the mountains of Colorado. They are determined to make it into a first class ski resort, but they must contend with a greedy banker. It's full of hilarious happenings, including some crazy skiing antics and a runaway snowmobile race. The whole family will enjoy this full length Disney film.

### SNOWS OF KILIMANJARO, THE  RATING 3.2
**1952    NR    Adventure-Drama    Age 12+    117 min.    Color**

Interesting story about a renowned writer living his last days in Africa. He takes the time to reflect on his life to determine if it had any meaning. Gregory Peck stars in this film version of the Hemingway novel.

### SON OF FLUBBER                                                    RATING 2.8
1963        NR        Comedy              Age 06+        100 min.        B&W

In this sequel to Disney's *Absent Minded Professor*, Fred MacMurray again stars as the inventor of "flubber," a substance which can bounce at great heights and make his Model-T fly. This time he invents "flubber gas" and "dry rain." A good family comedy ending with an unusual football game.

### SON OF THE MORNING STAR                                            RATING 3.3
1986        PG-13     Western             Age 17+        186 min.        Color

A different view of General George Custer who was sent to the Dakota territory to bring peace. There, he discusses the possibility of a Sioux nation with Sitting Bull. Custer, instead of fighting with the Indians, wants to be their representative in Washington. His ill-starred and ill-equipped battle is blamed on the leaders above him. Some violent fighting and two moderate crudities in this interesting retelling of Custer's last stand.

### SON OF THE PINK PANTHER                                            RATING 2.1
1993        PG        Comedy              Age 12+        93 min.         Color

A film reminiscent of the old Peter Sellers' hits of the '60s and '70s. Inspector Clousseau's son (Roberto Benigni) takes over where his dad left off, with his bumbling, clumsy ways and his talent for getting into trouble. His first mission is to rescue a beautiful Arabian princess kidnapped by a ruthless gang of mercenaries. Zany stunts are unfortunately mixed with the mildly suggestive movements of a bellydancer and some slapstick violence.

### SONG OF BERNADETTE                                                 RATING 3.7
1943        NR        Drama               Age 12+        156 min.        B&W

Religious drama about a French girl who experiences numerous visions of the Virgin Mary at Lourdes. She finds herself the object of local hostility as a result of her experiences. Lengthy, but exceptional in quality. Four Oscars were awarded as a result of the film quality and acting. Adapted from the book by Franz Werfel.

### SOS TITANIC                                                        RATING 3.2
1979        TVM       Docudrama           Age 12+        105 min.        Color

When survivors of the Titanic are rescued, their vivid flashbacks tell the story of that fateful voyage in 1912. Good presentation of the facts surrounding the Titanic, coupled with fine acting by David Janssen and Cloris Leachman. The story vividly recreates the sinking of that great luxury liner.

### SOUND OF MUSIC                                                     RATING 3.7
1965        NR        Musical             Age 06+        185 min.        Color

One of the most popular musicals in the history of cinema, *Sound of Music* depicts the life of the real Von Trapp family in 1938 Austria. Julie Andrews plays the governess who goes to care for the Von Trapp children and ends up marrying the wealthy widower Baron Von Trapp. When the Nazis invade Austria, the family must flee the country. A delightful Rodgers and Hammerstein musical score, including "Do Re Mi" and "My Favorite Things".

### SOUNDER                                                            RATING 4.0
1972        G         Drama               Age 06+        105 min.        Color

Moving and exceptional story of a black sharecropper family in Depression era Louisiana. The family endures severe hardships when the father is imprisoned for stealing a ham and the mother (Cicely Tyson) must care for the family. Both the happy and sad experiences of the young black son and his beloved hound, Sounder, are compelling and touching. One of the most profound and enjoyable family films ever made.

### SOUTH PACIFIC                                                      RATING 2.7
1958        NR        Musical             Age 12+        171 min.        Color

The exciting love story between a U.S. Navy nurse (Mitzi Gaynor) and a French planter (Rossano Brazzi) in the South Pacific during World War II. Numerous Rodgers and Hammerstein songs make this a wonderful musical with splendid scenery and romance. Popular songs from this film include "Some Enchanted Evening," "Bali Hai," and "Happy Talk."

### SOUTHERNER, THE — RATING 3.8
**1945  NR  Drama  Age 12+  81 min.  B&W**
Moving, realistic story of a Southern tenant farmer who struggles against man and nature to get his land to produce adequately to provide for his family. Tries to maintain his dignity during these difficult times. Beautiful film story starring Zachary Scott, Betty Field and J. Carol Naish.

### SPACED INVADERS — RATING 1.8
**1990  PG  Comedy-Science Fiction  Age 12+  100 min.  Color**
A group of little green misfit Martians land on earth and go into town to kill the "earthscum". The local yokels mistake them for children dressed for Halloween. The conversations among the Martians are usually humorous and sometime hilarious. The special effects and costumes are great fun. At times, the dialogue and jokes are hard to understand. Contains a number of "hells" and "damns".

### SPENCER'S MOUNTAIN — RATING 2.5
**1963  NR  Drama  Age 12+  118min.  Color**
Henry Fonda is Clay Spencer, the rough patriarch of a large Wyoming family. His nine children are the apple of his eye, especially Clay Boy, his oldest. When Clay Boy wants to go to college, Spencer has to find a way to pay the expenses. The minister lends his help, and even gets Spenser to start coming to church. A heart-warming story unfortunately containing many mild crudities. Basis for TV's popular *Waltons*.

### SPIRIT OF ST. LOUIS, THE — RATING 3.2
**1957  NR  Docudrama  Age 12+  138 min.  Color**
James Stewart stars in this fine story about the life of American aviation hero Charles Lindberg, giving particular attention to his famous trans-Atlantic solo flight. This is an above average film that is quite helpful in presenting viewers with this great event in American history.

### SQUANTO: A WARRIOR'S TALE — RATING 3.0(e)
**1994  PG  Drama-Adventure  Age 12+  102 min.  Color**
Squanto is an Indian tricked into slavery by a corrupt European. Once in England, he escapes his cruel master and is befriended by a Catholic priest. Squanto learns English and European ways in time to help negotiate peace between the Indians and the Puritans of the Mayflower. Unfortunately, religious lines between paganism and Christianity are blurred in an otherwise fine film containing a few violent scenes.

### STAGECOACH — RATING 1.7
**1986  TVM  Western  Age 06+  100 min.  Color**
Made for TV western featuring numerous country music stars such as Willie Nelson, Johnny Cash, and Waylon Jennings. They team with their wives in this story about several persons who take a stagecoach trip through Indian territory to Lordsburg, Arizona. Their tension filled trip is full of unusual experiences. The acting and script lack professionalism, but the story is entertaining.

### STAGECOACH — RATING 4.0
**1939  NR  Western  Age 12+  96 min.  B&W**
John Wayne was plunged into stardom with this John Ford western. A high action western that offers a fine character study. Portrays the emotional stress and reactions of various stagecoach passengers as they travel through Indian territory and experience a severe Indian attack. Incredible filming and stunt work. Cast includes Claire Trevor, Andy Devine, John Carradine and Louise Platt.

### STALAG 17 — RATING 4.0
**1953  NR  Adventure-Comedy  Age 12+  120 min.  B&W**
World War II drama in which William Holden gives one of his best performances as an American POW in Germany who is suspected of spying on his fellow prisoners. The movie does an outstanding job of dealing with the daily grind POWs went through, as well as the extreme measures used by the Germans to keep tabs on prisoner activities. The ending is quite good. Cast includes Robert Strauss, Harvey Lembeck, Peter Graves and Neville Brand. Inspiration for TV's *Hogan's Heroes*.

### STAR TREK—THE MENAGERIE                                                    RATING 4.0
**1967        TVM        Science Fiction-Adventure        Age 06+        100 min.        Color**
This is one of the best of the original *Star Trek* shows. Spock learns that his former commander, Capt. Pike, is a mere vegetable surviving via a machine on another planet. He places his career on the line by forcing the Enterprise to return to aid the commander. They travel to his planet where reality is altered and illusion is used to create an environment acceptable to the observer. Stars William Shatner and Leonard Nimoy.

### STAR TREK—THE MOTION PICTURE                                               RATING 2.0
**1979        G        Science Fiction-Adventure        Age 06+        132 min.        Color**
Spectacular special effects highlight this first in a series of *Star Trek* movies. Kirk and crew are off to intercept a lethal force field that is on a collision course with Earth. Avid Star Trek fans will enjoy the return of the cast. The film is entertaining and keeps the viewer intrigued throughout with its subtle plot.

### STAR TREK VI                                                               RATING 3.5
**1991        PG        Science-fiction        Age 12+        109 min.        Color**
Intense, action-packed science fiction thriller with Captain Kirk (William Shatner) and Mr. Spock (Leonard Nimoy) confronting their deadly archenemies, the Klingons. Suspicion falls on Kirk after some Klingon representatives are assassinated. Will Spock unravel the mystery in time to save his friend's life? Suspense and high adventure combine to entertain sci-fi fans in the on-going Star Trek adventure. Several mild crude words and some violent battles.

### STAR TREK: GENERATIONS                                                     RATING 3.7
**1994        PG        Science-Fiction        Age 12+        118 min.        Color**
Captain Kirk (William Shatner) meets Captain Picard (Patrick Stewart) in this time travel tale which unites two Star Trek TV series. Kirk and Picard work together to spoil the plans of evil Dr. Soran who wants to destroy the inhabitants of a planet for his own selfish gain. Contains several mild crude words, one severe obscenity, and some violent war scenes. One of the best of the Star Trek movies.

### STAR WARS                                                                  RATING 3.7
**1977        PG        Science Fiction-Adventure        Age 06+        121 min.        Color**
This is the first in the Star Wars series directed by George Lucas. Rebel forces led by daring ship pilot Mark Hamil battle the evil Empire, defended by a hoard of men commanded by the ominous, dark suited Darth Vader. With robots and human friends, Hamill rescues a princess taken captive by Darth Vader. Some eastern mystical concepts are portrayed favorably. Great story, space age action and terrific special effects.

### STARGATE                                                                   RATING 2.7
**1994        PG-13        Science-fiction-Action        Age 17+        115 min.        Color**
Army colonel (Kurt Russell) leads an Egyptologist through a space warp to a world light years away. There, the team discovers a replica of the Great Pyramid. They also discover an alien trying to pass himself off as the sun god Ra. Has one sexually suggestive incident, several mild crudities and some moderately violent scenes, and a strong depiction of an evil power. Reasonably decent, exciting adventure story for teenagers and adults.

### STARS FELL ON HENRIETTA, THE                                               RATING 2.5 (e)
**1995        PG        Drama        Age 12+        106 min.        Color**
During the 1935 oil boom, Henrietta, Texas becomes a center of commerce. The poor Day family is approached by a stranger who can just "smell" the oil beneath the Day's dirt farm. Can Don Day raise the $5,000 to finance a well without the risk of losing his wife and farm? Two profanities and a few moderate crudities slightly mar this film about God-fearing folks in a kinder and gentler era.

### STATE FAIR                                                                 RATING 3.0
**1945        NR        Musical        Age 12+        100 min.        Color**
Very good musical featuring numerous Rodgers and Hammerstein songs as "Good Night for Singing," and "It Might As Well Be Spring." This story deals with a farm family's experiences at the Iowa State Fair. Some romantic mix-ups add zest to the plot. Many feel that this 1945 version is superior to the remake of 1962. It's fun with much nostalgic appeal.

### STILL OF THE NIGHT, THE — RATING 2.7
1982    PG    Mystery    Age 17+    91 min.    Color

This suspenseful tale stars Roy Scheider as a psychiatrist whose patient is murdered. The police suspect his girl-friend, played by Meryl Streep, an art curator. Quite a suspenseful tale that does not rely on gore to make its point. A film definitely for adults with its implication of an implied affair, near nudity (breast) and partial rear nudity, along with two moderate crude words.

### STRANGERS ON A TRAIN — RATING 4.0
1951    NR    Mytery-Suspense    Age 12+    101min.    B&W

One of Hitchcock's most exciting and darkly quirky movies. When Guy Haines meets Bruno Antony, their lives are changed forever. Antony, mentally unbalanced, concocts a plan. If he kills Haines' estranged wife, Haines could kill Bruno's father. No one could ever solve either murder. Bruno murders Haines' wife and begins pressuring an unwilling Haines to do his part. Suspenseful with no objectionable elements other than a partially obscured killing scene.

### STRANGERS: THE STORY OF A MOTHER AND DAUGHTER — RATING 3.3
1979    TVM    Drama    Age 17+    88 min.    Color

Focus of this story is the strained relationship between a mother and her daughter. Abigail Mason returns home after a 21 year absence. Her mother, Lucy (Bette Davis), is still bitter over her daughter's leaving, aggravated by the fact that her daughter never contacted her during the absence. The mother eventually begins to soften. Moderate crude language once. Superb acting. Enjoyable movie, especially for women.

### STRATEGIC AIR COMMAND — RATING 2.5
1955    NR    Drama-Adventure    Age 12+    114 min.    Color

A baseball player (James Stewart) returns to active duty flying B-52 bombers for the Strategic Air Command. It interrupts his career and poses complications for himself and his wife (June Allyson). An interesting story of the men who flew these huge bombers that were some of the first aircraft to carry the atom bomb. Military aviation buffs will particularly enjoy the story, especially the fine footage of the aircraft.

### STRAWBERRY SHORTCAKE STORY SERIES — RATING 3.0
1982    NR    Adventure    Age +04    15 min.    Color

Delightful animated collection of cartoons about a lovable little girl named Strawberry Shortcake and her colorful friends. A dastardly villain called the Purple Pie Man also gets into the act to make life difficult for Strawberry Shortcake. The music and rhymes integrated with the cartoons are creative and appealing. Pre-schoolers will enjoy these clever videos.

### STRIKE UP THE BAND — RATING 2.7
1940    NR    Comedy-Musical    Age 06+    120 min.    B&W

Teenage musical comedy featuring youthful Mickey Rooney and Judy Garland who sings such tunes as "Do the Conga," "Our Love Affair," and "Nell of New Rochelle." Rooney is the leader of a high school band that competes in a nationwide radio contest. Delightful enthusiastic teenagers in small-town middle America. Paul Whiteman and his orchestra with their big band music provide the background for innocent young romantics.

### SUMMER MAGIC — RATING 2.8
1963    NR    Drama    Age 12+    116 min.    Color

Entertaining Disney story of a widow who moves her family to a home in Maine and seeks to scratch out a living. An uppity cousin comes to visit and creates havoc. Fine cast includes Darrin McGavin, Hayley Mills, Burl Ives. Disney remake of *Mother Carey's Chickens*. Pleasant and enjoyable.

### SUMMER OF MY GERMAN SOLDIER — RATING 3.5
1978    TVM    Drama    Age 12+    100 min.    Color

Touching story about a young Jewish girl (Kristy McNichol) in Georgia during World War II who encounters an escaped German POW (Bruce Davison). First a friendship, then romance develops as the girl realizes the soldier is anti-Nazi. It is refreshing to see a story featuring a German soldier with high morals and ideals. Excellent acting by McNichol and Davison. Emmy award winning role played by Esther Rolle.

### SUMMER SOLSTICE    RATING 3.0
**1981    TVM    Drama    Age 17+    56 min.    Color**
Brief, interesting story about a crusty individualist (Henry Fonda) and his wife (Myrna Loy) of 50 years. In this film, Fonda plays a staunchly autonomous artist. Both reflect on the joys and sorrows of their marriage, which was not without its rocky periods. They reaffirm and recognize the value of their love for each other.

### SUMMER TO REMEMBER, A    RATING 3.0
**1985    TVM    Drama    Age 06+    104 min.    Color**
Heartwarming story about a female Orangutan that escapes from captivity and is befriended by a deaf boy. Fortunately, both know sign language and are able to communicate with each other. Like most animals, this orangutan is vulnerable to cruelty, and has been abused by a circus hustler. How the young handicapped boy saves his animal friend will show children the need to love and respect animals.

### SUNDOWNERS, THE    RATING 4.0
**1960    NR    Drama    Age 17+    113 min.    Color**
Outstanding story of the arduous life of an Australian family (Robert Mitchum and Deborah Kerr) who raises sheep for a living. During one of their drives, they are befriended by a writer-teacher (Peter Ustinov). Realistic scenes of driving, herding and shearing the sheep as well as drinking and gambling among the shepherds. The family has its disagreements, but they show love for each other and sacrifice. One husband-wife bedroom scene.

### SUNRISE AT CAMPOBELLO    RATING 3.3
**1960    NR    Docudrama    Age 12+    143 min.    Color**
Story about Franklin Roosevelt's (Ralph Bellamy) pre-presidential political struggles as well as his bout with crippling polio. The focal point of the movie is FDR's walk on stage at the Democratic convention to nominate Al Smith. Those who remember the Roosevelt era will be reminded of the "good old days." Others will get a look at one of the political giants of the 20th century. Also stars Greer Garson and Hume Cronyn.

### SUPERMAN    RATING 3.3
**1978    PG    Science Fiction-Adventure    Age 12+    143 min.    Color**
Fine performance by Christopher Reeves as the man of steel. The story traces his life from the point of origin to his life with human parents and on to Metropolis. There, bespectacled reporter Clark Kent fools his friends, co-workers and the world when his alter-ego Superman takes on such master criminals as Lex Luthor. Special effects won the movie an Oscar. Humorous, satirical epic of a universal childhood hero.

### SUPERMAN IV: THE QUEST FOR PEACE    RATING 2.5
**1987    PG    Science Fiction-Adventure    Age 12+    90 min.    Color**
This fourth installment of the popular *Superman* movie series has the man of steel (Christopher Reeve) engaged in a desperate fight to rid the world of nuclear weapons. His arch enemy, Lex Luthor, is a greedy arms profiteer and creates Nuclear Man to challenge Superman. This video will thrill those who admire this All-American comic book hero. Fun for all.

### SUPPORT YOUR LOCAL SHERIFF    RATING 3.7
**1969    G    Comedy-Western    Age 12+    93 min.    Color**
Profoundly funny western featuring James Garner as a not-so-brave gold hunter who stumbles into a lawless town and is appointed sheriff. Garner eventually breaks every rule in the law books. The fun begins as he uses his wits to bring the gold rush town under control and it doesn't end until every western cliche is turned upside down. Walter Brennan and Jack Elam add to the hilarity of this good family comedy.

### SUTURE    RATING 3.0
**1994    NR    Mystery-Drama    Age 17+    93 min.    B&W**
Vincent, a white man suspected of killing his father, switches identities with Clay, a black man that he's attacked and left for dead. He escapes jail, while Clay assumes his place. Can the amnesia-suffering Clay remember his past? Mystery-lovers will enjoy trying to figure out this bizarre, cinematic puzzle, complete with a Freudian psychologist. Implied intercourse once with no nudity.

### SWAN PRINCESS, THE                                                           RATING 3.1
**1994        G            Fantasy-Adventure          Age 06+         88 min.           Color**
A cartoon fairy-tale, based on the story of the Swan Lake ballet. Odette is a beautiful princess who is turned into a swan by the evil magician Ruthbart. Prince Derek must find Odette in spite of her swan form, to show that he loves her for more than her beauty. An enjoyable touching story with no objectionable elements. However, some fighting scenes may scare younger children.

### SWISS FAMILY ROBINSON                                                        RATING 3.3
**1960        NR           Adventure                  Age 06+         128 min.          Color**
Outstanding remake of the 1940 classic. The Robinson family leaves Switzerland for New Guinea only to find themselves shipwrecked on an island paradise. Daunted at first by their twist of fate, they soon discover how to build sophisticated treehouses, acquire wild animals for pets, and stave off pirates in an exciting climax. Outstanding cast includes John Mills, Dorothy McGuire and James MacArthur.

### SYBIL                                                                        RATING 3.0
**1977        TVM          Drama                      Age 12+         122 min.          Color**
This is the story of Sybil, a young woman who developed multiple personalities as a way to deal with her childhood suffering at the hands of a psychotic parent. It's a touching film about her struggle to overcome her past. Sally Field won an Emmy for her fine performance as Sybil. Joanne Woodward plays the psychiatrist who treats her.

### TALE OF TWO CITIES                                                           RATING 3.7
**1935        NR           Drama-Adventure            Age 12+         121 min.          B&W**
Outstanding blockbuster based on classic Dickens novel. Setting is 1780s French Revolution era with Ronald Coleman as Sydney Carton, a lawyer who tries to redeem his past failures by helping victims during the Reign of Terror. Madame Defarge knits as she waits by the guillotine for the next head to roll. A notable sequence is the storming of the notorious French prison Bastille. Basil Rathbone of Sherlock Holmes fame also stars.

### TALE OF TWO CRITTERS                                                         RATING 3.5(e)
**1967        NR           Adventure-Drama            Age 04+         48 min.           Color**
Bear cub and baby raccoon are accidentally cast adrift down a swollen river away from their immediate homes. They form a team in their struggle to survive their strange wilderness surroundings. Baby bear and raccoon are shown in bear's den as he prepares for hibernation. Excellent outdoor scenery and animal photography make this nature film a must for children.

### TALL TALE                                                                    RATING 3.0
**1995        PG           Adventure-Fantasy          Age 06+         96 min.           Color**
A young, imaginative boy dreams of a life of adventure away from his remote farm in the early West. When an evil railroad baron tries to take their land, the boy imagines a fantasy land complete with his Wild West heroes. An entertaining film for the whole family with only a few moderate crude and two moderate obscene words and some violent fighting scenes.

### TARZAN, THE APE MAN                                                          RATING 3.8
**1932        NR           Adventure                  Age 12+         99 min.           B&W**
The best of all Tarzan movies features Johnny Weissmuller an Olympic medalist, as Tarzan. Maureen O'Sullivan stars as Jane. Tarzan swings through the jungle with the greatest of ease while coping with danger and protecting his beloved mate, Jane. This adventure story about an orphan raised by apes in the African jungles continues to entertain audiences with excitement and wild animal life.

### TEN (10) RILLINGTON PLACE                                                    RATING 3.3
**1971        PG           Drama-Suspense             Age 17+         111 min.          Color**
A suspenseful movie based on the notorious Christy-Evans case that shocked England in the 1940's. Richard Attenborough gives a brilliant performance as the slimy murderer Christy, who frames a young husband for the murder of his wife. Filmed in the actual neighborhood where the crime took place, the subject matter is definitely for older teens and adults. One profanity and some mild violence.

### TESTAMENT  RATING 3.5
1983   PG   Drama   Age 12+   89 min.   Color

Following a nuclear holocaust, a small town must now contend with the problems brought about by the radiation fallout. Particular attention is given to a single mother and her children who struggle to sustain their lives. The film focuses on their daily efforts to deal with the tragedy. Starring William DeVane and Jane Alexander. Very touching and engrossing film.

### THAT DARN CAT  RATING 2.7
1965   NR   Comedy-Suspense   Age 06+   116 min.   Color

Hilarious Disney comedy featuring Dean Jones as an FBI agent who depends on the help of a saucy Siamese kitty in trailing a kidnapped woman. The kitty even helps sniff out the bad guys. Many comical situations, a cute story and a fast pace make this a great family film. Good cast (Roddy McDowell, William Demarest of *My Three Sons* fame, Hayley Mills and Frank Gorshin).

### THAT'S DANCING  RATING 3.0
1985   G   Musical-Documentary   Age 12+   105 min.   Color

Numerous guests help host this collection of clips from the great musicals in Hollywood history. Sequences from the best of Fred Astaire and Ginger Rogers to *West Side Story* offer an outstanding tribute to the great Hollywood musicals. Narrations by Gene Kelly, Liza Minelli, Mikhail Baryshnikov, Ray Bolger, Sammy Davis, Jr. Includes a dance number by Ray Bolger which was cut from the famous *Wizard of Oz*.

### THAT'S ENTERTAINMENT  RATING 3.8
1974   G   Musical-Documentary   Age 12+   132 min.   Color

Judy Garland, Bing Crosby, Frank Sinatra, Elizabeth Taylor, Fred Astaire, and many others are showcased in this tribute to the great Hollywood musicals that were made between 1929 and 1958. High on nostalgia and profile of great stars, it presents scenes from some 100 MGM musicals. Includes several surprises such as Esther Williams, Clark Gable singing and dancing, Eleanor Powell and Jimmy Durante.

### THAT'S ENTERTAINMENT II  RATING 3.8
1976   G   Musical-Documentary   Age 06+   133 min.   Color

Outstanding sequel to *That's Entertainment*. More spectacular footage is taken from 75 great Hollywood productions. Features new footage of hosts Fred Astaire and Gene Kelly together for the first time in decades. Includes comedy and drama of the Marx Brothers, Spencer Tracy and Katherine Hepburn.

### THAT'S ENTERTAINMENT III  RATING 3.8
1994   G   Musical-Documentary   Age 12+   108 min.   Color

Another nostalgic extravaganza of stars, music, and dancing that chronicles MGM's Golden Age of filmmaking, from the inception of the "talkie" until the late 1950's. Features lavish costumes, casts of thousands and elaborate dance routines. Clips of Hollywood's best will delight older musicals fans and those interested in film history. Includes some obscured nudity in a shower scene and dancers in skimpy and form-fitting costumes.

### THEY WERE EXPENDABLE  RATING 3.8
1945   NR   Adventure-War   Age 12+   135 min.   B&W

Produced during World War II when Hollywood was making good films to support the war effort. Story depicts the bravery of Navy personnel in the Philippines who fought the Japanese with PT boats early in the war. Excellent acting and good footage make this a significant war picture. John Wayne and Donna Reed star.

### THIN MAN, THE  RATING 3.8
1934   NR   Mystery-Comedy   Age 12+   93 min.   B&W

This Depression Era film was so popular that it led to the production of five more *Thin Man* pictures. William Powell and Myrna Loy play Nick and Nora Charles, a happily married, successful couple who find excitement and adventure on detective capers. It contains a light-hearted blend of murder mystery and comedy. This is one of the more outstanding detective series to be found. Although dated, it still provides fine entertainment.

### THIRTY SECONDS OVER TOKYO — RATING 3.3
**1944 NR Drama-War Age 12+ 138 min. B&W**

Classic World War II film dealing with the famed Doolittle bombing raid on Tokyo in 1942. Spencer Tracy plays General Doolittle and Robert Mitchum and Van Johnson portray air crew leaders. This suspenseful story follows the crews through their training period, the exciting bomb raid, and their trek home on foot through China. One of the best World War II films made and still great entertainment.

### THIS IS THE ARMY — RATING 3.0
**1943 NR Musical Age 12+ 121 min. Color**

Entertaining World War II musical featuring Ronald Reagan, Irving Berlin, and many others. Entire cast consists of men in uniform performing mainly songs and skits. This is a good example of Hollywood's positive contribution to the American war effort. Patriotic and lots of fun.

### THOSE CALLOWAYS — RATING 3.2
**1964 G Drama-Comedy Age 06+ 130 min. Color**

This classic Disney story focuses on a fur trapper and his son who struggle to protect wild geese and their habitat from the encroachment of greedy, scheming land developers. The promotion of a healthy respect for nature and natural resources enhance the entertainment value of this film. The virtues of those who care for animals is highlighted against the backdrop of those who only love money.

### THOUSAND PIECES OF GOLD, A — RATING 4.0(e)
**1992 NR Drama Age 17+ 105 min. Color**

A Cantonese sheep rancher sells his daughter to a gambler in Oregon during the 1890's gold rush. Her new master plans to offer her to sex-starved miners, but she steadfastly refuses to take part in his schemes. She courageously overcomes monumental obstacles to take charge of her own destiny. A true story that shines with integrity, courage, and hope. Adult subject matter, implied sex, a few moderate obscenities, and one regular profanity.

### THREE COINS IN THE FOUNTAIN — RATING 2.8
**1954 NR Drama-Comedy Age 12+ 102 min. Color**

Romantic yarn about three secretaries on vacation in Rome. Looking for love, they each toss a coin into the Fountain of Trevi. Their wishes come true but with comic results as each experiences a romantic encounter. Rome provides a picturesque background for this light-hearted romantic adventure. Dorothy McGuire and Jean Peters star.

### THREE FACES OF EVE — RATING 2.8
**1957 NR Drama Age 12+ 91 min. B&W**

A gripping psycho-drama based upon the true story of a woman (Joanne Woodward) who has three distinct personalities that cause her to lead three separate lives. Her mental condition baffles her psychiatrist (Lee J. Cobb) who tries to help her. Narrated by Alistair Cooke. The film describes her struggle to overcome her childhood phobia caused by her grandmother's death.

### THREE LIVES OF THOMASINA, THE — RATING 3.1
**1964 G Drama Age 06+ 98 min. Color**

Patrick McGoohan plays a veterinarian in Scotland who must contend with his daughter's mental anguish when her cat runs away. He encounters a mysterious and bewitching young woman who has unusual powers over wild and domestic animals. This phenomenon baffles his scientific mind. Animals star along with people and love grows between father and daughter. Delightful Disney movie.

### THUMBELINA — RATING 3.3
**1994 G Fantasy Age 04+ 86 min. Color**

Modernized animated adaptation of Hans Christian Andersen fairy tale classic about a tiny girl born from a flower. She feels lonely in a large world until she meets Prince Cornelius and falls in love. A lovely film about being true to one's dreams. Great Spielberg touches, along with the distinctive voices of Charo, Carol Channing, and John Hurt make this film enjoyable family fare. Nothing objectionable.

### TIGER TOWN                                                        RATING 3.0
1983        G        Drama-Comedy        Age 06+        76 min.        Color

Billy Young is the aging right fielder for the Detroit Tigers who is going to hang up his cleats after this season. Alex is a young Tigers fan whose father recently died. Because of advice his father gives him, Alex believes that by "wishing hard enough" he can help Billy Young and the Tigers win the baseball pennant. Encourages children to believe in their abilities. Particularly good Disney film for young boys.

### TILL THE CLOUDS ROLL BY                                             RATING 2.5
1946        NR        Musical        Age 12+        137 min.        Color

Pleasant film with a star-studded cast featuring Judy Garland, Lena Horne, Van Johnson, Dinah Shore, Frank Sinatra, and others. Story is a biographical sketch of songwriter Jerome Kern. The musical scores and plethora of stars make this production a winner. The story barely does justice to the talent, but the musical scores are enjoyable.

### TIME FOR MIRACLES, A                                                RATING 3.0
1980        TVM        Docudrama        Age 12+        97 min.        Color

Kate Mulgrew, John Forsythe and Lorne Greene help recount the story of the great faith and many hardships of St. Elizabeth Bayley Seton, founder of the Daughters of Charity in the United States. Amid trials and tribulation her perseverance and love for God made a tremendous impact on untold numbers of people. A century later the Pope declared her a saint.

### TIME MACHINE, THE                                                   RATING 3.3
1960        NR        Science Fiction-Fantasy        Age 12+        108 min.        Color

Rod Taylor stars in this fine adaptation of H.G. Wells' classic story of a scientist who invents a machine that can travel into the past or future. Leaving his friends behind, he searches for a better world, but discovers he must make a better world. Good special effects, a fine script, superb acting, and a provoking conclusion make this much more than a science-fiction film. It examines the changes in human culture and values wrought by time.

### TO BE OR NOT TO BE                                                  RATING 3.2
1983        PG        Comedy-Drama        Age 12+        108 min.        Color

In this hilarious comedy, Mel Brooks and Anne Bancroft play a Polish theatrical couple who become embroiled with the Nazis at the outbreak of World War II. They prevent the Gestapo from locating certain persons in the Polish underground movement. Some of the more comical scenes occur when Brooks masquerades as a professor-spy, a Gestapo chief and der Fuehrer himself.

### TO KILL A MOCKINGBIRD                                               RATING 3.7
1962        NR        Drama        Age 12+        129 min.        B&W

Gregory Peck gives an outstanding performance as a southern lawyer who must contend with a prejudicial town as he defends a black man accused of attacking a white woman. His problems are compounded by the fact that he must help his two children understand why he is working to help the accused. Peck's Oscar-winning performance captures the unique flavor of the pre-integration South. Excellent drama on American race relations.

### TO LIVE                                                             RATING 3.8
1995        NR        Drama        Age 17+        130 min.        Color

An epic film which follows the life of Fugui and his wife Jiazhen as they struggle to survive the momentous changes during the Communist takeover in China. Fugui's gambling problems break up the family, but his determination to be with his family bring them back together again. An intense and realistic drama, with some war violence, drinking and one severe obscenity and two regular profanities. A mesmerizing eye-opener.

### TO RACE THE WIND                                                    RATING 3.3
1980        TVM        Drama        Age 12+        104 min.        Color

Based on the hit play *Butterflies are Free*, this biographical sketch dramatizes the hardships faced by Harold Krents, a blind man who successfully worked his way through Harvard law school. Shows how people with handicaps can excel in an environment that favors sight. Inspiring entertainment for the whole family. A compassionate, moving film.

### TO SIR WITH LOVE                                                                 RATING 3.5
1967          NR          Drama                    Age 12+          105 min.          Color

Shot on location in England, this film examines the trials of a young black teacher who struggles to educate a group of unruly teens in London's East End. Sidney Poitier is outstanding as the caring teacher who must overcome both social and implied racial barriers. His gradual gain of respect, with a fine musical score sung by Lulu, makes this a must-see production. Cockney dialect and setting enhance this true-to-life drama.

### TO THE LIGHTHOUSE                                                                RATING 3.3
1984          TVM         Drama                    Age 17+          115 min.          Color

Virginia Woolf's novel comes to the screen and explores the thoughts and actions of the Ramsay family and their summer guests in Cornwall, England. This is an interesting character study — an exploration of people and relationships which is made more appealing through strong acting and a beautiful setting. It combines the best of traditional English novels with modern trends of psychological character development.

### TOBY TYLER                                                                       RATING 3.3
1960          G           Comedy-Drama             Age 06+          96 min.           Color

Kevin Corcoron (Moochie) of *Mickey Mouse Show* fame stars in a delightful story of an orphan boy at the turn of the century who joins the circus and engages in typical mischief. A period piece, this classic Disney film provides fine shots of circus activities. The whole family will thrill to the beat of the drums and excitement under the big top. Based upon a favorite children's book.

### TOM AND JERRY: THE MOVIE                                                         RATING 2.0
1993          G           Comedy                   Age 04+          84 min.           Color

Tom, the buffoon cat, and his miniature antagonist, Jerry the mouse, team up to help a little girl find her long-lost father. Thrilling adventures await them, such as a river raft escapade and an encounter with Captain Kiddie, owner of an amusement park. A fun show, especially for the younger ones. Based on the Hanna-Barbara cartoon characters, this amusing film has some moderate cartoon violence.

### TOM AND VIV                                                                      RATING 3.3(e)
1995          PG-13       Drama                    Age 17+          125 min.          Color

An unflattering look at the Anglican man of letters, T.S. Eliot (William Defoe), and his rocky relationship with his wife Vivian (Miranda Richardson). Eliot, though he loves his wife, is unable to really communicate with her and care for her. Vivian's free spirit is soon crushed as she abuses drugs and is sent to a mental institution. Not for the tender-hearted, but a moving film. Contains one severe obscenity.

### TOM BROWN'S SCHOOL DAYS                                                          RATING 2.7
1940          NR          Drama                    Age 12+          80 min.           B&W

Good cast and setting make this a delightful movie about a boy in Victorian England who must adjust to life in an exclusive boys' school. He finds the school quite brutal at times. This makes such an impact on him that he sets out to be a civilizing influence on the student population. Chronicles the development of a true English gentleman. Tom makes the transition from a rowdy boy to a good role model for his peers.

### TOM SAWYER                                                                       RATING 2.5
1973          G           Adventure                Age 06+          104 min.          Color

Faithful production of the Mark Twain classic. Johnny Whitaker (Jody of *Family Affair*) plays the mischievous Tom Sawyer who finds himself in one problem after another. Most of the important situations found in the book are recounted here, along with Huck Finn and Becky Thatcher. A priceless reflection on school boy antics within the confines of the Mississippi River town culture of the 19th century.

### TOM THUMB                                                                        RATING 3.3
1958          NR          Fantasy                  Age 06+          98 min.           Color

This delightful fairy tale comes to life as an excellent children's movie featuring the tiny boy who finds comfort in the home of a kindly couple. Terry Thomas and Peter Sellers are quite entertaining as villains who seek to exploit Tom Thumb. A fine cast and good production of the classic story by Grimm will please the entire family. It teaches valuable lessons contrasting noble virtues and wicked exploitation.

## TOMORROW'S CHILD     RATING 2.5
1981     TVM     Drama     Age 12+     95 min.     Color

Dr. James Spense is asked to participate in a special project at the Steslund Institute. He and his wife Kay are to have their child conceived and allowed to develop outside the womb. After the procedure begins, they must deal with the issues surrounding their decision. A doctor opposed to the research threatens to stop the experiment. Entertaining and thought provoking.

## TOPKAPI     RATING 3.8
1964     NR     Mystery-Adventure     Age 12+     120 min.     Color

Outstanding film about jewel thieves who devise a remarkable plan to break into the famed Topkapi Museum in Istanbul, Turkey, and steal a priceless jeweled dagger. Humorous escapades, an excellent cast, superb script, and flawless suspense make this a must-see for anyone who relishes adventure movies on the lighter side. Peter Ustinov, Melina Mercouri and Maximillian Schell.

## TOY STORY     RATING 4.0(e)
1995     G     Fantasy-Adventure     Age 04+     80 min.     Color

Toys come to life and experience exciting adventures when their owner is away. The toys' leader, Cowboy Woody (voice of Tom Hanks) becomes second fiddle when high-tech spaceman Buzz Lightyear (voice of Tim Allen) moves into the toy room. The two eventually become friends as they find themselves held captive by a mean little boy. This film broke new ground with its computer-animated technology that will delight the whole family.

## TRAIN, THE     RATING 3.8
1965     NR     Adventure     Age 12+     113 min.     B&W

This action-packed World War II yarn tells about French Resistance fighters who must prevent a German train from transporting precious French art treasures into Germany. Burt Lancaster leads the Parisians against the wily German commander played by Paul Scofield. This is a highly entertaining war adventure. Excessive violence is avoided in this struggle to save the cultural heirlooms from destruction.

## TRAPEZE     RATING 2.8
1956     NR     Drama     Age 12+     105 min.     Color

Above average circus drama about a former aerialist (Burt Lancaster) who helps a young aerialist achieve success and fame. His efforts are complicated when he engages Tony Curtis in a contest for the affections of Gina Lollobrigida. Short of going to see a real circus, this European version will do just fine with thrilling scenes of death-defying action.

## TREASURE OF SIERRA MADRE, THE     RATING 4.0
1948     NR     Adventure-Drama     Age 12+     126 min.     B&W

Greed does not pay in this highly acclaimed story about three prospectors (Humphrey Bogart, Walter Huston, and Tim Holt) who seek their fortunes in gold. The highlight of the film is an examination of the weak character that each possesses and how it affects their work and relationships. Numerous Oscars awarded for acting in this epic story of desperate men seeking fortune and turning against each other.

## TREE GROWS IN BROOKLYN, A     RATING 4.0
1945     NR     Drama     Age 06+     128 min.     B&W

Dorothy McGuire, Joan Blondell and Lloyd Nolan star in this marvelous story about a young girl who must deal with an alcoholic father and other family problems. At the same time, she seeks to improve herself so she can escape the hard life that comes with living in a tenement environment in turn-of-the-century Brooklyn. Portrays the best efforts of a young girl to make something out of her life. Classic drama.

## TRIBES     RATING 3.3
1970     TVM     Drama-Military     Age 12+     74 min.     Color

Marine Thomas Drake prides himself in turning raw recruits into tough Marines. He has his job cut out for him when flower child Adrian Stone shows up on the bus as a new recruit. Many funny, sad and serious situations arise from the combination of these two people. Adrian preserves his values even when the world is trying to change them. Good presentation of how men are trained for military duty.

### TRIP TO BOUNTIFUL, THE — RATING 3.2
1985   PG   Drama   Age 12+   106 min.   Color

Geraldine Page won an Oscar for this emotionally charged story about an energetic elderly woman who comes to find life with her son and daughter-in-law unbearable. She takes a bus trip back to her former home in Bountiful, Texas. Along the way, she meets some interesting people and has some unusual experiences. What she finds is a place in ruin, but it manages to bring a positive change to everyone's lives. One of the best films of the 1980's.

### TROUBLE WITH ANGELS, THE — RATING 2.8
1966   NR   Comedy   Age 06+   112 min.   Color

The peace of mind and routine of the good sisters are disrupted at St. Francis convent in this funny story about two rambunctious girls living in a Catholic convent. Causing much grief for the sisters, and especially mother superior, Hayley Mills and June Harding star as the not so angelic little "angels." You'll have to laugh at the good-natured hi-jinx of these delightful pixies.

### TRUE GRIT — RATING 3.3
1969   G   Western   Age 12+   128 min.   Color

John Wayne stars as Rooster Cogburn, a ruffled, over-the-hill marshal who comes to the aid of a young girl seeking revenge on those responsible for her father's death. His efforts end in a final shoot-out with the villain, played by Robert Duvall. This film came near the end of Wayne's acting career, so fans of his will appreciate its historical significance. All the larger than life elements are combined to bring you the best of the Duke.

### TUCKER: THE MAN AND HIS DREAM — RATING 3.5
1988   PG   Drama   Age 12+   130 min.   Color

Superb account of the life and dreams of Preston Tucker who sought to develop the car of the future in the 1940's. His efforts are resisted by the major auto manufacturers, as well as the political machine. Tucker is admirable in his fight to build a better car against hopeless odds. More of a promoter than a mechanic, Tucker frequently gets himself into tight jams. Some mild and moderate crude language and one profanity.

### TWELVE ANGRY MEN — RATING 3.8
1957   NR   Drama   Age 12+   95 min.   B&W

Emotionally charged and stirring story about one man's (Henry Fonda) efforts to persuade eleven fellow jurors to change their verdict. He argues that their decision to pronounce a young man guilty of murdering his father should be reconsidered. The tolerance of one juror is pitted against the prejudice of his peers. All-star cast and good script make this courtroom drama exceptional entertainment.

### TWELVE O'CLOCK HIGH — RATING 3.7
1949   NR   Drama-War   Age 12+   132 min.   B&W

Gregory Peck is superb as a Patton-type World War II Army Air Corp officer who must apply tough rules to B-17 pilots and crew. The desire to get the job done is a strain on Peck as he becomes too compassionate toward his fellow airmen in this high drama. The beginning and ending set a unique tone for the film and instill a feeling of what it would be like to experience such a conflict, survive it, and reflect back on it.

### TWENTY THOUSAND LEAGUES UNDER THE SEA — RATING 3.8
1954   NR   Adventure-Fantasy   Age 12+   122 min.   Color

Men battle a deadly giant octopus surrounded by undersea beauty in this fabulous Disney version of Jules Verne's classic novel. Kirk Douglas plays a sailor who teams with scientist Paul Lukas to explore the ocean. They get involved with Captain Nemo (James Mason) and his sophisticated submarine. Once in the clutches of the power-hungry captain, they find adventure. Great special effects. Cast also includes Peter Lorre.

### TWO BITS — RATING 3.5(e)
1995   NR   Drama   Age 12+   93 min.   Color

This emotional story about a touching relationship of a dying grandfather and his young grandson centers around the price of admission to the movies, two bits. It's set in 1933 Philadelphia when 25 cents was hard to come by, especially for a child. The boy wants to go to the movies, and his grandfather promises him a quarter if he dies that day. Al Pacino gives his usual great performance as the grandfather.

### TWO OF A KIND — RATING 3.3
**1982  TVM  Drama  Age 12+  100 min.  Color**

A heartwarming story about two different people with a common problem. In this dramatic story, a withdrawn old man in ill health finds love and acceptance from his retarded grandson. Together they develop a close relationship and the old man regains a sense of value concerning life in general. A very touching family film depicting the value of handicapped people and their need to contribute to society.

### UNCLE TOM'S CABIN — RATING 2.7(e)
**1987  NR  Drama  Age 12+  100 min.  Color**

This fine adaptation of Harriet Beecher Stowe's classic, chronicles the life of Uncle Tom, a strong, pious black slave. Sold to a slave trader, when his owner finds himself under a mountain of debt, things turn dismal when Tom is finally sold to the evil Simon LeGree. Tom's Christian faith is portrayed positively, and helps him endure the mistreatment of LeGree. Some violent scenes of mistreatment may trouble youngsters.

### UNDERGRADS, THE — RATING 3.0
**1985  TVM  Comedy  Age 12+  102 min.  Color**

The generation gap in reverse is examined in this comedy. Art Carney gives an entertaining and likeable performance as an energetic grandfather who decides to enroll in college with his grandson. He proves to be quite a challenge for his grandson, who has to compromise his prim and proper attitude for the sake of Gramps. The plot reflects the growth of love between the grandfather and grandson. Good family viewing.

### UNNATURAL CAUSES — RATING 3.5
**1986  TVM  Drama  Age 17+  96 min.  Color**

Vietnam vet Frank Coleman is fighting a losing battle with cancer due to Agent Orange defoliant. He works with a Veteran's Administration worker to uncover the connection between Agent Orange and the problems suffered by many vets. They struggle against overwhelming odds as the Veterans Administration tries to cover up their findings. One vulgarity referring to breast prosthesis.

### UNSINKABLE MOLLY BROWN — RATING 3.0
**1964  NR  Musical  Age 12+  128 min.  Color**

In this true story of an orphan raised in the back woods of Colorado, Molly Brown (Debbie Reynolds) is a high-spirited woman who knows what she wants and heads for Denver to find it. She manages to amass wealth, experience romance, and attain a high social position. But later she settles for the true values of friendship and love. A rowdy parody on those who acquired wealth during the Rocky Mountain gold rush.

### UNSTRUNG HEROES — RATING 2.5(e)
**1995  PG  Drama  Age 17+  94 min.  Color**

A poignant, funny and uplifting story about a 12-year-old boy facing his mother's terminal illness. He goes to live with two very eccentric uncles whose junk collecting lifestyle creates some hilarious situations. But the young boy is also introduced to religion and learns to accept his mother's death. This bittersweet story contains a few crudities and one obscenity.

### VELVETEEN RABBIT, THE — RATING 4.0(e)
**1985  G  Fantasy  Age 04+  20 min.  Color**

Christopher Plummer (Sound of Music) narrates this cartoon version of the classic children's story. A stuffed toy rabbit arrives in the nursery, mocked by toy soldiers and toys that can do tricks. But a wise toy horse tells him that other toys will never become real like the rabbit can. He learns what the horse meant when the boy gets sick. A wonderful fantasy about the power of a boy's imagination.

### VERTIGO — RATING 4.0
**1958  NR  Mystery-Suspense  Age 12+  128 min.  Color**

An Alfred Hitchcock thriller with outstanding suspense throughout. Jimmy Stewart's excellent acting makes this a classic. Stewart is a retired detective who agrees to keep tabs on the wife of a friend. Spine-tingling danger lurks behind every corner and the various twists within the story make it virtually impossible to predict. Stewart ends up falling in love with his friend's wife (Kim Novak) and the plot thickens.

### VIVA ZAPATA!          RATING 3.8
1952     NR     Docudrama     Age 12+     113 min.     B&W

John Steinbeck's screenplay depicts the life of Mexican revolutionary Emililiano Zapata and his rise from a mere nobody to the presidency and back again to political obscurity. This historical period piece reflects the turmoil of the early 20th century in Mexico. Outstanding acting by Marlon Brando as Zapata and Anthony Quinn as his brother. Brando fans will enjoy this as an early example of his talent. Several Oscars were awarded for acting.

### VON RYAN'S EXPRESS          RATING 3.3
1965     NR     Adventure-War     Age 12+     117 min.     Color

Frank Sinatra gives a fine performance in his role as a World War II POW who leads a band of men on a daring escape attempt out of Germany into neutral Switzerland. Their means of escape is a hijacked train. The suspense puts one on the edge of his seat as the escapees find themselves in numerous tight situations. The ending is especially riveting.

### VOYAGE OF THE YES          RATING 2.3(e)
1972     TVM     Adventure     Age 12+     73 min.     Color

Cal is a California boy with a talent for sailing. He plans to sail to Hawaii before he enters college, and convinces black hitchhiker Orlando Parker to join him. But he does not know that Orlando is on the run for accidentally killing a drug pusher. All kinds of experiences develop as these two men from different backgrounds battle the elements and each other on the trip. In the process they learn what true friendship is all about.

### VOYAGE TO THE BOTTOM OF THE SEA          RATING 2.8
1961     NR     Science Fiction     Age 12+     105 min.     Color

Much better than the TV series, this fun underwater adventure features Walter Pidgeon as an overbearing admiral aboard an atomic submarine. He must contend with various problems on ship as well as strive to save the Earth from a burning radiation belt. Exciting sea photography. Good entertainment.

### WACKIEST SHIP IN THE ARMY, THE          RATING 2.9
1960     NR     Comedy     Age 12+     99 min.     Color

As the name implies, this is a hilarious World War II story about a group of misfit sailors who decide to make a broken down ship seaworthy and embark on a secret mission. Jack Lemmon and the late music star Ricky Nelson (of Ozzie and Harriet fame) are featured. It's a madcap look at the lighter side of the Navy in the Pacific.

### WAGONMASTER          RATING 3.5
1950     NR     Western     Age 12+     86 min.     B&W

Great scenery enhances this fine John Ford western. Two cowboys sign-on with a wagon train full of Mormons and help guide the religious pioneers to the Utah frontier. James Arness, who goes on to star as Matt Dillon in the *Gunsmoke* series, stars along with Harry Carey and Ben Johnson. This film spawned the television series, *Wagon Train*. A great western classic.

### WAIT TILL YOUR MOTHER GETS HOME          RATING 3.0(e)
1983     TVM     Comedy     Age 06+     96 min.     Color

High school football coach Bob Peters loses his summer job of teaching drivers education. At the same time, his wife Pat accepts a job as school secretary. Thinking that caring for the children and home is a minor issue, Bob draws up a contract with Pat stating that he will take over all household duties for the summer. The fun begins when Bob tries to "coach" the house. Theirs is a loving family with healthy husband-wife relationship.

### WALK IN THE CLOUDS, A          RATING 3.5(e)
1995     PG-13     Drama     Age 17+     97 min.     Color

Exquisite romantic film about Paul Sutton, a young soldier, who agrees to pose as the husband of a pregnant Spanish girl, for her to gain approval of her strict father. When circumstances delay Paul's departure, they soon find themselves in love. A beautifully photographed treat for the eyes. Due to the adult subject matter and one brief sex scene without nudity, this film is only appropriate for mature teenagers and adults. A few crude words.

### WAR, THE           RATING 3.3(e)
**1994    PG-13    Drama    Age 17+    126min.    Color**

Kevin Costner's look at a Mississippi family and the things they do to live with dignity against hatred and prejudice. The Simmons children learn to love their enemies and forgive others in this touching movie about war, specifically the conflict between them and some antagonistic neighbor kids. An outstanding film, but it has many mild and moderate crude words, several obscenities, two regular profanities and some violent fights.

### WAR OF THE WORLDS, THE           RATING 3.5
**1953    NR    Science Fiction    Age 12+    85 min.    Color**

A superior film version of H.G. Wells' classic story about the Martian invasion of Earth. Exciting battles between the Martian space ships and human ground forces wreak havoc on earth. But the all-powerful creatures from space fall prey to some lowly microbes on earth. For its day, the special sound effects were outstanding and won the picture an Oscar.

### WAR WAGON, THE           RATING 3.0
**1967    NR    Western    Age 12+    101 min.    Color**

Another shoot-em up with a novel vehicle, the War Wagon. John Wayne stars as a vagabond ex-con out to get villain Bruce Cabot who stole his gold mine and framed him. Wayne tries to steal back his gold from the armored stage Cabot is using to transport it. He manages to enlist the help of Kirk Douglas and his gang. But unknown to him, Douglas has been hired by Cabot to kill Wayne. Interesting twist of events and action make this an outstanding western. Much violent shooting and fighting.

### WATERSHIP DOWN           RATING 3.5
**1978    PG    Adventure-Fantasy    Age 12+    92 min.    Color**

Fine, animated story of a family of rabbits in search of a safe location in which to raise their family. Their search is complicated by dangerous encounters with humans, automobiles and other animals. This film, though animated, is not designed primarily for children. Entertaining rabbits' eye view of the world.

### WEST SIDE STORY           RATING 3.8
**1961    NR    Musical    Age 12+    155 min.    Color**

Rival Anglo and Puerto Rican gangs are the back-drop for this outstanding modern day musical Romeo and Juliet romance. Features such stars as Natalie Wood, Robert Wise, John Astin, and Simon Oakland. Great choreography and musical scores such as "America", and "Maria", by Bernstein and Sondheim. Some undesirable lifestyles are portrayed, but not glorified. The film ends with a dramatic, traumatic event.

### WHALE FOR THE KILLING, A           RATING 2.8
**1981    TVM    Drama    Age 12+    145 min.    Color**

Charles Landon takes his wife and two sons on a vacation sailing trip to the North Atlantic. During a storm, their boat is disabled, leaving them stranded in a fishing village off the coast of New Foundland. They discover a trapped whale in a lagoon near the village. The townpeople want to sell it to pirate whalers, but they and a few others fight to save it.

### WHAT'S UP DOC?           RATING 3.0
**1972    G    Comedy-Adventure    Age 12+    94 min.    Color**

Barbra Streisand plays a mischievous woman who can't seem to let college professor Ryan O'Neal and his fiance (Madeline Kahn) enjoy a normal relationship. She manages to get O'Neal involved with stolen jewels and into some very difficult situations. Car chases and general madness are featured in this outlandish comedy. The laughs keep rolling in this old-time Keystone Kops type humor.

### WHEN THE WHALES CAME           RATING 2.5
**1989    PG    Drama    Age 12+    90 min.    Color**

In 1914 on an island off England, two children establish a relationship with an old recluse called the "Birdman". Although the rest of the islanders believe he is evil and wicked, to the children he is a loving friend. The two children, along with the Birdman, try to return a beached whale to the sea before other whales come along and are beached as well. Excellent acting. Wonderful tale of love and hate, courage and cowardice.

### WHERE ANGELS FEAR TO TREAD  RATING 3.0
**1992    PG    Drama    Age 17+    112 min.    Color**

A Victorian widow shocks her relatives when she marries a young Italian she meets on vacation in southern Italy. Although the English aristocracy tries to dissuade her from staying with him, she refuses, to their astonishment. A refreshing love story with a wholesome message on values. Adults will appreciate this beautifully photographed social satire about hypocritical snobbery. Many drinking scenes, one suggestive scene between husband and wife, and one moderate crudity.

### WHERE THE RED FERN GROWS  RATING 3.2
**1974    G    Drama    Age 06+    90 min.    Color**

One of the best family films ever made, this poignant drama tells the story of a young Oklahoma boy who raises hounds and trains them to be excellent coon hunters. In this grand adventure, he learns much about responsibility and life in general. This is the kind of material that is typically found in Disney films. Great for adults and children. There won't be a dry eye in the house at the heart-rending conclusion.

### WHISTLE BLOWER  RATING 3.3
**1987    PG    Mystery-Adventure    Age 17+    100 min.    Color**

Suspenseful thriller starting with the relationship between Frank Jones and son Bob who is one of three British government employees suspected of being a Russian spy. Bob is mysteriously killed and Frank joins a journalist and war buddy in an effort to uncover the facts surrounding Bob's death. Two murders, an extra-marital affair and a few profanities.

### WHILE YOU WERE SLEEPING  RATING 3.2(e)
**1995    PG    Comedy-Romance    Age 12+    100min.    Color**

This charming movie follows Lucy (Sandra Bullock), a train tolltaker in Chicago, whose humdrum life becomes exciting when she's mistaken for the fiance of a man in a coma. As she grows to love the man's family, she also falls in love with his brother (Bill Pullman). A wholesome, romantic comedy with a few moderate crudities and three regular profanities. A true Cinderella story, complete with a gracious prince and lovable princess.

### WHITE CHRISTMAS  RATING 2.7
**1954    NR    Musical    Age 12+    120 min.    Color**

Bing Crosby and Danny Kaye play ex-army buddies who try to revive a winter resort operated by their former commanding officer (Dean Jagger). Numerous Irving Berlin musical scores are performed. Crosby and Kaye are at top form as they help their beloved friend. Crosby croons his famous "White Christmas" melody. A partial remake of the 1942 *Holiday Inn*.

### WHITE FANG  RATING 3.3
**1991    PG    Adventure    Age 12+    107 min.    Color**

Jack London's classic book comes to the screen as an exciting drama filmed in Alaska. A half-wolf dog and a young man fight for survival during the gold-rush craze. Together, they face man-killing wolves, incredible arctic cold, and vicious outlaws in a desolate wilderness. Vintage Disney entertainment for the whole family. Some dogfight scenes, however, may upset young children. One moderate and several mild, crude words.

### WHITE FANG 2: MYTH OF THE WHITE WOLF  RATING 2.3
**1994    PG    Adventure    Age 12+    107 min.    Color**

Set in early 1900's Alaska, this thrilling sequel features a young gold prospector and his half-wolf dog threatened by a gang of greedy gold miners hungry for the Indians' land. Meanwhile, he falls in love with a lovely Indian maiden who has rescued him from an accident. Outstanding film with plenty of excitement and spectacular wilderness scenery. Some moderately violent scenes and Indian mysticism.

### WHITE MAMA  RATING 3.2
**1980    TVM    Drama    Age 12+    96 min.    Color**

B.T., a sixteen-year-old black youth, must live with aging widow Mrs. Malone (Bette Davis) until his probation is completed. Mrs. Malone needs B.T.'s rent money to maintain her home. In time they develop a friendship which compels them to help each other in numerous ways. The relationship between two generations is expressed very well. Stresses the need for love and respect. Contains one regular profanity.

### WHO'S MINDING THE MINT                                                    RATING 3.3
1967        NR        Comedy              Age 06+        97 min.            Color

Jim Hutton stars in this wonderful comedy about a U.S. mint employee (Hutton) who accidentally destroys a substantial amount of currency. Desperate to replace the money, he acquires the help of a zany band of crooks who make the situation anything but better. Great cast of people including Bob Denver, Walter Brennan, Milton Berle, Joey Bishop, and Victor Buono. Really great side-splitting comedy.

### WILBUR AND ORVILLE—FIRST TO FLY                                           RATING 4.0
1973        NR        Docudrama           Age 06+        47 min.            Color

Superb historical film about the exploits of Wilbur and Orville Wright and their work to be the first to fly. Dramatizes the importance of completing a task and following your dreams, even when stiff criticism seems to be unbearable. A good film for presenting the achievements of the Wright brothers to younger people.

### WILD AND THE FREE, THE                                                    RATING 2.5(e)
1980        TVM       Comedy              Age 06+        96 min.            Color

Dr. Linda Davenport is studying chimpanzees in East Africa. In the U.S., Dr. Doug Rayferson teaches chimps to communicate by means of sign language. The hospital at which Dr. Rayferson works wants to perform inhumane experiments on his primates. So he and his chimps flee to Africa to join Davenport. The fun begins when the civilized chimps meet up with the chimps in the wild. Humorous happenings and beautiful African scenery.

### WILD HEARTS CAN'T BE BROKEN                                               RATING 3.3
1991        G         Drama               Age 12+        88 min.            Color

A young orphan girl with an indomitable spirit overcomes poverty and hardship to become a daring horse show star. Even when she falls and is severely injured, she refuses to succumb to her circumstances. This adaptation of a real-life drama demonstrates how individual determination and courage, triumphs over disaster and heartbreak. Refreshing story that will warm your heart and that of your children.

### WILD WOMEN                                                                RATING 2.5(e)
1970        TVM       Western-Comedy      Age 12+        90 min.            B&W

Killion leads a wagon train in the 1840's which is secretly carrying weapons to help the Texans fight the Mexican army. To avoid suspicion, five women convicts are promised their freedom if they will pose as the wives of the men driving the wagons. Jean Marsheck (Anne Francis) and Maude (Marilyn Maxwell) star as two strong willed women ready to face the dangers of the west to gain their freedom. Comical, entertaining western.

### WILLY WONKA AND THE CHOCOLATE FACTORY                                     RATING 2.8
1971        G         Fantasy-Adventure   Age 06+        98 min.            Color

Five lucky kids win special gold tickets to see inside Wonka's famous chocolate factory. The kids, except for Charlie, are spoiled by modern influences. Whimsical Willy Wonka (Gene Wilder) warns them to behave in the factory, but one by one they disobey. Will Charlie also mess up his chance? This delightful film entertains adults and children alike, and hopefully teaches them as well. One scary boat ride may frighten very young viewers.

### WIND AND THE LION, THE                                                    RATING 3.2
1975        PG        Adventure           Age 12+        120 min.           Color

A true story about the kidnapping of an American woman (Candice Bergen) and her children by a North African Berber chieftain, played with energy by Sean Connery. When President Roosevelt hears of the kidnapping, he calls out the Marines to rescue the family. Fine acting compliment a suspenseful plot. Some fighting violence along with two moderate crudities are the only detractors to this film.

### WINDS OF KITTY HAWK, THE                                                  RATING 3.0
1978        TVM       Docudrama           Age 06+        98 min.            Color

Chronicles the endeavors of Wilbur and Orville Wright to win the race for the sky. Through diligence and hard work the brothers manage to construct a machine that becomes the first manned flying machine. Excitement and drama develops as they fight financial distress, frustration and the ridicule of the public.

### WINNIE THE POOH AND THE HONEY TREE — RATING 3.0
1966　　NR　　Adventure　　Age 04+　　24 min.　　Color

Excellent animated cartoon about the loveable but occasionally inept bear Winnie the Pooh. It follows Winnie's exploits as he searches for his favorite snack — honey. Young children will enjoy this one — and probably their parents too.

### WINSLOW BOY, THE — RATING 3.8
1948　　NR　　Drama　　Age 12+　　117 min.　　B&W

Engrossing courtroom drama about a lawyer (Robert Donat) who must defend and prove the innocence of a Naval cadet (Neil North) who has been accused of theft. Based on an actual case in 1912, it captures the pomp and propriety of Edwardian England. The disregard of the crown for the rights of an innocent youth makes for a telling tale.

### WITHOUT A CLUE — RATING 2.8
1988　　PG　　Comedy-Mystery　　Age 12+　　107 min.　　Color

In this comedy spoof on the adventures of Sherlock Holmes, Michael Caine plays a very inept Sherlock Holmes who depends on his companion, Dr. Watson, for all his sleuthing expertise. When Watson and Holmes take on the job of locating a stolen British currency engraving plate, a lively string of comical episodes get underway. This clever, slapstick comedy is an enjoyable, laugh-filled experience. One mildly suggestive keyhole peeping scene.

### WIZARD OF OZ, THE — RATING 4.0
1939　　NR　　Fantasy-Adventure　　Age 06+　　101 min.　　Color

In depression era Kansas, Dorothy and her dog are transported by a tornado into the land of Oz. There she meets three fascinating companions who join her in a great adventure. They visit a comical wizard and battle a wicked witch who tries to destroy them. Her colorful friends are a cowardly lion, a tin man, and a silly scarecrow. This wonderful fantasy features many lively musical numbers. An all-time great.

### WOMAN HUNTER, THE — RATING 2.5(e)
1988　　PG　　Drama-Adventure　　Age 12+　　100 min.　　Color

Dina and Jerry Hunter are millionaires visiting Acapulco so Dina can recover from the trauma of killing a man in a car accident. Dina thinks she is being stalked by Paul Carter, whom she believes to be a ruthless international jewel thief. Because of the trauma she is experiencing, she cannot convince anyone she is in danger, including her husband. Intriguing story with an unexpected twist at the end.

### WOMAN OF THE YEAR — RATING 3.7
1942　　NR　　Comedy　　Age 12+　　114 min.　　B&W

This amusing comedy brought Katherine Hepburn and Spencer Tracy together for the first time. Hepburn plays an internationally popular political commentator who is put in her place by salty sportswriter Tracy. The fun gets underway when love at first sight turns into mayhem as they recognize and resolve their different personalities. But their conflict eventually brings them to love and marriage. One of the best from yesteryear.

### WORLD WAR III — RATING 3.3
1982　　TVM　　Drama-War　　Age 12+　　183 min.　　Color

The president of the United States has instituted a grain embargo against the Soviet Union. The USSR feels it must seize a portion of the Alaskan pipeline and use it as a bargaining chip against the United States. The Soviets send a strike force into Alaska and two U.S. intelligence agents are commissioned to stop them during an Alaskan blizzard. High action entertainment. Many "hells" and "damns" and moderate violence.

### WORLD'S GREATEST ATHLETE, THE — RATING 2.9
1973　　G　　Comedy　　Age 06+　　89 min.　　Color

Two college coaches flee their troubles at Merrivale College in this comedy farce. In their attempt to forget it all they go to Africa, where they run into Nanu, a super athlete. Tim Conway is particularly funny in several sequences as these two losers find the solution to their problems. This typical Disney feature will keep you laughing.

### WRONG ARM OF THE LAW, THE RATING 3.5
1962 NR Comedy Age 12+ 94 min. Color

Those who appreciate the antics of Peter Sellers will enjoy this comedy about a trio of gangsters who manage to disguise themselves as police officers. They cleverly manage to confiscate loot from other thieves. Sellers plays one of the gang leaders who is out to get the trio beating the gangsters at their own game. Good fun.

### YANKEE DOODLE DANDY RATING 3.8
1942 NR Musical Age 12+ 126 min. B&W

James Cagney appears in this wonderful song and dance biographical tribute to entertainer George Cohan. Cagney won an Oscar for his rare performance. This exceptional film is full of great music, coupled with fine performances by numerous entertainers, including Eddie Foy, Jr. Uplifting and patriotic.

### YEARLING, THE RATING 3.8
1946 NR Drama Age 06+ 128 min. Color

Star-studded adaptation of Marjorie Rawling's great novel. Young boy develops a strong attachment to a fawn he has acquired and cared for. Unfortunately, his father feels he must destroy the beloved pet. A very sensitive and emotionally charged film. Gregory Peck and June Lockhart star in this poignant tale. One of the best pictures of all time.

### YOGI'S GREAT ESCAPE RATING 2.5(e)
1987 NR Adventure-Comedy Age 04+ 96 min. Color

In this colorful, fast-paced animated cartoon, the government decides to shut down Jellystone Park and move Yogi Bear to a zoo. But Yogi and his friend Bo-Bo take off on an exciting adventure trying to elude the park ranger. It's great fun with many positive values and no excessive violence.

### YOUNG AT HEART RATING 3.2
1954 NR Musical-Drama Age 06+ 117 min. Color

This exciting boy-meets-girl musical is a remake of Fannie Hurst's *Four Daughters*. A music teacher has four winsome daughters who experience problems in their competitive pursuit of male companionship. Frank Sinatra attempts to romance Doris Day. The musical scores and romance are light-hearted and enjoyable.

### YOUNG EINSTEIN RATING 2.1
1989 PG Comedy Age 12+ 91 min. Color

This Australian comedy follows the crazy exploits of a brilliant young scientist who splits the atoms of beer. He gets a patent on his invention, but it's stolen and he must go to Paris to rescue it. In the meantime, he falls in love with young Marie Curie and with rock and roll. This weird film may appeal to youngsters, but not many others. One prolonged scene with rear views of nude boys in a shower is included.

### YOU'RE IN LOVE CHARLIE BROWN RATING 3.3(e)
1967 NR Comedy Age 04+ 26 min. Color

This delightful animated Peanuts short feature finds Charlie Brown depressed and confused. It seems he is hopelessly in love with a little red-headed girl at his school. His friend Linus isn't much help, so he asks Peppermint Patty for assistance. But she only makes matters worse. Really clever, enjoyable show.

### YUMA RATING 2.2
1970 TVM Western Age 06+ 73 min. Color

U.S. Marshall Dave Harmon comes to Yuma to clean-up the town that is infested with crooked businessmen and brawling cowboys. Harmon is forced to kill the brothers of Arch King, a tough cattle driver. To complicate his situation, the Indians have been cheated out of cattle by local businessmen. An explosive conclusion has Harmon trying to bring Yuma under control.

### ZORRO RATING 3.3
1975 G Adventure Age 12+ 88 min. Color

In a South American country, the cruel Colonel Huerta controls the country and oppresses the people. But the dashing swordsman Don Diego dons the mask of Zorro to rescue the people from his corrupt domination. The action includes many sword fights, but only a few fatalities. Exciting version of this classic tale.

# RECOMMENDED CHRISTIAN MOVIES

### ADVENTURES IN ODYSSEY — RATING 3.0
1993     NR     Adventure     Age 06+     30 min.     Color

Produced by Focus on the Family, this colorful, animated series covers the escapades of young Dylan and his friends. The exciting, fast-paced episodes deal with such issues as faith, friendship, and truth. Segments include Shadow of a Doubt, Star Quest, Once Upon an Avalanche, and Electric Christmas. [BBS; FOF; GF; HFL; JD; VV]

### ADVENTURES OF THE FLYING HOUSE — RATING 3.0
1981     NR     Adventure-Biblical     Age 04+     45 min. each     Color

While playing in the forest, three inquisitive youngsters discover a unique old house that really is a time machine. Angie, Justin, and Corky, together with Professor Bumble and his robot SIR, whiz back in time to relive New Testament Biblical events. Children will enjoy this excellent series of animated cartoons. Tapes are each 45 minutes in length with two episodes per tape. [FBS; TP]

### AGONY AND THE ECSTASY, THE — RATING 3.0
1965     NR     Drama     Age 12+     139 min.     Color

This loosely historical account of Michelangelo's painting of the Sistine Chapel is a moving dramatization of the artist's fight, both a religious and moral one, with Pope Julius II (Rex Harrison). An all-star cast including Charlton Heston as Michelangelo brings to life the struggle that gave birth to one of the greatest paintings of Christian art in the world. [BBV; GF; VV]

### ALL THE KING'S HORSES — RATING 3.5
1986     NR     Docudrama     Age 12+     80 min.     Color

Based on a true story, this heart-wrenching film features a motocross racer and his determined wife struggling to restore their marriage. Facing the possibility of divorce, they finally turn to God to restore their union. Viewers will be captivated by the high intensity of this life-changing drama. Fine acting and a strong salvation message. [RD]

### ANCIENT SECRETS OF THE BIBLE-PART II — RATING 3.0
1993     NR     Docudrama     Age 06+     30 min.     Color

This excellent series gives an introduction to some of the events of the Old Testament. Biblical characters such as David and Goliath battle for the supremacy of their nations and, in effect, God Himself. Other videos highlight the Ark, the Red Sea miracle and Noah's Ark. Complete with dialogue and narration, this is a well-done presentation perfect for the whole family [GP; JD]

### ANGEL ALLEY — RATING 3.5
1984     NR     Drama-Comedy     Age 06+     61 min.     Color

This inspiring Kuntz Brothers film features Nick, a young athlete who is trying to determine God's best for his life. The lure of a lucrative boxing career is dangled before him and he has to come to grips with a decision. Christian youth will identify with Nick's dilemma in this fast-paced film.[GTF; HFL]

### ANGEL OF SARDIS — RATING 3.5
1986     NR     Drama     Age 12+     62 min.     Color

Courageous Pastor Robert Ingstrom battles to rescue his apathetic church from the worst fate imaginable - spiritual death. The stiff resistance he encounters from his congregation and the opposing spiritual principalities makes for an intriguing tale. Christians will find their spiritual sensitivities awakened by this entertaining film. One of the best in the genre. [EF; HFL]

### BAMBOO IN WINTER — RATING 4.0
1991     NR     Drama     Age 12+     58 min.     Color

A young woman in a small Chinese village converts to Christianity despite the protests of her boyfriend and father. The Communist government threatens her to give up her newfound faith. A few violent torture scenes may be too intense for young children, but the message of the life-giving power of the Gospel will make you cheer for this brave girl. Voted best Christian film of 1991. [GF; HFL; JD]

### BEHIND THE SUN — RATING 3.5
**1995    NR    Drama    Age 12+    56 min.    Color**

Samir Majan has just graduated from a university in Chicago and has abandoned his Muslim faith to become a Christian. When he returns to his home in the Middle East, his father discovers his son has become a Christian and banishes Samir from the family. Samir is taken in by a group of underground Christians, but he finds his troubles are just beginning. This is an intriguing film with superb acting and dramatic realism. [ODI]

### BELONGING GAME — RATING 3.0
**1985    NR    Drama    Age 06+    30 min.    Color**

Wendy, a newcomer to a small town, desperately craves acceptance from the popular girls at school. When the "in group" tests Wendy's loyalty through actions she knows are wrong, she faces a tough decision - to give in to the pressure or to stand on her Christian convictions. Entertaining video on teen struggles. [CF; HFL]

### BEYOND THE NEXT MOUNTAIN — RATING 2.5
**1984    PG    Docudrama    Age 12+    98 min.    Color**

In 1908 in northeast India, a young boy leaves his remote village to study languages in an urban university in India. His father, who is the village pastor, has encouraged him to translate the Bible into their native tribal tongue. He continues his studies in Scotland and the U.S. while courting his girlfriend back home by correspondence. After many years he rejoins his father. This is an interesting, professionally produced true story. [GTF]

### BIBLE, THE — RATING 3.0
**1966    NR    Docudrama-Biblical    Age 12+    174 min.    Color**

Peter O'Toole and Ava Gardner star in this lavish spectacle presenting the first twenty-two chapters of Genesis, including the stories of Adam and Eve, Cain and Abel, and Noah. Although the retelling of Biblical stories is somewhat overdone, the sterling acting performances deserve a long look. [BBV; GF; VV]

### BIBLEMAN SHOW: THE BIG BIG BOOK — RATING 2.5
**1995    NR    Musical-Drama    Age 06+    40 min?    Color**

One of a fast-paced, rollicking series featuring a new kind of superhero, The Bibleman. Empowered by the limitless might of the Scripture, he offers encouragement and shares God's message of strength and hope. Preteens planning a musical show for their neighborhood lack confidence to perform until Bibleman appears and explains that God's strength is made perfect in their weakness. Music, adventure and laughter are key ingredients. [FBS]

### BIG MONEY MIX-UP — RATING 3.0
**1982    NR    Comedy-Adventure    Age 06+    35 min.    Color**

In this hilarious comedy-adventure, five kids find a bag stuffed with $75,000 that accidentally fell out of a bank truck. While they struggle with what to do with their new-found loot, the bumbling truck drivers disguise themselves to search for the money. Children will learn the importance of turning over big decisions to God. [GF; GTF; HFL; VV]

### BROTHER SUN, SISTER MOON — RATING 4.0
**1973    PG    Docudrama    Age 12+    121 min.    Color**

This magnificent, historical film by Zeffirelli portrays the self-sacrificing lifestyle of Francis of Assisi, one of the patron saints venerated by the Catholic Church. He gives up the wealth of a loving family in favor of deeper spiritual communion with God. Starting with a few followers, he rebuilds a chapel in the French country side and ministers to the poor and diseased. Artistically beautiful and moving film. [BBV; VV]

### CAMP, STEVE: SOLD OUT — RATING 3.0
**1993    NR    Concert    Age 06+    60 min.    Color**

The energy of Steve Camp is now on video. Steve combines sincere, heart-felt lyrics with catchy music to touch both our minds and hearts. Hear some of his best-known songs such as "Stranger to Holiness," "He is Able," and "The Love I Found in You." Steve's music and testimony will hopefully minister to you and call you to a deeper commitment to serve the Lord. [FBS]

## Christian Movies

### CARMAN - COMIN' ON STRONG
**RATING 3.0**
1985　　NR　　Concert　　Age 06+　　60 min.　　Color

Carman, a dynamic Christian musician, ministers to a packed house in this live concert with his usual verve and vigor. He dramatically performs such songs as "Lazarus, Come Forth," "Sunday's on the Way," and "God Don't Care What the Circumstance." Carman's outspoken approach, combined with light humor, effectively communicates the Gospel to youth and adults. [FBS]

### CARMAN LIVE - RADICALLY SAVED
**RATING 3.0**
1988　　NR　　Concert　　Age 06+　　71 min.　　Color

Carman, popular contemporary Christian singer and musician, is video taped live at his concert at the Brady Theatre in Tulsa, Oklahoma. He sings high energy inspirational songs to the delight of all. These include "I Been Delivered," "No Way," "Radically Saved," "Celebrating Jesus," "Shout of Victory," "I Feel Jesus," "Revive Us Again," and "Lord of All." Great Christian musical entertainment. [FBS]

### CARMAN: THE STANDARD
**RATING 3.0**
1995　　NR　　Concert　　Age 06+　　70 min.　　Color

If you have never experienced one of Carman's emotion-packed concerts, now is your chance. Part rapper, part ballad singer, Carman sings with energy to the youth of today. His words and his strong witness for the Lord will undoubtably impact both you and your children. This concert footage includes the songs "Revive Us, O Lord," "Radically Saved," and "Great God," among others. [BBS; FBS]

### CASH, JOHNNY - THE GOSPEL ROAD
**RATING 3.0**
1972　　NR　　Concert　　Age 06+　　62 min.　　Color

The unmistakable voice of country singer Johnny Cash set against the spectacular backdrop of the Galilean countryside provides delightful viewing for the whole family. Cash takes audiences back 2,000 years to the time of Jesus Christ's ministry. Spiritually uplifting tunes and marvelous scenery make this film a treasure to see again and again. [BBV; WWP]

### CAUGHT IN TIME
**RATING 2.5**
1985　　NR　　Drama-Adventure　　Age 06+　　55 min.　　Color

Two teenage boys are taken back magically in time to the Roman Biblical period. There, they get involved with a non-violent Christian group. The Christian alternative to *Back to the Future*, this film is a fast moving drama with a touch of comedy and a strong Christian message. A clever, well-produced idea. [HFL]

### CHINA CRY
**RATING 3.5**
1990　　PG-13　　Docudrama　　Age 12+　　103 min.　　Color

A moving, dramatic true story about a young Chinese girl living in pre-World War II Shanghai. She survives both the brutal 1941 Japanese occupation and the 1949 Communist takeover. Subjected to brutal beatings by the Communists because of her Christian education, she begins a harrowing pilgrimage of terror, hope and ultimately faith. It clearly proclaims the saving gospel of Jesus Christ through a heroic woman who unexpectedly finds God. [BBV; GF; GTF]

### CHRISTIAN MUSIC DIET, THE
**RATING 3.0**
1996　　NR　　Educational　　Age 06+　　　　Color

This outstanding new video was produced by Al Menconi Ministries. It is a concept which should be taught in every home and Sunday School in America. This video takes the important principles of Al's seminar on popular music and combines them with a strong challenge for Christian music. It includes Michael W. Smith's "Secret Ambition" music video, as well as a leader's guide to stimulate discussions in your home or classroom. [AMM]

### CHRISTMAS IS...
**RATING 3.0**
1987　　NR　　Drama-Animated　　Age 04+　　30 min.　　Color

This animated holiday feature focuses on Benji, a small boy trying to discover the meaning of Christmas. After learning that he is to play a shepherd in the school musical for the second year in a row, he daydreams about the first Christmas and finally understands the reason for the season. Cute story for kids. [CF; GF; HFL; VV]

### CITY THAT FORGOT ABOUT CHRISTMAS, THE     RATING 3.0
1987     NR     Drama-Animated     Age 06+     30 min.     Color

Young Benji, who stars in this animated video, declares "Sometimes I wish there wasn't a Christmas because all the hustle and bustle causes my parents to be irritable." So grandfather tells Benji the story of a town which has completely forgotten Christmas and how a carpenter, Matthew, brings back the magic and meaning of Jesus to the gloomy town. Entertaining movie with an important reminder. [GF; HFL; VV]

### CLIMB A TALL MOUNTAIN     RATING 2.8
1977     NR     Drama-Adventure     Age 06+     55 min.     Color

In this excellent Gospel Films release set in the Swiss Alps, three young children struggle with bitterness, hatred, and disappointment over the loss of their family dog. Their grandfather, a godly woodcarver, teaches them to forgive each other. This is a beautiful, poignant tale of living out one's faith, even in the toughest times. [GF; GTF; HFL; VV]

### CLIMB, THE     RATING 4.0
1975     NR     Drama-Adventure     Age 12+     55 min.     Color

A team of four, including an atheist, a magazine writer and a godly couple, try to successfully climb a high mountain. The writer, a novice climber, almost causes the deaths of the others. A suspenseful rescue mission adds appeal to the story. This exhilarating film combines a strong but natural evangelistic message with an exciting adventure. [GF]

### COACH     RATING 3.5
1984     NR     Drama-Sports     Age 06+     78 min.     Color

This Christian version of "Hoosiers" features a new basketball coach at a Christian high school who turns some losers into a winning team through discipline, commitment, and strong moral convictions. Although he lacks actual experience, he uses the word of God for success. Youth groups will enjoy the award-winning, exciting plot and the challenging message to strive for excellence. [HFL; RD; WP]

### COLBY'S MISSING MEMORY     RATING 3.0
1985     NR     Musical-Children     Age 04+     54 min.     Color

This charming children's film deals with the value of friendship in a child's life. The kids dance and sing while they build a club house and repair their friend Colby. Colby, the adorable chubby computer, sings "Love is the Greatest Gift," "Give It Away!" and "It's a Good Thing to Give Thanks." Children will be delighted by the bright, colorful characters and upbeat tunes. [FBS]

### COLBY'S PLACE - SKATEBOARD FOR SALE     RATING 2.5
1989     NR     Musical-Children     Age 04+     24 min.     Color

Featuring a friendly, scripture-quoting robot and some adolescent children, this children's film tells about a boy's desire for a new skateboard and the strong influence of peer pressure on young people. The importance of standing alone against the crowd when necessary is clearly presented. Contains some very lively music and fantastic skateboarding scenes. [FBS]

### COLSON: RELUCTANT PROPHET     RATING 3.5
1995     NR     Documentary     Age 17+     41 min.     Color

In this profound and intriguing documentary, the political career and imprisonment of Chuck Colson, special advisor to President Nixon, is presented. Also, the founding of his prison ministry after being released from prison and his work among prisoners around the world is chronicled. Both in narration and in Colson's own words, the film indicates how Colson has become one of the most perceptive and respected leaders in the Christian community. [WWP]

### COME THE MORNING     RATING 3.0
1993     NR     Drama     Age 12+     61`min.     Color

A determined woman moves her children from Texas to L.A. after her husband leaves and moves there. Unfortunately, things are much harder in L.A. than expected and she ends up in a street shelter. A kind restaurant owner and a fellow resident of the shelter befriend the family, helping them track down the delinquent husband. A touching story of enduring love and acceptance. Another good movie from the Billy Graham Association [BH; WWP]

## CONCERT OF THE AGE: PHILLIPS, CRAIG AND DEAN  RATING 3.5
1994  NR  Concert  Age 06+  90 min.  Color

Join the Christian group Phillips, Craig and Dean as they sing their upbeat songs of faith such as the title song, "A Wing and a Prayer," and "Favorite Song of All." Phillips, Craig and Dean are joined by other Christian singers as well to indeed make this The Concert of the Age. A good, energetic music video for teenagers. [FBS]

## CROSS AND THE SWITCHBLADE  RATING 3.5
1969  PG  Docudrama  Age 06+  105 min.  Color

This riveting biographical film features David Wilkerson (Pat Boone), a fearless evangelist from the rural parts of Pennsylvania, who takes the Gospel to violent gangs in the New York ghettos. He shows Nicky Cruz, the merciless leader of a hated mob, that the only hope for his life is in Jesus. Powerful, life-changing message. [GF; GTF; HFL; JD; VV]

## CROSS CURRENTS  RATING 3.0
1979  NR  Adventure-Drama  Age 06+  30 min.  Color

Three mischievous children disobey their camp counselors by attempting to navigate a canoe down some dangerous rapids. After some near misses with death, two of the kids ask Josh, the Christian, how to be saved. Children viewing the film will identify with the playful antics of kids at camp. Clear evangelistic message. [GF; GTF; HFL; JD; VV]

## CROSSFIRE  RATING 3.5
1979  NR  Drama-Adventure  Age 12+  56 min.  Color

Based on a true story, set in a Middle East country, this suspenseful adventure film deals with a young American girl who is attracted to both a terrorist and a missionary. Although strangely drawn to them because of their idealism, she soon realizes their values are poles apart. This relevant, award-winning film is packed with romance, realism and daring excitement. [HFL]

## DARK VALLEY  RATING 3.0
1961  NR  Drama  Age 17+  40 min.  B&W

Trapped in a coal mine cave-in, a father and son experience healing in their family relationship through the tragic death of a friend. The rebellious young son realizes he needs to surrender his life to the Lord. *Dark Valley* is a poignant story with a good evangelistic message that speaks powerfully to hearts everywhere. [GF]

## DATING MOVIE, THE  RATING 3.0
1983  NR  Educational-Comedy  Age 12+  60 min.  Color

Well known Christian comedian and youth worker, Pat Hurley, humorously treats the awkward subject of self-acceptance for the teenager in this entertaining video. Dramatic episodes focus on agonizing emotions that accompany a young boy's first date. Hurley describes hummingbird lovers and M&M lovers with good-natured appeal. Light fun for youth. [WP]

## DATING - TURNING YOUR LOVE LIFE OVER TO JESUS  RATING 3.0
1982  NR  Educational-Comedy  Age 12+  48 min.  Color

Tony Campolo, a Christian sociologist, handles the subject of teenage dating with his unique brand of tongue-in-cheek humor and insight in this educational video. He emphasizes the importance of maintaining high moral standards and respecting the self-worth of others. Youth will appreciate Campolo's straightforward approach to a serious topic. [WP]

## DEGARMO AND KEY: DESTINED TO WIN  RATING 3.5
1993  NR  Concert  Age 12+  30 min.  Color

One of the first Christian rock bands, DeGarmo and Key compile some of their great music videos. "Are You Ready" and "Rock Solid Medley" offer a sampling of their biggest hits. Included is the video once banned by MTV, "Six, Six, Six," because of its supposed violence in depicting hell, which may not be appropriate for younger children. [FBS]

### DEGARMO AND KEY: VISION OF THE LIGHT BRIGADE  RATING 3.0
1984   NR   Concert   Age 12+   30 min.   Color

The musically talented DeGarmo and Key present several concept videos in this vibrant production. Triumphant songs such as "Destined to Win" and "Alleluia, Christ is Coming" highlight a visually powerful video. Also, the prophetic message of "Six, Six, Six" is graphically portrayed. Youth who prefer hard-driving sound will enjoy this one. [FBS]

### DISTANT THUNDER, A   RATING 3.0
1986   NR   Drama-Prophecy   Age 12+   77 min.   Color

This shocking sequel to *A Thief in the Night* depicts the nightmarish times faced by a young woman and her friends during the Tribulation period. They are pursued and captured by the evil Antichrist forces. The seven seal judgments described in Revelations 6, 7, and 8 are graphically portrayed. Christians will want their unsaved friends to see this evangelistic film. [GTF; HFL; JD; RD]

### DOOG'S GARAGE THEATER-VOL. I.   RATING 3.0
1987   NR   Drama-Musical   Age 04+   30 min.   Color

Doog, one of Agapeland's Sloops and a lovable member of the Music Machine Club, has decided to host his own professional variety show in his dad's garage. Trouble arises in several areas, but Doog refuses to quit. Children will learn valuable lessons about courage, joy, self-acceptance, and kindness. [FBS]

### DOOG'S GARAGE THEATER-VOL. II   RATING 3.0
1988   NR   Drama-Musical   Age 04+   30 min.   Color

Doog, the lovable Agapeland favorite, interviews Hearty the Sloop, the distinguished president of the Music Machine Club. During the filming of the show, technical problems arise on the set, stretching Doog's patience to the limit. Volume II will teach children the principles of self-control, friendship, contentment, and faith. A creative idea. [FBS]

### DRAVECKY: A STORY OF COURAGE AND GRACE   RATING 2.5
1994   NR   Docudrama   Age 12+   61min.   Color

Dave Dravecky is the major league pitcher who threw 19 scoreless innings for the San Francisco Giants in the 1987 World Series. He is also the man who, the next year, found a cancerous lump in his pitching arm, which led doctors to amputate it. Hear Dave's encouraging story of faith in God and God's faithfulness during these trying times in his life. A great film to share with a non-believing sports fan. [GF; GTF; HFL; JD]

### DUNCAN, BRYAN: MERCY ALIVE   RATING 3.0
1994   NR   Concert   Age 06+   50min.   Color

The former lead singer of Sweet Comfort Band has now established himself as a good artist and singer on his own. This video is taken at Bryan's performance at a Christian concert in the Netherlands. His wonderful voice and upbeat lyrics keep you entertained as well as stimulating your thought. Songs performed include "When It Comes to Love," "Mercy Me," and "Step by Step." [WP]

### EARLY WARNING   RATING 3.5
1981   NR   Drama-Adventure   Age 12+   86 min.   Color

Sam Jensen, a skeptical newspaper reporter, gets a hold of a once-in-a-lifetime scoop. Through intense investigation, he discovers a link between currency devaluation, global computerization, and survivalist camps. All these are associated with the One World Foundation, a group determined to control the world. This prophetic film dramatically illustrates signs of God's final judgment. Lots of action and excitement. [GF; HFL; JD]

### EDGE OF EVIL, THE   RATING 3.0
1989   NR   Educational   Age 12+   60 min.   Color

Occult expert Jerry Johnston warns young people about the dangers of dabbling in Satanism and psychic phenomena in this startling new video. In addition, Johnston presents a clear-cut evangelistic message that counters the attractive lies told to today's youth. Viewers will appreciate this fresh candor about a troubling but timely topic. [WP]

## ENTER AUNT JENNY — RATING 3.5
**1987 NR Drama Age 12+ 30 min. Color**

In this video produced by Family Films, a world-weary man whose wife has just died discovers the secret of true happiness from his daughter-in-law's wise aunt. At first it appears a romance may develop, but she has something even more important to share! *Enter Aunt Jenny* is a touching story that deals with accepting God's love. [CF]

## FACE IN THE MIRROR — RATING 3.0
**1987 NR Drama Age 12+ 65 min. Color**

This thought-provoking film deals with a teenage boy who attempts suicide after realizing that he is lost and doesn't know how to find salvation. Youth can readily identify with the troubled teenager and his problems. An excellent treatment of a relevant issue and fine acting makes this worth a look. [RD]

## FALSE GODS OF OUR TIME: IN THE BEGINNING — RATING 3.0
**1988 NR Documentary Age 17+ 25 min. Color**

One in a good series of helpful films hosted by Christian theologian and philosopher Norman Geisler. Dr. Geisler helps us understand the difference between atheism, pantheism and theism. He also discusses the errors involved in evolution and explains how only having God as Creator makes good sense. Not a boring lecture, the video uses different scenes and formats to make this an enjoyable and educational experience. [GTF; HFL]

## FATHER, SON, AND A THREE MILE RUN — RATING 2.5
**1986 NR Drama Age 06+ 65 min. Color**

Inspiring, compassionate story of a father's unfailing love for his son who most say will be a failure in life. Shows fathers how to be fathers and parents how to love with an unconditional love. A touching story, it will entertain and motivate audiences of all ages. [EF; GTF; HFL]

## FIESTA — RATING 3.0
**1975 NR Drama Age 12+ 30 min. Color**

This moving Family Film production presents a modern-day Hispanic version of the prodigal son story. Manuel, the younger son, squanders his father's fortune in the bars of Chicago and becomes a drunken bum. Penitent and sorrowful, he returns home to seek forgiveness from his father. The father celebrates his homecoming with a fiesta. [BH]

## FILLING STATION TEACHING SERIES — RATING 3.0
**1984 NR Educational-Drama Age 04+ 15 min. each Color**

This set of instructional videos for children uses fast paced, attention keeping stories along with pictures to illustrate Biblical truths. Topics such as love, obedience, forgiveness, and patience are covered. Children will love this Christian form of "Sesame Street" and will learn some important lessons along the way. [TP]

## FINISH LINE — RATING 3.5
**1985 NR Drama Age 12+ 30 min. Color**

When death strikes a loved one as well as a friend of Jeff's, he becomes concerned about his own health and begins exercising. Jeff meets a minister dying with cancer who helps him see death in a different light. He also tells him how to obtain eternal life. This video contains a strong evangelistic message related in a natural manner. Pleasant and meaningful. [CF]

## FOR PETE'S SAKE — RATING 3.5
**1966 NR Adventure-Drama Age 06+ 108 min. Color**

This fast-paced drama tells how one family copes with the little irritations that occur throughout daily life. Filled with humor, excitement, and spiritual truth, *For Pete's Sake* offers a unique perspective on the daily grind. The whole family will enjoy this fun-filled adventure story. [HFL; WWP]

### FOURTH WISE MAN, THE — RATING 2.5
1985　　TVM　　Drama　　　　　　　　Age 12+　　72 min.　　Color

Martin Sheen portrays Artaban, a wise man who, like the other three wise men, discovers that heavenly signs foretell the coming of the Messiah. Unlike the other wise men, however, Artaban just misses presenting his gifts to the Messiah time and again. For 33 years, he follows after the Lord, only to miss him every time. His patience and love for the Lord is rewarded Easter Sunday. An unforgettable movie [BBV; GF; VV]

### FRIENDSHIP'S FIELD — RATING 3.0
1996　　NR　　Drama　　　　　　　　Age 06+　　94 min.　　Color

Ira, an 11-year-old tomboy on a farm in Idaho, is a mischievous, imaginative little girl enjoying her last summer of childhood. Next year she will be working the fields alongside her family. She befriends Oscar, the young son of a migrant worker, and they learn about each other's culture as they share many adventures. Prejudice among the neighbors, however, creates problems. This well done drama has enough humor and pathos to entertain the whole family. [FFF]

### FRONT ROW: CHARLIE PEACOCK — RATING 4.0
1990　　NR　　Concert　　　　　　　Age 06+　　60 min.　　Color

It is just like you are there listening to the vocal artistry of Charlie Peacock, backed up by the soulful voice of Vince Ebo and the wonderful acoustic guitar of Jimmy Abegg. Hear Charlie's unique brand of infectious music and his straightforward commitment to Jesus Christ. An excellent musical treat including songs like "Big Man's Hat," "Dear Friend," and "One Thing." [GF]

### FRONT ROW: MICHAEL CARD — RATING 3.5
1990　　NR　　Concert　　　　　　　Age 06+　　60 min.　　Color

Spend an intimate evening with Michael Card and his music. With him on the guitar, John Catchings on the cello, and Scott Brasher on the keyboard, you'll enjoy hearing songs such as "Joy in the Journey," "The Final Word," and "That's What Faith Must Be." This is a good video to introduce someone to the rich melodies and lyrics of the man who penned "El Shaddai." [GF]

### FURY TO FREEDOM — RATING 3.0
1985　　NR　　Docudrama　　　　　　Age 17+　　78 min.　　Color

To his high school friends and those who fought alongside him in Vietnam, Raul Ries stood for fear, fighting and fury. To his family he was a time bomb about to explode. Then, one evening, he was converted to Christ and he now preaches love and forgiveness to his buddies. Raul Ries went from black rage to inner peace, never to be the same again. Includes some violent fighting. [GF]

### GAITHERS - DREAM ON — RATING 3.0
1987　　NR　　Musical-Testimony　　Age 06+　　49 min.　　Color

In their simple, down-home manner, Bill and Gloria Gaither talk about the dreams God places within the hearts of Christians and the ways He fulfills them. The music of Sandi Patti, Don Francisco, Carman, Amy Grant, David Meece, and Joni is featured. Viewers will love this memorable look at the past and the future.[GV]

### GERBERT - GOD KNOWS MY FEELINGS — RATING 3.5
1988　　NR　　Variety　　　　　　　Age 04+　　30 min.　　Color

This Christian version of *Sesame Street* features the colorful puppet Gerbert, who has a rotten day. He is comforted, however, to learn that God understands his feelings. Children will enjoy a fun story and learn an important lesson at the same time. Produced by *Home Sweet Home* Educational Media Company. [FBS; WWP]

### GERBERT - HOP TO IT — RATING 4.0
1989　　NR　　Variety　　　　　　　Age 04+　　30 min.　　Color

Entertaining object lessons are offered by Gerbert, our little muppet-like friend, along with Biblical instruction. Gerbert learns the value of perseverance in life as he attempts to master a pogo stick. Colorful segments are included on counting, early flight history, and firemen. Excellent music adds appeal to this high quality video. [FBS]

### GERBERT - SAFE IN HIS ARMS    RATING 4.0
1988    NR    Variety    Age 04+    30 min.    Color

Gerbert, the energetic muppet-like character, uses story and song to teach that we are safe in God's arms. Gerbert's father fixes his scooter and advises Gerbert not to ride unless he wears his safety equipment. Against his advice, he rides it anyway unprotected and gets hurt. The message is that if we follow our "Father's" advice, we will also be safe. Lively, entertaining video for all ages. [FBS]

### GERBERT - THE CAT'S MEOW    RATING 4.0
1989    NR    Variety    Age 04+    30 min.    Color

In this offering of the *Gerbert Curriculum* series, our little muppet-like friend eagerly awaits a new pet cat. After its arrival, things are much different than Gerbert had expected. A quality lesson in loving even when the object of love is unlovable. Vignettes on patience, forgiveness and animals are included. [FBS]

### GERBERT - THE WORLD AROUND US    RATING 3.5
1987    NR    Variety    Age 04+    35 min.    Color

A musical adventure starring the lovable puppet Gerbert and his baby sitter. Featuring a colorful set and warm music, this video encourages children in imaginative play and healthy personal development. Includes six musical numbers and a special guest appearance by Courtney. Excellent quality and very enjoyable. [FBS]

### GINGERBROOK FARE    RATING 4.0
1982    NR    Musical-Educational    Age 04+    42 min.    Color

This delightful children's musical produced by Word features clown students learning the importance of obedience. A story within a story enhances the film's appealing charm. The clowns discover that "obedience is cheerfully doing what I'm asked to do and doing it quickly because I love you." Excellent and entertaining fare for kids. [WP]

### GOD ON TRIAL    RATING 2.5
1986    NR    Drama    Age 12+    60 min.    Color

Through a series of unexpected circumstances, Greg, a skeptical college student, questions the goodness of God. He asks, "How can I accept a God who would let a third of the world go hungry or permit the Holocaust in Germany to occur?" Greg puts God on trial and comes up with a verdict. Thought provoking.

### GOD'S GAME PLAN    RATING 3.0
1983    NR    Documentary-Testimony    Age 06+    33 min.    Color

Sports fans, have you ever wanted to go inside a major league baseball clubhouse? Now you can with *God's Game Plan*. Many ball players share real life experiences and the difference Jesus Christ has made in their lives. Youth groups will enjoy the exciting action clips and the testimonies from some of their favorite players. [GF]

### GODS OF THE NEW AGE    RATING 3.5
1987    NR    Documentary    Age 12+    100 min.    Color

This revealing documentary explores the deceptive and satanic roots underlying the eastern religions stemming from Hinduism. Part One discusses the history, basic tenets and practices of Hinduism, including Yoga, visualization, and transcendental meditation. *Part Two* features an in-depth look at the satanic basis of Hinduism. Features actual shots of Eastern religion practices and interviews with experts. [GTF; HFL]

### GOLD THROUGH THE FIRE    RATING 3.0
1987    NR    Drama    Age 12+    79 min.    Color

A 17-year-old Russian boy, Peter Smyslov, escapes from religious persecution in Russia and comes to live with a Christian family in the United States. However, he is disappointed in the commitment of Christians in America, and cannot freely share his faith at his high school. All the while, Russian KGB agents are spying on him. He also is enticed by American materialism. Dealing with these challenges makes for an interesting, sometimes humorous, story. [McD; GTF]

### GOLDEN DOLPHIN, THE  RATING 2.0
1986　　NR　　Drama　　Age 06+　　52 min.　　Color

An American family has inherited an expansive English country estate. Unfortunately, a disinherited claimant makes trouble when he tries to assert his false claims. Mark, the young son, discovers the life-giving strength of the Scriptures after he is kidnapped. This film portrays Christians using faith to overcome their difficulties. [GTF; HFL; KA]

### GOOSEHILL GANG & THE GOLDRUSH TREASURE MAP  RATING 3.5
1985　　NR　　Mystery-Adventure　　Age 06+　　30 min.　　Color

A group of kids find an 1850 diary at a yard sale that contains a treasure map. They eagerly dream about what they will do with the hidden gold and set out to find the treasure. Greed gets the best of them, and they quarrel. Children and adults will learn a valuable lesson from this family film. [BH; CF; WP]

### GOOSEHILL GANG & THE MYSTERIOUS STRANGERS  RATING 3.5
1985　　NR　　Mystery　　Age 06+　　30 min.　　Color

While seeking help for their diseased clubhouse tree at a local nursery, the Gang stumbles across a stolen necklace. After discussing the importance of being honest, they return the necklace to the jewelry store, not knowing the thieves heard their conversation. This video demonstrates the necessity of maintaining a good Christian testimony before the world. [BH; CF; WP]

### GOOSEHILL GANG & THE MYSTERY OF THE HOWLING WOODS  RATING 3.0
1980　　NR　　Mystery　　Age 06+　　30 min　　Color

The Goosehill Gang, two girls and three boys, are off on a camping trip with the parents of one of the boys. Their fun is interrupted by scary howling noises coming from deep within the woods. When two of the boys go to investigate, they come across a man with whom they share the Gospel. Though they apparently find the source of the howling, their troubles are just beginning. A fun movie with a worthwhile message. [BH; CF; WP]

### GOOSEHILL GANG & THE MYSTERY OF THE TREEHOUSE GHOST  RATING 3.0
1985　　NR　　Mystery　　Age 06+　　30 min.　　Color

In this episode of the *Goosehill Gang* series, Michael is fascinated by ghosts and reads a great deal about the subject, disobeying his parents. He is thoroughly convinced a ghost is stealing food from their clubhouse, so he sets a trap for it. Children watching this film will learn the importance of obeying their parents.[BH; CF; WP]

### GOOSEHILL GANG & THE VANISHING SCHOOLMATE  RATING 3.5
1985　　NR　　Mystery　　Age 06+　　30 min.　　Color

To find out why their soda pop bottles are missing, the gang trails Trudy, a new friend. They learn that she is stealing bottles to support her family. The gang responds by sending work to her father, an unemployed electronics technician. This gives them an opportunity to share the Gospel with him. Excellent message. [BH; CF; WP]

### GOSPEL MUSIC LIVE-PUBLIC PERFORMANCES  RATING 3.0
1992　　NR　　Concert　　Age 12+　　60 min.　　Color

Some of the best talents who have provided music for Billy Graham's crusades come together on this video. This all music program includes memorable performances by George Beverly Shea, Johnny Cash, Sheila Walsh and many others singing such favorites as "How Great Thou Art," and "I'd Rather Have Jesus." Enjoy this mix of classic and contemporary Christian music together as a family. [WWP]

### GRANT, AMY - AGE TO AGE CONCERT  RATING 3.0
1985　　NR　　Concert　　Age 06+　　90 min.　　Color

A youthful Amy Grant sings several of her timeless hits in this exciting concert video. Such tunes as "I Have Decided," "My Father's Eyes," "Sing Your Praise to the Lord," "In His Hand" and "Finally" will inspire viewers. They will encourage all ages to draw closer to God and serve Him with whole hearts. Excellent. [WP]

### GRANT, AMY - CIRCLE OF LOVE — RATING 3.0
1980  NR  Documentary-Testimony  Age 06+  44 min.  Color

Join Amy Grant at home with her family in this charming, homespun video. She shares her personal testimony and allows fans to get a glimpse of some aspects of her individual life in relation to the Lord, family, and friends. Viewers will appreciate her fresh candor and wholesome spiritual outlook. [WP]

### GRANT, AMY - FIND A WAY — RATING 3.0
1985  NR  Concert  Age 06+  20 min.  Color

The vibrant energy of Amy Grant explodes with light, color, and sound in this exciting video presentation. She performs five classic hits: "Find A Way," "Wise Up," "It's Not a Song," "Angels," and "Don't Run Away." This sensitive Christian singer ministers to both youth and adults through the dynamic power of her music. [WP]

### GRANT, AMY - HEART IN MOTION — RATING 3.0
1991  NR  Concert  Age 06+  22min.  Color

See and hear some of Amy's biggest hits from her Grammy-nominated album, *Heart in Motion*. Amy's upbeat songs appeal to the romantic in all of us while still reminding us of the importance of our relationship with God. A good video for a youth party. Amy selects five videos from her album, including videos for the songs "Baby Baby," "Every Heartbeat," and "That's What Love Is For." [WP]

### GREAT BANANA PIE CAPER — RATING 3.0
1979  NR  Comedy-Adventure  Age 06+  28 min.  Color

A group of kids attempt to deliver 75 banana cream pies while being chased by a gang of bullies in this hilarious comedy. Children will enjoy the zany, fun story blended with a natural evangelistic message. A winner of the "Best Children's Film of the Year" award, this video is ideal for ages six to thirteen. [GTF]

### GREAT ROCK RIVER RAFT RACE — RATING 3.0
1987  NR  Adventure  Age 06+  34 min  Color

Paul, Baxter, Joey and D.J. (Jane) decide to design and build a raft for the big Fourth of July raft race. After recovering their stolen plans, they build the raft which incorporates a secret weapon for speed. The competition, Eddie's gang, kidnaps Baxter to get the secret weapon, but he escapes in time for the race. The day of the big race arrives and they're off down the river! This film is packed with fun, adventure and spiritual values. [GTF; HFL]

### GREATER THAN GOLD — RATING 4.0
1983  NR  Drama  Ages 12+  63 min.  Color

Highly professional, engrossing drama about a pregnant, unmarried teenager agonizing over whether to have an abortion. Story includes a too-busy father and a lack of communication that threatens the family. Speaks out on standing firm in the faith, the consequences of premarital sex and on the sanctity of life. Superb video. One of the best. [EF; HFL]

### GREATEST ADVENTURE BIBLE STORY SERIES (Hanna Barbera) — RATING 3.5
1986  NR  Adventure-Biblical  Age 06+  30 min.  Color

Hanna-Barbera, the famed animated cartoon producers, present Biblical episodes seen through the eyes of three young children. Familiar characters such as Noah, Moses, Daniel, David, and Samson spring to life in this imaginative animated video series. Kids will delight in this unique production of well-known Bible stories. Well done, popular videos. Eight cassettes, 30 min. each. [BBV; FBS; GF; HFL; JD]

### GREEN, STEVE - FOR GOD AND GOD ALONE — RATING 3.0
1987  NR  Concert  Age 06+  54 min.  Color

This inspirational concert video features the magnificent tenor voice of Steve Green. He sings some of his best known hits, including "People Need the Lord," "He Holds the Keys," "Enter In," and "For God and God Alone." Experience the wonder of God's majestic presence through the messages of these powerful songs. [SCG]

**GUESS WHO'S COMING TO AMERICA**     **RATING 3.0**
1992     NR     Drama     Age 12+     58 min.     Color

T.J., a writer for a Christian magazine, travels to Africa to report on a famine. In Mali, he meets Mohammed, a devout Muslim, and the two become friends. Mohammed plans a trip to America and T.J. wants to share the gospel with him. But T.J. discovers his own life needs renewal from God before he can witness to Mohammed. A thought-provoking look at the need for faith in Jesus Christ alone. [GF; GTF; JD]

**HAPPINESS IS...**     **RATING 3.5**
1987     NR     Drama     Age 06+     67 min.     Color

In this *Mark IV* film, three young boys start a secret "guys only" club in a partially condemned building. Their efforts to keep the neighborhood tomboy out of their club leads to a series of humorous but harrowing escapades. Through a series of unusual happenings, the boys become converted to Christ. Children will enjoy the action packed plot and the dominant message of love and forgiveness. [HFL; RD]

**HARLEY**     **RATING 3.5**
1985     NR     Drama     Age 06+     63 min.     Color

Lou Diamond Phillips plays a juvenile delinquent sent to work on a Texas ranch for rehabilitation. There he encounters a Christian family who showers him with the love of God. One of the local boys makes life difficult for Harley. Also, the rancher's teenager doesn't get along with Harley, but that changes. First rate, entertaining video. Teenagers will like it. [GTF; HFL]

**HEALING, THE**     **RATING 3.0**
1983     NR     Drama     Age 12+     79 min.     Color

In this *Mark IV* production, a bright young physician nearly destroys his life through alcoholism after the death of his wife. He ends up in a skid-row mission, where some of the residents and staff help him regain a sense of purpose and hope for his life. A compelling film combining laughter and sorrow. [RD]

**HEART OF STONE**     **RATING 3.5**
1994     NR     Drama     Age 12+     137 min.     Color

This gripping movie follows two black men, Richard and Michael, who decide to leave their high-powered jobs and live in an impoverished black community. They move into the neighborhood in order to help reduce crime and gang violence. Their efforts are met with resistance but one young gang member comes to believe in the transforming power of Christ. A well-acted, quality movie appropriate for older children and adults.

**HEAVEN'S HEROES**     **RATING 3.5**
1986     NR     Docudrama     Age 06+     72 Min     Color

This heart-stopping drama features Hill, a former war hero turned cop who refuses to compromise his Christian convictions. His partner doesn't understand what makes Hill tick until a tragic event gets his attention. Viewers will be moved by this inspiring tale of heroic courage. An outstanding piece of work. [HFL; RD]

**HIDING PLACE, THE**     **RATING 3.5**
1975     G     Docudrama     Age 12+     145 min.     Color

This gripping, awe-inspiring film traces the courageous activities of the Ten Boom family in Holland during World War II, including their assistance to persecuted Jews and their subsequent imprisonment in a Nazi concentration camp. Through all the trouble they experience, they discover "there is no pit so deep that He is not deeper still." [BBV; BH; GF; VV]

**HITOPS**     **RATING 3.5**
1986     NR     Musical     Age 06+     102 min.     Color

Two angels take on youthful human form to experience the same emotional traumas teenagers face in this whimsical musical-drama. Peer pressure, temptation, and moral issues are handled quite well. Youth will enjoy the light-hearted story and bright, syncopated music. *Hitops* encourages kids to reach for God's best. [BBS]

## HOLDING ON
**RATING 3.0(e)**
1992     NR     Drama     Age 12+     ???     Color

Compelling story about a teenager afraid to tell her parents that she is pregnant. Instead, she confides in her two friends, who advise her to have an abortion. Her boyfriend, a devout Christian, strongly discourages her from taking this action. This film has a dramatic message that life in the womb is sacred, but unfortunately includes a few moderate crudities and obscenities [GF; GTF].

## HOLLYWOOD: LIGHTS, CAMERA, BLASPHEMY
**RATING 3.0**
1995     NR     Documentary     Age 17+     110 min.     Color

Eric Holmberg, noted critic of the entertainment media, has produced a series of videos attacking the moral decline of movies, TV and music. This one focuses on Hollywood's blatant anti-Christian, anti-religion movies and television programs. Movie clips illustrating the industry's negative treatment of religion flash on the screen intermittently. An excellent tool for youth group meetings, churches and schools. [APF]

## HOLLYWOOD VS. RELIGION
**RATING 3.0**
1994     NR     Documentary     Age 17+     59 min.     Color

Michael Medved, author of the popular book, *Hollywood vs. America*, presents a powerful indictment of the film industry's ongoing attack on religion and people of faith. With an introduction by Dr. James Dobson and a closing by Chuck Colson, Medved uses clips from films illustrating the increase of anti-religion content in films since the mid-1960s. Especially suitable for parents, youth leaders and church groups. [CHF]

## HOLM, DALLAS - AGAINST THE WIND
**RATING 3.0**
1987     NR     Concert     Age 06+     24 min.     Color

Dallas Holm, one of the pioneers in the contemporary Christian music field, sings seven tunes from his recent album by the same title. The settings vary from a live concert atmosphere to an informal recording studio. Holm's loyal following will greatly enjoy his hard-hitting songs and his thoughts behind the music. [WP]

## HOOMANIA
**RATING 3.0**
1986     NR     Fantasy-Adventure     Age 06+     37 min.     Color

After breaking a family window, Kris Atwood wants to run away. Sam Weatherfield, an inventor, befriends him and magically zaps them both onto a fantasy game board full of crazy characters. They either help or hinder Kris on this way to Mt. Wisdom, and he soon learns to make responsible choices. Entertaining animated adventure.[GF; GTF; HFL]

## HOUSE DIVIDED, A
**RATING 3.3**
1985     NR     Drama     Age 12+     58 min.     Color

Committed Christian teenager Paul Parker has lately taken his relationship with God for granted. When his brother Johnny comes home from med school and tells him about his upcoming marriage to an unbeliever, Paul becomes bitter and self-righteous. This touching film shows how life's complexities can blind us to our weaknesses. [GF; HFL]

## HUMPTY
**RATING 3.0**
1969     NR     Fantasy-Educational     Age 04+     30 min.     Color

This delightful animated film features Humpty, a rebellious egg who breaks the rules of the kingdom by getting too close to the wall. Laviathan, an evil dragon, convinces him that he's a better egg than all the rest and deserves a higher class life. *Humpty* teaches the importance of obedience and submission to authority. [GF; HFL; JD]

## IMAGE OF THE BEAST
**RATING 3.0**
1987     NR     Drama-Prophecy     Age 12+     93 min.     Color

This third film in the *Mark IV* end-time series deals with the mid-years of the Great Tribulation when the Antichrist sets up his one-world government. A small rebel band of fugitives struggle to stay alive amid spectacular and devastating heavenly judgments. Viewers will be kept on the edge of their seats.[GTF; RD]

## IMPERIALS - 20TH ANNIVERSARY CONCERT
**RATING 3.0**
1985    NR    Concert    Age 06+    45 min.    Color

This marvelous concert features the peerless Christian musical group belting out some of their classic hits, like "Praise the Lord," "The Trumpet of Jesus," "Stand by the Power," "Sound His Praises," and "What Can I Do for You." Imperials fans will treasure this memorable collection of some of the best in Christian music. [WP]

## IN MY WILDEST DREAMS
**RATING 3.0**
1991    NR    Drama    Age 12+    85 min.    Color

White-collar crime drama about a small electronics company that develops the first robot with a high intelligence level. A young stockbroker plans to get rich off this exciting innovation by gaining control of the company stock. His plans run amuck, however, when a high school student beats him to the punch. Appealing story for teenagers and adults. [FFF]

## IN SEARCH OF MORGAN AVERY
**RATING 3.5**
1983    NR    Drama    Age 17+    30 min.    Color

Morgan Avery, a wealthy financier, is advised by his physician to take a vacation for his health's sake and see a world that he knows nothing about. En route he is befriended by Nellie and her friends at a trailer park. There he discovers Christian kindness. This appealing film has a natural evangelistic message that viewers will appreciate. [CF]

## INNOCENT AGAIN
**RATING 3.0**
1992    NR    Drama    Age 17+    30 min.    Color

Jamie struggles with the dilemma of protecting his father, who has sexually molested him, or telling the truth in court. The young man is hesitant to risk embarrassing himself and discrediting his father in public. This thought-provoking movie opens up the issue of abuse for discussion, but its emotional nature is for older teenagers only. A Christian singer concludes Jamie's story by initiating discussion among the viewers and sharing the Gospel [GF].

## INTRUDER, THE
**RATING 3.0**
1994    NR    Drama    Age 12+    58 min.    Color

The Bartons, a quiet Christian family living in England, become disconcerted when Kevin, a rambunctious cousin, comes to live with them. The Barton children don't know how to respond to the stranger intruding on their comfortable lives. However, when Kevin and the children discover some mysterious goings-on at an abandoned house, they all learn how to deal with adversity and the value of perseverance [GF; VV]

## JESUS FILM, THE
**RATING 3.5**
1979    NR    Drama    Age 12+    83min.    Color

Following the book of Luke, *The Jesus Film* is the most widely viewed movie in history. This excellent evangelistic film has been translated into some 260 languages because of its powerful portrayal of the life, death and resurrection of the Lord Jesus. Follow Jesus and his disciples as they walk the countryside healing the sick, raising the dead, and proclaiming the kingdom of God.[BBV; GF; JD; VV]

## JESUS OF NAZARETH(Parts 1,2,3)
**RATING 3.0**
1976    TVM    Docudrama-Biblical    Age 12+    371 min.    Color

Franco Zeffirelli's crowning directorial achievement never gets old; instead, this film just gets better with each viewing. Meticulous research lends realism to a fine portrayal of the life of Jesus. A renowned international cast that includes Robert Powell, Olivia Hussey, and Anne Bancroft enhances the serious nature of the film. [BBV; GF; VV]

## JIMMY AND THE WHITE LIE
**RATING 3.0**
1985    NR    Drama-Educational    Age 06+    54 min.    Color

Jimmy and Harold are playing a great game of baseball catch when the ball goes through Mr. Cranshaw's window. How was Jimmy to know that a "harmless little lie" would grow and grow. Great story about asking God for forgiveness and making things right with someone you've harmed. Amusing, animated story. [CF; JD]

## JOAN OF ARC — RATING 3.0
1948　　NR　　Drama　　Age 12+　　100 min.　　Color

Opulent version of the maid from Orleans, Joan of Arc, played by Ingrid Bergman. Joan of Arc, a poor French girl, believes she has been chosen by God to help the French defeat the English. She overcomes the skepticism of the French leaders and drives the British out of much of France. A compelling story about the risks of faith and the courage of one faithful woman [BBV; GF; VV]

## JOHN HUS — RATING 3.0
1985　　NR　　Docudrama　　Age 12+　　55 min.　　Color

This courageous defender of the faith died singing! One hundred years before the Reformation, John Hus introduced the novel idea of teaching the Bible in everyday language to the people. Resenting this intrusion, the religious establishment burned him at the stake. Viewers will be inspired to take a stand for their beliefs. [GF; GTF; HFL; JD; VV]

## JONI — RATING 3.5
1980　　G　　Docudrama　　Age 06+　　108 min.　　Color

At 17, Joni Eareckson was paralyzed from the neck down because of a diving accident. The story of the trial of her fragile faith is retold in this touching film. She meets several people who show her that God has a special plan for her life. Joni is a story of courage and triumph over adversity. It is one of the most captivating Christian films ever made. [BBV; BH; GTF; HFL; VV; WWP]

## JUDAS PROJECT, THE — RATING 3.5 (e)
1993　　PG-13　　Drama　　Age 17+　　97 min.　　Color

How would Jesus be received if he appeared on earth for the first time today? This interesting movie explores this hypothetical question in an allegorical account of Jesus' life. Jesus becomes Jesse, who attracts followers along the beaches of North Carolina. Jesse is persecuted by a powerful politician and a religious leader. Dramatic special effects bring the movie to life. Rated PG-13 for the graphic crucifixion scene. Several mild crude words as well [GF; CGF]

## JUST LAST SUMMER — RATING 2.5
1977　　NR　　Drama　　Age 06+　　50 min.　　Color

Filmed on the California coast, this teenage drama deals with Cheryl, a young Christian girl who starts dating a non-Christian guy. Although Cheryl experiences inner conflict about letting him go, she decides to follow the Lord's will. *Just Last Summer* presents a fairly good treatment of a controversial issue. [GF]

## KID'S PRAISE 4 — RATING 3.0
1985　　NR　　Musical-Children　　Age 06+　　45 min.　　Color

This Maranatha children's classic teaches the Biblical principle of servanthood, using bright musical tunes and lovable animated characters. Psalty the Singing Songbook and Charity Churchmouse join in on "Make Me a Servant" and "Jesus Put the Song in My Heart." Kids will enjoy this exciting video time and again. [FBS]

## KID'S PRAISE 5 — RATING 3.0
1986　　NR　　Musical-Children　　Age 06+　　58 min.　　Color

Psalty the Singing Songbook, his dog Blooper, and the one-winged Farley McFirefly take a group of kids on a singing camping trip. Along the way, they teach them that every hardship they face is an opportunity for the Lord to move in their lives. Kids will love the fun story and the bouncy songs. [FBS]

## KING OF KINGS — RATING 3.5
1961　　NR　　Docudrama-Biblical　　Age 06+　　168 min.　　Color

This deeply moving film portrays the life of Christ with simple, but powerful dramatic strokes. The memorable scene featuring the Sermon on the Mount rates as one of the best. Narrated magnificently by Orson Welles, *King Of Kings* is truly one of the greater films on the life of Christ. [BBV; GF]

### LAST CHANCE DETECTIVES: ESCAPE FROM FIRE LAKE — RATING 3.5
1995     NR     Adventure     Age 06+     50 min     Color

In this Last Chance Detective adventure, Mike, one of the adolescent detectives, is taken hostage by some desperate bank robbers, then left to die in the Arizona desert. While Mike is fighting to survive, his friends and the sheriff launch a search for him. Mike's strength comes from scriptures he remembers from his childhood. This Focus on the Family series is first rate entertainment. [FOF; GF; HFL; JD; VV]

### LAST CHANCE DETECTIVES: LEGEND OF THE DESERT BIGFOOT — RATING 3.5
1995     NR     Adventure     Age 06+     50 min     Color

Fast moving adventure about four adolescents known as the Last Chance Detectives. Sightings of a large gorilla in the desert near their small Arizona town prompt the group to investigate. This leads to some very tense and suspenseful adventures as they are confronted by the ferocious creature and encounter an escaped criminal. They also learn lessons about making difficult choices. [FOF; GF; HFL; JD; VV]

### LAST CHANCE DETECTIVES: MYSTERY LIGHTS — RATING 3.5
1994     NR     Adventure     Age 06+     50 min.     Color

Three young boys and a girl become the "last chance detectives" who discover an old airplane which becomes their new headquarters. They begin hearing strange voices from the airplane's radio and seeing mysterious lights on the Navajo Mesa. Will these detectives be able to solve the mystery of Navajo Mesa? Your children will love to find out in this well-produced film from Focus on the Family [BBS; FOF; GF; HFL; JD; VV].

### LAST RODEO, THE — RATING 2.8
19??     NR     Drama     Age 17+     30 min.     Color

In this poignant film, an aging ex-rodeo performer longs for the old days when he supported himself. Believing that he is a burden on his family, he runs away to find work. A Christian cowboy convinces him to go home and receive his daughter's love as a gift. Good, evangelistic message. [CF]

### LEARN TO DISCERN — RATING 3.0(e)
1993     NR     Documentary     Age 12+     100 min.     Color

Focus on the Family youth culture specialist Bob DeMoss uses rapid-fire visual effects to demonstrate how much influence the entertainment media has on America's youth. He discusses sexually suggestive magazine ads, the gruesome scenes in horror films, and the obscene lyrics of today's rock music. Parents must view this shocking video. Some explicit content may not be suitable for younger children. [ETI; HFL]

### LIFE FLIGHT — RATING 3.0
1987     NR     Adventure-Drama     Age 06+     83 min.     Color

This absorbing film explores the challenging field of emergency helicopter service. One of the pilots grapples for control of his life and seeks help from a Christian paramedic trying to live out his beliefs on the job. *Life Flight* deals with crucial decision making and how it affects the destinies of individual lives. [GF; GTF; HFL; VV]

### LIFETIME CONTRACT — RATING 2.0
1986     NR     Drama-Fantasy     Age 06+     55 min.     Color

Satan's forces grapple with God's angelic servants over the destiny of a young teenage boy in this creative film. The demons dangle the lure of riches and fame before his eyes in exchange for his eternal soul. *Lifetime Contract* teaches the importance of surrendering one's life to God. [WP]

### LION, WITCH AND THE WARDROBE — RATING 3.0
1985     TVM     Fantasy-Animated     Age 06+     95 min.     Color

In this delightful animated adaptation of the beloved C.S. Lewis classic, a group of four friends are magically transported to the fantasy land of Narnia. They experience many harrowing adventures as they contend with the evil White Witch. This unique allegory of Christ's salvation for sinners will be appreciated by teens and adults. A beautiful tale that hasn't lost its power. [BBV; GF; GTF; VV]

### LITTLE TROLL PRINCE
**RATING 3.8**
1988   TVM   Drama-Animated   Age 06+   45 min.   Color

A little troll prince discovers that he is a misfit in a land where right is wrong and wrong is right. After his fellow trolls trick him into going to Peopleland, he meets two little girls who tell him about Christ's love. This animated film features the voices of Vincent Price, Cloris Leachman, and Don Knotts. [GF; FBS]

### MCGEE AND ME - A STAR IN THE BREAKING
**RATING 3.5**
1989   NR   Drama   Age 06+   30 min.   Color

Another well done story for children featuring Nicolas and his animated buddy McGee. Young Nicolas wins a chance to appear on a kid's TV game show contest. Along the way he learns some lessons about humility. Good music and performances teach Christian morals. [BBS; FOF; GF; HFL; JD; VV]

### MCGEE AND ME - NOT SO GREAT ESCAPE
**RATING 3.0**
1989   NR   Drama   Age 06+   30 min.   Color

Two adolescent boys want to see the new horror film, but Nicholas' parents believe that viewing sadistic or crude films will adversely affect his spiritual life. Nicholas sneaks out and goes to the movie anyhow, but later realizes they were right. While pointing out the drastic decline in moral content of movies, young people are urged to be selective. McGee, a cartoon character, livens up the show. [BBS; FOF; GF; HFL; JD; VV]

### MCGEE AND ME - SKATE EXPECTATIONS
**RATING 4.0**
1989   NR   Drama   Age 06+   30 min.   Color

Nick Martin and his cartoon character friend McGee must come up with a way to help the school nerd before he is beaten up by the school bullies. Nick challenges the bully to a dangerous skateboard race which will decide the fate of the nerd. Entertaining Good Samaritan story about showing love and kindness to others no matter who they are. [BBS; FOF; GF; HFL; JD; VV]

### MINE EYES HAVE SEEN THE GLORY
**RATING 4.0(e)**
1993   NR   Documentary   Age 12+   165 min.   Color

Outstanding three-part video series produced for PBS that discusses the origins, nature, and growth of the evangelical Christian movement in America. Professor Randall Balmer of Columbia University gives his analysis of its development, beginning with the contributions of fiery frontier preachers to Christian revivalists such as Whitfield and Moody, and leading to the developments in modern day evangelical churches. Fascinating, informative, and well-produced [GF; VV]

### MIRACLE OF FATIMA
**RATING 3.2**
1952   NR   Docudrama   Age 12+   102 min   Color

Dramatic account of actual events in the village of Fatima, Portugal, in the early 1900's. Three children of a poor villager see a vision, presumably the Virgin Mary. She speaks to them but only Lucia hears her clearly. After repeated occurrences, many of the townspeople also believe in the visions. Eventually thousands converge on the pasture where some very unique events occur. [BBV; VV]

### MITCH AND ALLEN
**RATING 3.5**
1988   NR   Comedy-Variety   Age 06+   49 min.   Color

This hilarious stand-up Christian comedy duo uses modern day parables and unlikely situations to communicate vital Biblical truths. Broad farce, sight gags, comical sound effects and subtle wit will tickle every viewer's funny bone. Particularly appealing to young people. [VV]

### MOLDER OF DREAMS
**RATING 3.5**
1989   NR   Docudrama   Age 12+   90 min.   Color

Guy Doud, a renowned teacher recognized for excellence by President Ronald Reagan, tells of his humorous and touching experiences as a teacher. You will be reminded that a good teacher must be a "molder of dreams" as you laugh and cry over his experiences as a teacher and as a student. A good, motivating film for teachers or learners; we are all one or the other [GF; HFL; JD; VV]

### MOMENT OF TRUTH — RATING 3.0
19??  NR  Drama  Age 12+  30 min.  Color

This follows the story of Norman and his "moment of truth." The prayers of believers give Norman a chance to see the consequences of choices he has made and gives him a chance to hear the gospel. After Norman's father leaves the house because of a divorce, angels decide it is time for Norman to be brought before the truth of God. A compelling story told with a futuristic touch. [GF; HFL; JD]

### MOMS, DADS, AND OTHER ENDANGERED SPECIES — RATING 2.8
1983  NR  Educational-Comedy  Age 06+  29 min.  Color

In this amusing teaching video, Pat Hurley, a well known youth speaker, shares the five things parents want from their kids: respect, honesty, communication, gratitude, and love. Teenagers will enjoy watching this video because Hurley presents the material in an informal, encouraging way. Parents will learn new ways to communicate with their children. [CF; WP]

### MOORE, GEOFF AND THE DISTANCE — RATING 3.0
1993  NR  Concert  Age 06+  46min.  Color

On his Life Together video collection, gospel singer Geoff Moore does what he does best—challenge young people to a greater commitment to the Lord. In this collection he tackles such topics as evolution in "Evolution Redefined." Other songs include "When All Is Said and Done" and "A Friend Like U." A more rock sound than many contemporary Christian artists, Geoff's strong relationship with the Lord comes through clearly. [BBS; WP]

### MOSES — RATING 2.5
1975  TVM  Docudrama-Biblical  Age 06+  141 min.  Color

Innovative interpretation of the life of Moses from his birth in Egypt until his death prior to the Jews entering the Holy Land. Moses stands as their sometimes troubled leader. Portrays the bitter, childish complaints of the Jews. Sympathetic to Moses, but shows some of his weaker moments. Burt Lancaster gives excellent portrayal of Moses. [BBV; GF; HFL; JD]

### MOUNTAIN MAN GO HOME — RATING 2.8
1984  NR  Drama  Age 06+  30 min.  Color

A woman whose aging, uncouth father comes to live in her home learns a lesson about unconditional love from her young son, Josh. Even though she resents her father's crudeness, Josh and his friends accept him into their group. Viewers will be moved by this film dealing with Christian mercy and kindness. [CF]

### MUSIC BOX — RATING 3.5
1980  NR  Musical-Fantasy  Age 06+  30 min.  Color

An assembly line worker is given a music box to relieve the monotony of his daily grind. The magical box comes with a group of gospel singing angels who delight the worker with their lively gospel songs. Gradually, he learns the joy of sharing his gift with his family, and then the entire city. *Music Box* is a lively musical story with a great message about spreading the Good News. [GTF; HFL; WP]

### MUSIC MACHINE, THE — RATING 3.0
1990  NR  Musical-Children  Age 04+  25min.  Color

A clever, animated musical for young children. A dastardly crook and his three comical cohorts attempt to steal a music machine from Agapeland. Fortunately, two young kids are hot on their trail. Lots of lively music and a clever story combine to make this a fun-filled adventure for children. [FBS]

### MYSTERY OF WILLOUGHBY CASTLE, THE — RATING 3.0
1980  NR  Mystery-Drama  Age 06+  35 min.  Color

Three adventuresome youngsters believe they can solve the age-old mystery of Willoughby Castle. They encounter scary surprises and thrills along the way when they discover a secret laboratory filled with unusual inventions. Kids of all ages will love this spellbinding mystery thriller and come back for more. [HFL]

## NATHANIEL THE GRUBLET             RATING 3.0
1987      NR      Musical-Children      Age 06+      30 min.      Color

This cute Agapeland musical video features Nathaniel, the smallest grublet of the group, who is faced with the choice of stealing or obeying his conscience. Light, bouncy songs and a clear message against the sin of stealing make this children's video a good teaching tool. Kids will certainly appreciate this one.[FBS]

## NEWSONG: ALL AROUND THE WORLD             RATING 3.0
1993      NR      Concert      Age 06+      30 min.      Color

The hopeful and catchy songs of Newsong are a great addition to your Christian music collection. Now you can watch them on video as well. This collection includes "All Around the World," "Field of Faith" and "Got Me Going." The whole family will enjoy Newsong with their contemporary pop sounds and challenging lyrics .

## NITE SONG             RATING 2.5
1978      NR      Drama-Adventure      Age 06+      65 min.      Color

Joe and Pete, two teenage boys, battle Satan in the city and minds of their friends in their virtuous attempt to rid the neighborhood of drug abuse. A suspenseful plot builds to an exciting climax that will leave a vivid impression on the viewer. *Nite Song*, like most *Mark IV* films, imparts a strong, evangelistic message. [HFL; JD; RD]

## NO LONGER ALONE             RATING 3.0
1955      NR      Docudrama      Age 12+      55 min.      Color

Joan Winmill, a hot new talent in England, has all she could ever wish for — wealth, beauty, fame, and friends. Yet, she still feels a deep loneliness in her soul that would not go away. After being converted to Christ at a Billy Graham London crusade, her life is changed and she is freed from her suicidal tendencies. Triumphant message for those who suffer from doubt and loneliness. [WWP]

## ORDINARY GUY             RATING 3.0
1979      NR      Drama      Age 12+      90 min.      Color

Tired of living a half-hearted Christian life, Guy decides to take his commitment to God seriously. Persecution erupts when his fiancee and her father fail to understand Guy's radical lifestyle. Despite the trouble he experiences, Guy stands firm for the Lord. Although just an ordinary guy, his total commitment to Jesus produces extraordinary results. [GTF; HFL]

## PARADISE TRAIL             RATING 4.0
1987      NR      Drama-Western      Age 12+      68 min.      Color

Two outlaw brothers kidnap a blind preacher and his family in this exciting western drama. The villains get angry at the preacher for his bold sermonizing and his unwavering faith. When their hate finally explodes, an unusual climax results. Filled with suspense and action, this Christian western is highly professional and entertaining. [HFL; RD]

## PARIS, TWILA: Sanctuary             RATING 3.5
1992      NR      Concert      Age 06+      48 min.      Color

Twila Paris is one of the best lyricists in Christian music today. Having written such favorites as "We Bow Down" and "Lamb of God," Twila now makes these songs available on a video tape. The tape includes appropriate video images that bring across the joy and peace of her songs. Other songs include "Sanctuary" and "Come Worship the Lord." A good tape for morning devotions. [SCG]

## PATTI, SANDI — "LIVE" CONCERT             RATING 3.5
1986      NR      Concert      Age 06+      55 min.      Color

Gospel Artist of the Year Sandi Patti presents the life-giving message of Jesus Christ in song throughout this vibrant concert. She sings such memorable tunes as "We Shall Behold Him" and "Because of Who You Are" with deep feeling and warmth. Also included is the award winning duet with Larnelle Harris, "More Wonderful." [WP]

### PATTI, SANDI — LET THERE BE PRAISE  RATING 3.5
1987　　　NR　　　Concert　　　　　　　　Age 06+　　　95 min.　　　Color

This spiritually uplifting concert combines the vibrant sound of Sandi Patti with spectacular special effects. Patti sings from her Easter album, "Was It a Morning Like This?" in her own inimitable way. First Call, a dynamic singing group, presents some of their music as well. Christian viewers will enjoy this professional, visually sophisticated production. [WP]

### PENELOPE GANG, THE  RATING 3.5
1982　　　NR　　　Comedy　　　　　　　　Age 06+　　　35 min.　　　Color

While playing soccer, a group of six kids find an old broken-down circus calliope. Hilarious fun erupts when two comic repairmen try to help them fix it. The kids learn some important lessons about commitment, discipline, and love along the way. This delightful comedy film presents the message of salvation in a light-hearted way. [GF; GTF; HFL; VV]

### PETER AND THE MAGIC SEEDS  RATING 3.0
1981　　　NR　　　Adventure-Educational　　　Age 04+　　　24 min.　　　Color

In this cute animated story, Peter thinks he's not worth anything because he's so small. At a mirage carnival run by the evil Mr. Zebble, he eats some magic seeds, hoping that they will make him grow. Children will learn the basis for a healthy self-image and how to trust God for salvation. [HFL; WP]

### PETRA: WAKE UP CALL  RATING 3.0
1993　　　NR　　　Concert　　　　　　　　Age 12+　　　52 min.　　　Color

Those who like the rock sounds of Petra will enjoy this video collection of some of their best, more recent songs. The vocals soar on ballads like "Creed" and "Love," and get down to business on others like "Sight Unseen" and "Just Reach Out." Petra's long witness as a group dedicated to Christ and reaching out to young people makes this an ideal video for a youth meeting. [FBS]

### PILGRIM'S PROGRESS  RATING 3.0
1985　　　NR　　　Drama-Animarted　　　　Age 12+　　　40 min.　　　Color

This animated version of John Bunyan's timeless classic features the journey of Pilgrim from the City of Destruction to the Celestial City. On the way, he encounters the Slough of Despond and the Hill of Difficulty. Viewers will enjoy an outstanding work that has ministered to people for three hundred years. [GF; TP; WP]

### PLACE CALLED HOME, A  RATING 3.0
1991　　　NR　　　Docudrama　　　　　　Age 12+　　　59 min.　　　Color

This fast-paced video follows the conversion stories of several well-known figures such as Noel Paul Stookey and Charles Colson. It also documents the journey towards faith of people dealing with AIDS or the trauma of past abortions and other difficult situations. Their touching stories of faith provide an excellent opportunity for evangelism. A clear presentation of the healing gospel of Jesus Christ, appropriate for teenagers and adults [GF; VV]

### POWERPLAY  RATING 4.0
1994　　　NR　　　Drama　　　　　　　　Age 17+　　　60 min.　　　Color

A hard-boiled business woman in Vancouver meets her match in Cody Harris, a dedicated Christian and talented hockey player. She tries to recruit him for the failing hockey team to convince investors to buy the team under her new direction. In the process, she learns that there is something more to life. The Billy Graham Association produced this fine film that young adults will particularly enjoy. [BBS; HFL; WWP]

### PRIZE, THE  RATING 3.0
1978　　　NR　　　Drama-Sports　　　　　Age 06+　　　73 min.　　　Color

Rick Jenkins, a newcomer to the freestyle stunt skiing circuit, nearly sacrifices everything, even his own soul, to win. He finds himself in trouble when he gets mixed up with the wrong crowd. An aging veteran skier shows Rick the futility of pursuing a prize that won't last. The talented young skier realizes that the real prize is a relationship with Jesus Christ. Contains spectacular shots of acrobatic and cross-country skiing. [GTF]

### PRODIGAL, THE — RATING 3.5
1983　　NR　　Drama　　Age 12+　　106 min.　　Color

An average, self-satisfied family attempts to live out the American dream by indulging in education, sports, fast cars, and hobbies. One of the sons in the family attends a seminary while the other "prodigal" son leaves home to live in a nearby wilderness. The prodigal eventually surrenders his life to Christ and is reunited with his family. [BH; GTF; WP]

### PRODIGAL PLANET — RATING 3.8
1988　　NR　　Drama-Prophecy　　Age 12+　　127 min.　　Color

In this *Mark IV* end-times film, the Believers' Underground Movement strives to destroy the communication network of the Antichrist, Brother Christopher. The judgments described in the Book of Revelation are depicted in graphic detail. Exciting cat and mouse action sequences add zest to this story with a science fiction flavor. Spellbinding action and an evangelistic message make this an outstanding video. [GTF; HFL; RD]

### PROSECUTOR, THE — RATING 3.5
1983　　NR　　Drama　　Age 06+　　54 min.　　Color

A modern-day attorney general attempts to prove in a court of law that Jesus' resurrection was a hoax. He cross-examines some of the disciples who witnessed several appearances of Jesus "two years ago." *The Prosecutor* is a probing courtroom drama that compels viewers to make a vital decision. [GF]

### PSYCHIC CONFESSIONS — RATING 3.0
1987　　NR　　Documentary　　Age 12+　　44 min.　　Color

This intriguing video shows how Danny Korem, a renowned magician and expert on deception, exposes the world's leading so-called psychic — James Hydric — as a fraud. Hydric himself confesses the trickery he uses to deceive millions and shares revealing details about his life. Viewers will learn the dangers of psychic frauds and occultism in this eye-opening demonstration. [GF; GTF; HFL; VV]

### QUIGLEY'S VILLAGE - BE KIND TO ONE ANOTHER — RATING 3.0
1987　　NR　　Drama-Educational　　Age 04+　　35 min.　　Color

Danny Lion and Spike Porcupine teach the Biblical principal of being kind to one another. Danny and Spike are competing in the world championship hide and seek contest. Danny breaks his arm prior to the contest, but Spike thinks it serves him right. Eventually they both learn what it means to be helpful and kind to one another. [GF; VV]

### QUIGLEY'S VILLAGE - THAT'S NOT FAIR — RATING 3.0
1988　　NR　　Musical-Educational　　Age 04+　　35 min.　　Color

Mr. Quigley, Molly and the puppets sing songs that teach the value of having a good attitude toward each other and toward life. Baby Lemon Lion learns to trust God when tempted to be discouraged by unfairness. Mr. Quigley teaches all the puppets through Biblical parable that God himself is never unfair. Wonderful for toddlers and tots. [GF; VV]

### REBA: HE GAVE ME MUSIC — RATING 3.0
1984　　NR　　Musical-Testimony　　Age 06+　　30 min.　　Color

Live performances and studio recording sessions by singer soloist Reba are featured in this unique video. Also included are intimate conversations with Reba and her songwriter husband Dony McGuire. This award winning, creative couple tell how their songs and performances are dedicated to the Lord. This video can serve as a worshipful experience or evangelism. [RMR]

### REFLECTIONS OF HIS LOVE — RATING 3.0
1981　　NR　　Documentary　　Age 12+　　42 min.　　Color

Joni Eareckson Tada, a vibrant Christian woman paralyzed at the age of 17, shares her thoughts and feelings during the filming of her life story in this inspiring documentary. Viewers will be challenged to experience the love of God, and to develop their ministry of reconciliation by sharing Christ's joy and peace with others. [WWP]

### REFORMATION OVERVIEW — RATING 3.5
1994　　NR　　Documentary　　Age 17+　　30 min.　　Color

This excellent series of two videos is divided into six 30-minute segments and covers the beginnings of the Reformation. You will learn about the great leaders of the Reformation, including Martin Luther, Calvin, Wycliffe, Zwingli and Tyndale. Their stories will make viewers appreciate the price these admirable bold leaders paid to bring new attention to the gospel message. [GF; VV]

### RESCUER, THE — RATING 2.5
1995　　NR　　Adventure-Drama　　Age 06+　　58 min.　　Color

Set in the beautiful English countryside, this story of three young siblings caught in a crisis will appeal primarily to young people. In an effort to locate some men who are destroying a vanishing flock of eagles, one of the girls draws her younger brother and sister into a dangerous area of rocky cliffs. They soon find themselves in serious trouble, but draw on their faith and learn to put others' needs before their own.[VV]

### REVIVAL — RATING 4.0
1995　　NR　　Musical　　Age 17+　　60 min.　　Color

Bill and Gloria Gaither lead an old-fashioned gospel singing celebration at a rural Methodist church. The celebration features musical presentations by outstanding gospel singers and the small congregation often sings along with the performers. The presentations, along with occasional commentary, range from the very lively to the very touching and make for one of the most enjoyable musical videos ever produced. It will particularly appeal to more mature audiences. [GV]

### REZ VIDEO — RATING 2.5
1986　　NR　　Concert　　Age 12+　　15 min.　　Color

The exciting husband and wife musical team discusses the ways REZ ministers with Christian songs and provides street shelter for the homeless. The *Rez* band also sings "Crimes" and "Love Comes Down." Youth as well as adults will be fascinated by the uniqueness of the *Rez* ministry and will be challenged to be fully committed to the Lord.

### RIGOLETTO — RATING 3.0(e)
1994　　NR　　Musical-Fantasy　　Age 12+　　???　　Color

Unique musical fantasy about a disfigured, small-town recluse who appears to menace the neighborhood children. His teen-age housekeeper, however, discovers that the man is really a kind-hearted, musical genius and draws him out of his self-centered existence. A beautiful film portraying the transforming power of genuine love and understanding [BBV; FFF].

### RISE AND WALK: THE DENNIS BIRD STORY — RATING 3.5
1995　　NR　　Drama　　Age 12+　　90 min.　　Color

Dennis Bird, a talented, professional football player for the New York Jets, becomes a strong and lovable witness to his teammates. But Dennis' convictions are truly tested when he becomes paralyzed from the neck down in a tragic collision with another player during practice. His inspiring story of perseverance and faith in God will touch every viewer, whether or not they are a football fan [GF; HFL].

### ROBE, THE — RATING 3.5
1953　　NR　　Drama　　Age 12+　　133 min.　　Color

This profound, intriguing epic features Richard Burton as Marcellius Gallio, a young Roman tribune present at the crucifixion of Jesus. His subsequent conversion occurs after a great moral struggle on his part. Viewers will enjoy the brilliant acting performances and heart-stopping action in this striking film produced in Hollywood. [BBV; GF; JD; VV]

### RUN TO THE SEA — RATING 3.2
1976　　NR　　Drama　　Age 12+　　55 min.　　Color

A difficult home situation and the resolute faith of a girlfriend forces a young man to ride the waves to find peace and solitude. Caught in a violent storm and separated from his boat, he is rescued by an old sea captain who helps him realize the only answer to life's storms: Jesus Christ. [GF]

### SAFE AT HOME                                                                RATING 3.0
1991        NR         Drama                    Age 12+         26 min.         Color

When Nathan, a young Little League baseball player, is hit hard by a line drive, he wakes up to find himself on a heavenly team. He goes back to earth to tell his skeptical friends, but they are now teenagers. How can he convince them that his experience was real? A funny and heart-warming movie about the importance of making a decision for Christ. A good film for youth groups [GF; GTF].

### SAMMY                                                                       RATING 3.0
1977        NR         Drama                    Age 06+         68 min.         Color

In this award-winning film produced in the Disney tradition, a crippled young boy captures the hearts of those around him through his courage and cheerful spirit. The plucky lad gets himself into a very threatening trap in an auto junk yard and his family must come to his rescue. His grateful family learns to trust God. Viewers will appreciate this charming film with a strong evangelistic message. [HFL; RD]

### SAMSON AND DELILAH                                                          RATING 3.0
1949        NR         Docudrama-Biblical       Age 12+         128 min.        Color

This extravagant version of the famous Biblical story tells of a beautiful temptress robbing the strength of Samson. It features classic scenes and other definitive Cecil B. DeMille touches. Victor Mature and Hedy LaMarr deliver realistic acting performances. Video viewers will enjoy this highly entertaining film just as much as viewers did in 1949. [BBV; GF; JD; VV]

### SAND CASTLES                                                                RATING 3.5
1980        NR         Drama                    Age 12+         80 min.         Color

The Morgans are a typical secure, affluent American family who appear cheerful and content on the surface. But underneath, they lack a sound spiritual foundation and their family life is near collapse. How they overcome their problems through faith in Christ is the theme of this engrossing, well done video. A good drama and message for the family or a church group. [EF; HFL]

### SCARS THAT HEAL: THE DAVE ROEVER STORY                                      RATING 3.0
1993        NR         Documentary              Age 12+         41 min.         Color

This moving story recounts the tragic accident that Dave Roever had in Vietnam when a grenade exploded and took part of his face. Dave shares with youth groups how he dealt with this sudden change in his life and how God has given him a unique, positive perspective about the accident. An uplifting film for older children about the wonder of God's grace. [BH; HFL; WWP]

### SEASONS OF THE HEART                                                        RATING 3.0(e)
1993        NR         Drama                    Age 12+         94min.          Color

An orphan boy attempts to find acceptance from a pioneer Oregon family in the 1890's. After many exasperating moments with the young boy, the embittered mother finally realizes how much he needs a family's love. A profound, heartwarming story that illustrates the wonder of God's love. Available only through Feature Films for Families. Winner of the Crown Award for best picture of 1993. [FFF]

### SECRET ADVENTURE SERIES                                                     RATING 2.5
1994        NR         Comedy                   Age 06+         30min.          Color

Drea, a teenager, solves her everyday problems in an animated, make-believe world based on Christian principles. In the segment titled "Truth," Drea seeks help from her animated friends to resist the temptation to discredit her haughty opponent in a school election. In another, "Snap," Drea learns the value of responsibility when a dog runs away from some children she is babysitting. Wholesome entertainment for young children on up. [BBS; BH; GF; JD]

### SECRET OF THE SECOND BASEMENT, THE                                          RATING 3.0
1985        NR         Drama                    Age 06+         30 min.         Color

Colorful puppets and actors tell the story of how young Nanny Feather becomes a part of Isaiah Bond's loving family of street people. Without the pastor's knowledge the family is living in the sub-basement of a church. But they can't keep their secret forever. A unique look at the struggles of street people and their search for Christmas joy and discovery of Jesus' love . [GF; HFL; JD]

### SHADOWLANDS (C.S. Lewis: Through the Shadowlands) — RATING 4.0
1985     NR     Docudrama     Age 12+     96 min.     Color

This moving biographical look at the life of renowned author C. S. Lewis focuses on his marriage relationship with Joy Davidman. He encounters the mystery of true love at a late period in his life. He also endures the depths of sorrow when his sweetheart dies. Viewers will gain fresh insights into this beloved Christian author whose stories impacted millions. One of the most moving, profound videos ever made. [GF; GTF; VV]

### SHEPHERD, THE — RATING 3.5
1984     NR     Drama-Adventure     Age 06+     79 min.     Color

This riveting film deals with the conflicts of the men who push the brink of supersonic danger in the Air National Guard. Aerial dogfights highlight an intense plot. When a veteran pilot accidentally brings tragic death to his best friend, he must deal with his own inner conflict. An uplifting film about love, forgiveness and true friendship. [GTF; HFL; RD]

### SMITH, MICHAEL W: BIG PICTURE CONCERT — RATING 3.0
1987     NR     Concert     Age 06+     80 min.     Color

Glitzy special effects combined with the powerful music of Michael W. Smith makes this an outstanding contemporary Christian concert. Smith sings some of his classic hits, including "Rocketown," "You Need a Savior," and "Be Strong and Courageous." Youth groups will enjoy this frazzle dazzle concert and find themselves challenged to follow Christ. [WP]

### SMITH, MICHAEL W: CHANGE YOUR WORLD — RATING 4.0
1993     NR     Concert     Age 06+     86 min.     Color

This video of Michael W. Smith's Change Your World Tour demonstrates Michael's energy and sincerity that have made him one of the top Christian singers today. The gospel message comes out clearly in songs like "Secret Ambition." Others, like "Picture Perfect," help teens struggling with poor self-image. Michael's lyrics and music in "Friends" and "Go West Young Man," among others, will lift your heart and energize your soul. [WP]

### SPARROW TV DINNERS — RATING 3.5
1994     NR     Concert     Age 06+     50 min.     Color

One of the only and perhaps the best compilation of recent music videos from a diversity of Christian singers. Enjoy videos from Steven Curtis Chapman, Lisa Bevill, Out of the Grey, PFR and Michael Card, among others. These are all Dove award nominated videos and the variety of contemporary, country and folk sounds makes this a good investment, as well as an enjoyable music experience. [SCG]

### SPLIT INFINITY — RATING 2.0(e)
1993     NR     Drama     Age 12+     ???     Color

A.J., ashamed of her parents' lack of money, discovers that her family might have been rich if her grandfather had not made an unwise investment. She becomes angry and retreats to the barn, pouting. A.J. hits her head which begins a dream about her grandparents during the Depression. A.J. learns the importance of family over possessions in this thought-provoking movie. [FFF]

### SPORTS CAPERS! — RATING 2.8
1985     NR     Comedy-Testimony     Age 06+     40 min.     Color

This highly entertaining sports video includes several film clips of amusing bloopers that actually occurred in various sporting events. Also, Christian athletes share their personal testimonies on how they came to know the Lord. Youth workers will want to show this video to teenage boys who are engrossed in the professional sports scene. [HFL]

### ST. JOHN IN EXILE — RATING 3.0
1987     NR     Docudrama-Monologue     Age 12+     95 min.     Color

Actor Dean Jones gives a one man dramatic interpretation of the eighty-six year old John of Patmos, the last living disciple of Jesus. The year is 96 A.D. when thousands of Christians are being killed by the Roman emperor Domitianus. John is imprisoned on the island of Patmos and we relive these eventful times through his eyes. A magnificent, humor-filled one man play. [GF; JD; VV]

*Christian Movies*

### STONEHILL, RANDY — LOVE BEYOND REASON     RATING 3.0
1985     NR     Concert     Age 06+     34 min.     Color

Randy Stonehill blends humor with the compelling Gospel message in this musical video. Concept videos illustrate important truths, especially "The Gods of Men," "Love Beyond Reason," and "Still Small Voice." He also sings "Until Your Love Broke Through" and "Hymn." Viewers will enjoy the ministry of one of the pioneers in contemporary Christian music. [WP]

### STORY KEEPERS SERIES     RATING 3.5
1995     NR     Drama-Adventure     Age 06+     30 min. each     Color

A colorful animated series of 30-minute dramatizations designed to introduce children to the Bible. Set in 64 A.D. in Rome, the church faces fierce persecution, and Christians hold secret meetings to learn about Jesus. Ben the Baker leads one group, telling young orphans stories of Jesus and his miracles. When the Roman soldiers capture one of Ben's group, Ben and the children conduct a hair-raising rescue. Plenty of excitement and humor. [GF; VV]

### STORY OF RUTH, THE     RATING 4.0
1960     NR     Docudrama-Biblical     Age 06+     132 min.     Color

A high action, intense drama of the life of Ruth and Naomi. Ruth (Elana Eden) and Naomi (Peggy Wood) must leave the land of Moab to save their lives after Ruth's husband is killed. Ruth meets Boaz and the rest of this Bible story depicts Ruth's love for Boaz and her devotion to Naomi. Entertaining and well produced. [GF; VV]

### STORYBOOK TREE, THE     RATING 3.0
1995     NR     Comedy-Musical     Age 04+     30 min. each     Color

Clever comedy-musical skits, each with an important lesson. All the characters are puppets, except for Henry, who's sort of in charge. One episode is about sharing. The Earl of Oats, a wealthy puppet, won't share the beautiful feathers in his hat. Another, set in the wild west, teaches that honesty is the best policy. Lively and appealing. [BH]

### SUPERBOOK BIBLE STORY SERIES     RATING 3.0
1982     NR     Adventure-Biblical     Age 06+     60 min. each     Color

This intriguing animated children's series features Chris and Joy, two adventurous youngsters who stumble onto a glowing Superbook that takes them back in time to witness many events in the Bible. Children will learn about various Biblical characters, including Joseph, Samson, and Ruth. Twenty-five tapes contain two exciting episodes each. Also includes nine *Superbook Delux* tapes. [FBS; HFL; TP]

### SURVIVAL     RATING 3.0
1987     NR     Adventure     Age 12+     73 min.     Color

In this action-packed *Mark IV* adventure film, a small plane carrying a wealthy family crashes in the middle of a desert. Surrounded by desolation, the family encounters numerous dangers from nature as well as a killer cougar. Not only does the panic-stricken family learn about physical survival, they also discover the meaning of spiritual survival as well. Strong evangelistic theme. [HFL; RD]

### TAKE FIVE     RATING 3.0
1985     NR     Concert     Age 06+     30 min.     Color

This musical sampler from Word Publishers features five of the top contemporary Christian singing artists and their unforgettable hits. They include: Amy Grant ("It's Not a Song"), Mylon LeFevre ("Stranger to Danger"), Randy Stonehill ("Still, Small Voice"), Michael W. Smith ("Away"), and Leon Patillo ("Love Calling"). Viewers will enjoy this unique collection. [WP]

### TAKE TWO     RATING 3.0
1987     NR     Drama     Age 12+     58 min.     Color

An ambitious young director struggles to make sense out of a mixed-up environment full of crazy people. During the filming of a comedy, he meets a young Christian actress who tells him that Jesus can put his life together. *Take Two* will appeal to viewers interested in a realistic look at the Hollywood lifestyle.

### TAYLOR, STEVE - LIMELIGHT     RATING 3.0
1986     NR     Concert     Age 12+     56 min.     Color

At the magnificent Castle Ashby in England, Steve Taylor puts on a fast moving Christian concert with colorful lighting, roving spotlights and simulated smoke. In between musical numbers, Taylor discusses various issues, such as the prosperity gospel, abortion, gay rights, racism, values clarification and holding to one's faith. Most of his high energy presentations also center around these issues. Good entertainment for young people. [GF]

### TEN COMMANDMENTS     RATING 3.5
1956     NR     Docudrama-Biblical Epic     Age 12+     219 min.     Color

Charlton Heston powerfully portrays Moses in this breathtaking Cecil B. DeMille extravaganza. Magnificent special effects such as the parting of the Red Sea and the writing of the tablets make viewing this film a memorable experience. An all-star cast features Yul Brynner, Edward G. Robinson and Anne Baxter. [BBV; GF; VV]

### THIEF IN THE NIGHT     RATING 3.0
1972     NR     Drama-Prophecy     Age 12+     69 min.     Color

This powerful *Mark IV* film portrays what life would be like immediately after the Rapture of the Church. Patty, an average young woman, finds herself left behind to face the terrible judgments of God in the Tribulation Period. Dramatic suspense and a graphic look at Biblical prophecy make this an exciting video to watch. It's somewhat amateurish, but has been a very popular Christian video. [GTF; HFL; JD; RD]

### TIME TO RUN     RATING 3.0
1978     NR     Drama     Age 06+     97 min.     Color

This moving drama set in today's society deals with a family struggling with internal conflicts and how they overcome them through a personal relationship with Jesus Christ. Viewers will be challenged to rely on the protective strength of the Lord and not on their own understanding. Well done. Produced by Billy Graham's World Wide Pictures.[WWP]

### TOUGH QUESTIONS ABOUT SEX     RATING 3.0
1985     NR     Educational     Age 12+     35 min.     Color

Youth worker Dawson McAllister answers questions about sex and dating with frankness and light humor. He offers reasonable guidelines for dating and explains how premarital sex diminishes one's commitment to Christ. He also offers advice on what to do when you've gone too far sexually. This enlightening video is the third part of the film series, "Straight Talk on Love, Sex, and Dating." Excellent for youth groups. [WP]

### TROCCOLI, KATHY — LIVE CONCERT     RATING 3.0
1986     NR     Concert     Age 06+     30 min.     Color

Kathy Troccoli sings some of her inspiring songs in this dynamic live concert, including "Once in a Lifetime Love," "Stubborn Love," "Holy, Holy," "I Belong to You," "There is a Redeemer," "Bittersweetness," "Long Distance Letter," and "Mighty Lord." Christians, especially the younger generation, will enjoy this dynamic singing artist.

### TUNNEL, THE     RATING 3.0
1985     NR     Adventure-Comedy     Age 06+     36 min.     Color

This charming Kuntz Brothers film deals with the disappearance of a prize show horse. A group of three youngsters attempts to unravel the mystery. The youngsters, along with two comical detectives, get involved in an intriguing adventure as they look for the stolen horse. In the process they learn some important lessons about respecting others, no matter what their age may be. *The Tunnel* offers quality entertainment for the whole family. [GF; GTF; VV]

### TWICE GIVEN     RATING 4.0
1985     NR     Docudrama     Age 12+     79 min.     Color

This film tells the heart-wrenching true story of Tom Williams, an evangelist whose wife contracts bacterial meningitis. He chooses to trust God in the face of suffering by taking care of her at home. A strong testimony of one man's love for his wife and his unwavering faith in God. Excellent. [HFL; RD]

## TWO A PENNY — RATING 3.0
1978　　NR　　Drama　　　　　　　　Age 12+　　65 min.　　Color

Cliff Richards is featured in this dramatic film about a young art student in London who gets caught up in drug dealings. His girlfriend tells him about her newfound relationship with Jesus Christ but he is very harsh and skeptical. Out of curiosity he attends a Billy Graham crusade, but still makes fun of Christianity. But there is more to the story. [WWP]

## TWO X 4 — RATING 2.5
1989　　NR　　Concert　　　　　　　Age 12+　　38 min.　　Color

Various Christian artists sing about issues of vital concern to Christians - from poverty and guilt to premarital sex. As they sing, dramatic scenes relating to their songs are interjected or shown in the background. Among the presentations are Rich Mullins singing "Other Side of the World," Chris Eaton with "Jerusalem," Bob Halligan and Rick Cua dramatizing "Young Boy, Young Girl" and Michael W. Smith with "Secret Ambition" and "I Miss the Way." [WP]

## UNHOLY HOLLYWOOD — RATING 3.0
1994　　NR　　Documentary　　　　 Age 12+　　30 min.　　Color

This seven-part series uncovers the dangerous messages inherent in many movies produced since the 1960's. The devaluation of human life is evident as the host, Eric Holmberg, shows specific and sometimes graphic examples of the ways Hollywood has desensitized audiences to violence, harmful sexual behavior and degenerate moral behavior. Series includes "Hollywood-License to Kill," "The Young and the Restless," and "War Games." Some scenes are too graphic for youngsters. [APF]

## WALSH, SHEILA — SHADOWLANDS — RATING 3.0
1986　　NR　　Concert　　　　　　　Age 06+　　66 min.　　Color

This live concert filmed in London features Sheila Walsh, a dynamic Scottish Christian musician, at her best. She performs "Triumph in the Air," "Big Boy Now," "What Do You Know (That I Don't)," "Christian," and "Ship of Love" with a unique blend of energy and depth. For youth and adults. [WP]

## WARLORD MEETS CHRIST, A: The Conversion Of Colonel Bottomly — RATING 4.0
1985　　NR　　Docudrama　　　　　Age 12+　　45 min.　　Color

Colonel Heath Bottomly, a rugged commander of one of the greatest U.S. Air Force strike teams in history, was sure that God was merely a mythical concept. When his career reaches its peak in Viet Nam, however, he is threatened by a court-martial. Through the bold witness of his son, he discovers new life and joy in Jesus Christ. Men in particular will relate to this outstanding film. [CF]

## WATSON, WAYNE - IN CONCERT - WATERCOLOR PONIES — RATING 4.0
1987　　NR　　Concert　　　　　　　Age 06+　　46 min.　　Color

Outstanding concert by Wayne Watson, one of the most popular Christian musicians of our time. The concert features songs from his albums "Watercolor Ponies" and "Giants in the Land." These include "I Still Believe," "Material Magic," "Is There No Harbor," "Peace that Passes Understanding," "Watercolor Ponies," "Somewhere in the World" and others. One of the best. [WP]

## WELCOME HOME — RATING 2.5
1978　　NR　　Drama　　　　　　　　Age 12+　　54 min.　　Color

A confused, worried drug pusher is being hunted by the police. After an auto accident, he's taken in by a Christian family who introduces him to the Gospel. Slowly he comes to believe and his life changes. He meets and becomes fond of a Christian girl. Eventually, he must decide whether to turn himself in to the law. This powerful message of God's love and forgiveness features the music of Dave Boyer, Debbie Boone and Andre Couch. [GF]

## WENDY AND THE WHINE — RATING 3.5
1987　　NR　　Fantasy-Educational　　Age 06+　　30 min.　　Color

In this amusing children's video, a young girl named Wendy asks God to help her stop whining. She doesn't realize how annoying her habit is until the whine actually comes out of her mouth and sails around the room. Children watching this film will learn the follies of whining and complaining. [CF]

**WHITCOMB'S WAR**   RATING 2.5
**1980**   **NR**   **Comedy-Drama**   **Age 06+**   **67 min.**   Color

David Whitcomb, a serious minded young preacher, battles the spiritual forces of darkness for control of a small mid-western town. He's joined by a stubborn businessman and a host of comic characters. Two demons who disrupt the town are portrayed in a light, satirical way for comic relief. Arm yourself with laughter and enjoy this warm and witty look at spiritual warfare. [HFL; RD]

**WOLFHUNTER**   RATING 3.0
**1983**   **NR**   **Adventure-Drama**   **Age 06+**   **34 min.**   Color

Twelve-year-old Josh is forced by a gang to go into "Maggie's Woods" to find and destroy a wild wolf creature. He also must contend with an old woman who roams about in the woods with a grave digger's shovel. This heart-stopping story, filmed in the beautiful Shenandoah Valley, deals with the vital issues of peer pressure and the consequences of sinful actions. A must-see for the whole family. [JD]

**YEARS OF THE BEAST**   RATING 3.3
**1981**   **NR**   **Adventure-Prophecy**   **Age 06+**   **96 min.**   Color

After the rapture, a group of persons in the northwest move to a remote rural area. They are pursued by the local sheriff who is working for the Antichrist. There's plenty of action and suspense as they try to elude the sheriff and his men. Professionally produced and believable, this is one of the better end times dramas. [GF; HFL; JD]

# SOURCES OF CHRISTIAN VIDEOS

As a service to our readers, after most of the film reviews we have given a source(s) for purchasing or renting the film through mail order. Also, some secular video stores carry a limited selection of Christian videos. Music concert videos are available in many Christian book stores, but we've also listed some mail order sources for them.

In the reviews, we have only given an abbreviation for the source company, but we have listed below their full names, locations and phone numbers, usually toll free. Some are distributors or dealers only, designated (D), who may be able to help you obtain copies of many Christian videos.

## MAIL ORDER SOURCES

|  |  |  |
|---|---|---|
| AMM | AL MENCONI MINISTRIES, SAN MARCOS, CA | 1-800-786-8742 |
| APF | AMERICAN PORTRAIT FILMS, CLEVELAND, OH | 1-800-736-4567 |
| BBS(D) | BAPTIST BOOK STORE CENTER, NASHVILLE, TN | 1-800-233-1123 |
| BBV | BLOCKBUSTER VIDEO | (NATIONWIDE SECULAR VIDEO STORES) |
| BH | BROADMAN AND HOLMAN, NASHVILLE, TN | 1-800-251-3225 |
| CF | CONCORDIA FILMS, ST. LOUIS, MO | 1-800-325-3040 |
| CGF(D) | CENTURY GOSPEL FILMS, SOUDERTON, PA | 1-800-523-6748 |
| CHF | CHATHAM HILL FOUNDATION | P.O. BOX 542647, DALLAS TX 75354 |
| EF | EVANGELICAL FILMS/GRACE PRODUCTS, RICHARDSON, TX | 1-800-527-4014 |
| ETI | ENTERTAINMENT TODAY, INC., COLORADO SPRINGS, CO | 1-719-635-3000 |
| FBS(D) | FAMILY BOOK STORES (ZONDERVAN), WYOMING, MI | 1-800-887-6555 |
| FOF | FOCUS ON THE FAMILY, COLORADO SPRINGS, CO | 1-800-232-6459 |
| FFF | FEATURE FILMS FOR FAMILIES, MURRAY, UT | 1-800-347-2833 |
| GF(D) | GOSPEL FILMS, MUSKEGON, MI | 1-800-253-0413 |
| GTF(D) | GTF MEDIA RESOURCES, MINNEAPOLIS, MN | 1-800-333-5344 |
| GP | GROUP PRODUCTIONS, LOVELAND, CO | 1-800-447-1070 |
| GV | GAITHER VIDEOS, ALEXANDRIA, IN | 1-800-561-7667 |
| HFL(D) | HERITAGE FILM LIBRARY, BOLIVAR, NY | 1-800-543-3456 |
| JD(D) | JD AUDIO VISUAL/CHRISTIAN FILMS, LA HABRA, CA | 1-800-336-3456 |
| KA | KEN ANDERSON FILMS, WINONA LAKE, IN | 1-800-458-1387 |
| MCD | MCDOUGAL FILMS, GLENCOE, IL | 1-847-835-5333 |
| ODI | OPEN DOOR INTERNATIONAL, FOUNTAIN VALLEY, CA | |
| RDF | RUSS DOUGHTEN FILMS, DES MOINES, IA | 1-800-247-3456 |
| TDP | TYNDALE PUBLISHING, WHEATON, IL | 1-800-323-9400 |
| VO(D) | VIDEO OUTREACH, MARRIETA, CA | 1-800-333-6475 |
| VV(D) | VISION VIDEO/GATEWAY FILMS, WORCHESTER, PA | 1-800-523-0226 |
| WP | WORD PUBLISHING, WACO, TX (ALSO CONCERT VIDEOS) | 1-800-933-9673 |
| WWP | WORLD WIDE PICTURES (BILLY GRAHAM), MINNEAPOLIS | 1-800-745-4318 |

## ADDITIONAL MAIL ORDER SOURCES FOR CONCERT VIDEOS

|  |  |  |
|---|---|---|
| MM | MARANATHA! MUSIC, LAGUNA HILLS, CA | 1-714-248-4000 |
| RMR | RAMBO-MCGUIRE MUSIC, NASHVILLE, TN | 1-615-327-3777 |
| SCG | SPARROW COMMUNICATIONS GROUP, BRENTWOOD, TN | 1-615-371-6800 |

# APPENDIX

# LISTING OF SECULAR MOVIES BY AGE GROUPS

| Title | Rating | Type | Age |
|---|---|---|---|

## AGE GROUP 04+

| Title | Rating | Type | Age |
|---|---|---|---|
| RACE FOR / LIFE, CHARLIE BROWN | 2.5 | Adventure | 04+ |
| YOGI'S GREAT ESCAPE | 2.5 | Adventure | 04+ |
| BIG RED | 2.8 | Adventure | 04+ |
| CHARLIE THE LONESOME COUGAR | 2.8 | Adventure | 04+ |
| CHARLOTTE'S WEB | 3.0 | Adventure | 04+ |
| MUPPETS TAKE MANHATTAN | 3.0 | Adventure | 04+ |
| STRAWBERRY SHORTCAKE STORY | 3.0 | Adventure | 04+ |
| WINNIE THE POOH / HONEY TREE | 3.0 | Adventure | 04+ |
| BON VOYAGE, CHARLIE BROWN | 3.2 | Adventure | 04+ |
| DOG OF FLANDERS | 3.2 | Adventure | 04+ |
| MR. MAGOO, MAN OF MYSTERY | 3.2 | Adventure | 04+ |
| MUPPET MOVIE, THE | 3.2 | Adventure | 04+ |
| BALTO | 3.5 | Adventure | 04+ |
| BAMBI | 3.5 | Adventure | 04+ |
| MR. MAGOO / SHERWOOD FOREST | 3.5 | Adventure | 04+ |
| ONE HUNDRED/ONE DALMATIONS | 3.5 | Adventure | 04+ |
| TALE OF TWO CRITTERS | 3.5 | Adventure | 04+ |
| DUMBO | 4.0 | Adventure | 04+ |
| RIKKI TIKKI TAVI | 4.0 | Adventure | 04+ |
| APPLE DUMPLING GANG RIDES | 1.7 | Comedy | 04+ |
| HERBIE GOES BANANAS | 1.8 | Comedy | 04+ |
| APPLE DUMPLING GANG | 2.0 | Comedy | 04+ |
| GUMBY THE MOVIE | 2.0 | Comedy | 04+ |
| TOM AND JERRY: THE MOVIE | 2.0 | Comedy | 04+ |
| HERBIE GOES TO MONTE CARLO | 2.5 | Comedy | 04+ |
| GUS | 2.8 | Comedy | 04+ |
| GOOFY MOVIE, A | 3.0 | Comedy | 04+ |
| HERBIE RIDES AGAIN | 3.0 | Comedy | 04+ |
| BUGS BUNNY-ROAD RUNNER | 3.2 | Comedy | 04+ |
| YOU'RE IN LOVE, CHARLIE BROWN | 3.3 | Comedy | 04+ |
| BABE | 3.8 | Comedy | 04+ |
| JETSONS: THE MOVIE | 2.3 | Drama | 04+ |
| BOY NAMED CHARLIE BROWN | 3.2 | Drama | 04+ |
| SNOOPY COME HOME | 3.3 | Drama | 04+ |
| BLACK BEAUTY | 3.5 | Drama | 04+ |
| PRINCESS WHO /NEVER LAUGHED | 3.5 | Drama | 04+ |
| PUSS IN BOOTS | 3.5 | Drama | 04+ |
| MR. MAGOO'S CHRISTMAS CAROL | 3.6 | Drama | 04+ |
| MR. MAGOO'S STORYBOOK | 3.6 | Drama | 04+ |
| LADY AND THE TRAMP | 3.8 | Drama | 04+ |
| MICKEY'S CHRISTMAS CAROL | 4.0 | Drama | 04+ |
| PIED PIPER OF HAMELIN, THE | 4.0 | Drama | 04+ |
| PEBBLE AND THE PENGUIN | 2.2 | Fantasy | 04+ |
| ONCE UPON A FOREST | 2.5 | Fantasy | 04+ |
| PETE'S DRAGON | 2.5 | Fantasy | 04+ |
| RUMPELSTILTSKIN | 2.5 | Fantasy | 04+ |
| JUNGLE BOOK, THE | 3.0 | Fantasy | 04+ |
| LITTLE NEMO / SLUMBERLAND | 3.0 | Fantasy | 04+ |
| BRAVE LITTLE TOASTER | 3.2 | Fantasy | 04+ |
| THUMBELINA | 3.3 | Fantasy | 04+ |
| BEAUTY AND THE BEAST | 3.8 | Fantasy | 04+ |
| CINDERELLA | 4.0 | Fantasy | 04+ |
| DR. SEUSS: THE CAT IN THE HAT | 4.0 | Fantasy | 04+ |
| HORTON HEARS A WHO | 4.0 | Fantasy | 04+ |
| PINOCCHIO | 4.0 | Fantasy | 04+ |
| SNOW WHITE/ SEVEN DWARFS | 4.0 | Fantasy | 04+ |
| SNOW WHITE/ SEVEN DWARFS | 4.0 | Fantasy | 04+ |
| TOY STORY | 4.0 | Fantasy | 04+ |
| VELVETEEN RABBIT, THE | 4.0 | Fantasy | 04+ |
| CHITTY CHITTY BANG BANG | 2.2 | Musical | 04+ |
| SESAME STREET: FOLLOW / BIRD | 2.8 | Musical | 04+ |
| NUTCRACKER | 3.0 | Musical | 04+ |
| ROCK-A-DOODLE | 3.0 | Musical | 04+ |
| FANTASIA | 4.0 | Musical | 04+ |

## AGE GROUP 06+

| Title | Rating | Type | Age |
|---|---|---|---|
| LIFE AND TIMES/GRIZZLY ADAMS | 1.5 | Adventure | 06+ |
| NEW ADVEN. PIPPI LONGSTOCKING | 1.5 | Adventure | 06+ |
| AGAINST A CROOKED SKY | 2.0 | Adventure | 06+ |
| GIANT OF THUNDER MOUNTAIN | 2.0 | Adventure | 06+ |
| PURPLE PEOPLE EATER | 2.0 | Adventure | 06+ |
| BRIGHTY OF THE GRAND CANYON | 2.2 | Adventure | 06+ |
| MOONCUSSERS | 2.2 | Adventure | 06+ |
| BENJI THE HUNTED | 2.3 | Adventure | 06+ |
| MOUNTAIN FAMILY ROBINSON | 2.3 | Adventure | 06+ |
| ACROSS THE GREAT DIVIDE | 2.5 | Adventure | 06+ |
| AMAZING PANDA ADVENTURE | 2.5 | Adventure | 06+ |
| MR. SUPERINVISIBLE | 2.5 | Adventure | 06+ |
| NIGHT TRAIN TO KATHMANDU | 2.5 | Adventure | 06+ |
| SEVEN ALONE | 2.5 | Adventure | 06+ |
| TOM SAWYER | 2.5 | Adventure | 06+ |
| LAST FLIGHT OF NOAH'S ARK | 2.7 | Adventure | 06+ |
| NIGHT CROSSING | 2.7 | Adventure | 06+ |

## Secular Movies — Appendix

| Title | Rating | Type | Age |
|---|---|---|---|
| BLACK STALLION RETURNS, THE | 2.8 | Adventure | 06+ |
| CASTAWAY COWBOY, THE | 2.8 | Adventure | 06+ |
| GENTLE GIANT | 2.8 | Adventure | 06+ |
| GREAT LOCOMOTIVE CHASE | 2.8 | Adventure | 06+ |
| MOONSPINNERS | 2.8 | Adventure | 06+ |
| SAVANNAH SMILES | 2.8 | Adventure | 06+ |
| NAPOLEON AND SAMANTHA | 2.9 | Adventure | 06+ |
| ADVEN. WILDERNESS FAMILY - II | 3.0 | Adventure | 06+ |
| CHEETAH | 3.0 | Adventure | 06+ |
| FIGHTING PRINCE OF DONEGAL | 3.0 | Adventure | 06+ |
| FLIGHT OF THE NAVIGATOR | 3.0 | Adventure | 06+ |
| FOR THE LOVE OF BENJI | 3.0 | Adventure | 06+ |
| HORSE WITHOUT A HEAD | 3.0 | Adventure | 06+ |
| LITTLEST HORSE THIEVES, THE | 3.0 | Adventure | 06+ |
| PRINCE OF CENTRAL PARK, THE | 3.0 | Adventure | 06+ |
| TALL TALE | 3.0 | Adventure | 06+ |
| ADVEN. WILDERNESS FAMILY | 3.2 | Adventure | 06+ |
| DAVY CROCKETT, KING / FRONTIER | 3.2 | Adventure | 06+ |
| FANTASTIC VOYAGE | 3.2 | Adventure | 06+ |
| FOX AND THE HOUND, THE | 3.2 | Adventure | 06+ |
| IN SEARCH OF THE CASTAWAYS | 3.2 | Adventure | 06+ |
| JASON AND THE ARGONAUTS | 3.2 | Adventure | 06+ |
| NIGHT THEY SAVED CHRISTMAS | 3.2 | Adventure | 06+ |
| PAINTED HILLS, THE | 3.2 | Adventure | 06+ |
| ADVENTURES OF MILO & OTIS | 3.3 | Adventure | 06+ |
| AROUND THE WORLD IN 80 DAYS | 3.3 | Adventure | 06+ |
| HOBBIT, THE | 3.3 | Adventure | 06+ |
| HOMEWARD BOUND | 3.3 | Adventure | 06+ |
| INCREDIBLE JOURNEY | 3.3 | Adventure | 06+ |
| MAN FROM SNOWY RIVER | 3.3 | Adventure | 06+ |
| SWISS FAMILY ROBINSON | 3.3 | Adventure | 06+ |
| ADVEN. GREAT MOUSE DETECTIVE | 3.5 | Adventure | 06+ |
| BENJI | 3.5 | Adventure | 06+ |
| BIRDS OF PREY | 3.5 | Adventure | 06+ |
| GOLD DIGGERS: SECRET/ BEAR MT | 3.5 | Adventure | 06+ |
| HONEY, I SHRUNK THE KIDS | 3.5 | Adventure | 06+ |
| PETER PAN | 3.5 | Adventure | 06+ |
| BLACK STALLION, THE | 3.7 | Adventure | 06+ |
| LION KING, THE | 3.7 | Adventure | 06+ |
| CHARLIE BROWN'S ALL STARS | 4.0 | Adventure | 06+ |
| GREAT ESCAPE, THE | 4.0 | Adventure | 06+ |
| GUNGA DIN | 4.0 | Adventure | 06+ |
| JUMANJI | 4.0 | Adventure | 06+ |

| Title | Rating | Type | Age |
|---|---|---|---|
| MAN FROM CLOVER GROVE | 1.3 | Comedy | 06+ |
| ERNEST RIDES AGAIN | 1.8 | Comedy | 06+ |
| MONKEY'S UNCLE, THE | 1.8 | Comedy | 06+ |
| GOING BANANAS | 2.0 | Comedy | 06+ |
| GORDY | 2.0 | Comedy | 06+ |
| SHAKIEST GUN IN THE WEST | 2.0 | Comedy | 06+ |
| SNOWBALL EXPRESS | 2.0 | Comedy | 06+ |
| LITTLE RASCALS | 2.1 | Comedy | 06+ |
| COMPUTER WORE TENNIS SHOES | 2.2 | Comedy | 06+ |
| KID WITH THE 200 IQ, THE | 2.2 | Comedy | 06+ |
| NOW YOU SEE HIM, NOW / DON'T | 2.2 | Comedy | 06+ |
| SHAGGY D.A., THE | 2.2 | Comedy | 06+ |
| CAT FROM OUTER SPACE, THE | 2.3 | Comedy | 06+ |
| ERNEST SAVES CHRISTMAS | 2.3 | Comedy | 06+ |
| GHOST AND MR. CHICKEN | 2.3 | Comedy | 06+ |
| HEAVYWEIGHTS | 2.3 | Comedy | 06+ |
| HOT LEAD AND COLD FEET | 2.3 | Comedy | 06+ |
| MILLION DOLLAR DUCK | 2.3 | Comedy | 06+ |
| NORTH AVENUE IRREGULARS, THE | 2.3 | Comedy | 06+ |
| BEETHOVEN | 2.5 | Comedy | 06+ |
| BOATNIKS | 2.5 | Comedy | 06+ |
| CANDLESHOE | 2.5 | Comedy | 06+ |
| WILD AND THE FREE, THE | 2.5 | Comedy | 06+ |
| BEETHOVEN'S SECOND | 2.6 | Comedy | 06+ |
| GNOME MOBILE, THE | 2.7 | Comedy | 06+ |
| MAN IN / SANTA CLAUS SUIT | 2.7 | Comedy | 06+ |
| MAN'S FAVORITE SPORT? | 2.7 | Comedy | 06+ |
| STRIKE UP THE BAND | 2.7 | Comedy | 06+ |
| THAT DARN CAT | 2.7 | Comedy | 06+ |
| FATHER GOOSE | 2.8 | Comedy | 06+ |
| FLINTSTONES, THE | 2.8 | Comedy | 06+ |
| GONE ARE THE DAYES | 2.8 | Comedy | 06+ |
| GREAT RACE, THE | 2.8 | Comedy | 06+ |
| MIGHTY DUCKS, THE | 2.8 | Comedy | 06+ |
| SON OF FLUBBER | 2.8 | Comedy | 06+ |
| TROUBLE WITH ANGELS | 2.8 | Comedy | 06+ |
| WORLD'S GREATEST ATHLETE | 2.9 | Comedy | 06+ |
| BISHOP'S WIFE, THE | 3.0 | Comedy | 06+ |
| ERNEST GOES TO JAIL | 3.0 | Comedy | 06+ |
| FOOTBALL FOLLIES | 3.0 | Comedy | 06+ |
| FOOTBALL FEVER | 3.0 | Comedy | 06+ |
| IT TAKES TWO | 3.0 | Comedy | 06+ |
| OPERATION DUMBO DROP | 3.0 | Comedy | 06+ |

# Appendix — Secular Movies

| Title | Rating | Type | Age |
|---|---|---|---|
| PRINCESS AND THE PIRATE, THE | 3.0 | Comedy | 06+ |
| RETURN TO MAYBERRY | 3.0 | Comedy | 06+ |
| SEND ME NO FLOWERS | 3.0 | Comedy | 06+ |
| SEVEN LITTLE FOYS, THE | 3.0 | Comedy | 06+ |
| WAIT TILL / MOTHER GETS HOME | 3.0 | Comedy | 06+ |
| MONKEY TROUBLE | 3.1 | Comedy | 06+ |
| ABSENT MINDED PROFESSOR, THE | 3.2 | Comedy | 06+ |
| DARBY O'GILL & LITTLE PEOPLE | 3.2 | Comedy | 06+ |
| FREAKY FRIDAY | 3.2 | Comedy | 06+ |
| ANGELS IN THE OUTFIELD | 3.3 | Comedy | 06+ |
| GREAT MUPPET CAPER, THE | 3.3 | Comedy | 06+ |
| LOVE BUG, THE | 3.3 | Comedy | 06+ |
| MY FAVORITE BRUNETTE | 3.3 | Comedy | 06+ |
| NUTTY PROFESSOR, THE | 3.3 | Comedy | 06+ |
| PALEFACE | 3.3 | Comedy | 06+ |
| PARENT TRAP, THE | 3.3 | Comedy | 06+ |
| TOBY TYLER | 3.3 | Comedy | 06+ |
| WHO'S MINDING THE MINT | 3.3 | Comedy | 06+ |
| ANDRE | 3.5 | Comedy | 06+ |
| AUNTIE MAME | 3.5 | Comedy | 06+ |
| CORRINA, CORRINA | 3.5 | Comedy | 06+ |
| HONEY, I BLEW UP THE KID | 3.5 | Comedy | 06+ |
| CHRISTMAS IN JULY | 3.7 | Comedy | 06+ |
| SANTA CLAUSE, THE | 3.7 | Comedy | 06+ |
| GOLDEN AGE OF COMEDY (silent) | 4.0 | Comedy | 06+ |
| HAIL THE CONQUERING HERO | 4.0 | Comedy | 06+ |
| NATIVITY, THE | 2.3 | Docudrama | 06+ |
| BARNUM | 2.5 | Docudrama | 06+ |
| OTHER SIDE OF THE MOUNTAIN | 2.5 | Docudrama | 06+ |
| NADIA | 3.0 | Docudrama | 06+ |
| WINDS OF KITTY HAWK, THE | 3.0 | Docudrama | 06+ |
| MIRACLE WORKER | 3.3 | Docudrama | 06+ |
| PISTOL: BIRTH OF A LEGEND | 3.3 | Docudrama | 06+ |
| PRIDE OF THE YANKEES | 3.8 | Docudrama | 06+ |
| WILBUR & ORVILLE - 1ST TO FLY | 4.0 | Docudrama | 06+ |
| SIXTEEN DAYS OF GLORY | 3.0 | Document. | 06+ |
| DAVID COPPERFIELD | 2.5 | Drama | 06+ |
| INTERNATIONAL VELVET | 2.5 | Drama | 06+ |
| LONELIEST RUNNER, THE | 2.5 | Drama | 06+ |
| MAGIC OF LASSIE, THE | 2.5 | Drama | 06+ |
| FOLLOW ME, BOYS! | 2.7 | Drama | 06+ |
| GREYFRIARS BOBBY | 2.7 | Drama | 06+ |
| PRINCE AND THE PAUPER | 2.7 | Drama | 06+ |
| BENIKER GANG, THE | 2.8 | Drama | 06+ |
| DREAM FOR CHRISTMAS, A | 2.8 | Drama | 06+ |
| KID FROM LEFT FIELD, THE | 2.8 | Drama | 06+ |
| ONE MAGIC CHRISTMAS | 2.8 | Drama | 06+ |
| BEST CHRISTMAS PAGEANT EVER | 3.0 | Drama | 06+ |
| BIG GREEN, THE | 3.0 | Drama | 06+ |
| CHRISTMAS LILIES OF THE FIELD | 3.0 | Drama | 06+ |
| DANNY | 3.0 | Drama | 06+ |
| FREE WILLY 2 | 3.0 | Drama | 06+ |
| KNUTE ROCKNE - ALL-AMERICAN | 3.0 | Drama | 06+ |
| LITTLE HOUSE ON THE PRAIRIE | 3.0 | Drama | 06+ |
| SAVING GRACE | 3.0 | Drama | 06+ |
| SKEEZER | 3.0 | Drama | 06+ |
| SUMMER TO REMEMBER, A | 3.0 | Drama | 06+ |
| TIGER TOWN | 3.0 | Drama | 06+ |
| THREE LIVES OF THOMASINA, THE | 3.1 | Drama | 06+ |
| COURAGE MOUNTAIN | 3.2 | Drama | 06+ |
| DRAGNET | 3.2 | Drama | 06+ |
| JOHNNY TREMAIN | 3.2 | Drama | 06+ |
| PRANCER | 3.2 | Drama | 06+ |
| THOSE CALLOWAYS | 3.2 | Drama | 06+ |
| WHERE THE RED FERN GROWS | 3.2 | Drama | 06+ |
| ALL CREATURES GREAT & SMALL | 3.3 | Drama | 06+ |
| ANNE OF GREEN GABLES | 3.3 | Drama | 06+ |
| BELLS OF ST. MARY'S | 3.3 | Drama | 06+ |
| FREE WILLY | 3.3 | Drama | 06+ |
| HEIDI | 3.3 | Drama | 06+ |
| HOMECOMING: CHRISTMAS STORY | 3.3 | Drama | 06+ |
| LITTLE PRINCESS, THE | 3.3 | Drama | 06+ |
| OLD YELLER | 3.3 | Drama | 06+ |
| ORPHAN TRAIN | 3.3 | Drama | 06+ |
| BORN FREE | 3.5 | Drama | 06+ |
| CHRISTY | 3.5 | Drama | 06+ |
| GIRL WHO SPELLED FREEDOM | 3.5 | Drama | 06+ |
| LASSIE | 3.5 | Drama | 06+ |
| LITTLE LORD FAUNTLEROY | 3.5 | Drama | 06+ |
| MIRACLE DOWN UNDER | 3.5 | Drama | 06+ |
| MIRACLE ON 34TH STREET | 3.5 | Drama | 06+ |
| POLLYANNA | 3.5 | Drama | 06+ |
| ANNE OF AVONLEA | 3.6 | Drama | 06+ |
| CHARIOTS OF FIRE | 3.7 | Drama | 06+ |
| CHRISTMAS TO REMEMBER, A | 3.7 | Drama | 06+ |
| DOLLMAKER, THE | 3.7 | Drama | 06+ |

## Secular Movies — Appendix

| Title | Rating | Type | Age |
|---|---|---|---|
| GREATEST SHOW ON EARTH, THE | 3.7 | Drama | 06+ |
| NATIONAL VELVET | 3.7 | Drama | 06+ |
| AMERICAN DREAM | 3.8 | Drama | 06+ |
| MIRACLE ON 34TH STREET | 3.8 | Drama | 06+ |
| OLIVER TWIST | 3.8 | Drama | 06+ |
| YEARLING, THE | 3.8 | Drama | 06+ |
| GREAT EXPECTATIONS | 4.0 | Drama | 06+ |
| IT'S A WONDERFUL LIFE | 4.0 | Drama | 06+ |
| LITTLE WOMEN | 4.0 | Drama | 06+ |
| SOUNDER | 4.0 | Drama | 06+ |
| TREE GROWS IN BROOKLYN, A | 4.0 | Drama | 06+ |
| DOCTOR DOLITTLE | 2.0 | Fantasy | 06+ |
| NEVER ENDING STORY PART II | 2.3 | Fantasy | 06+ |
| PAGEMASTER, THE | 2.3 | Fantasy | 06+ |
| KID IN KING ARTHUR'S COURT, A | 2.5 | Fantasy | 06+ |
| SANTA CLAUS: THE MOVIE | 2.7 | Fantasy | 06+ |
| AMER. TAIL: FIEVEL GOES WEST | 2.8 | Fantasy | 06+ |
| AMERICAN CHRISTMAS CAROL | 2.8 | Fantasy | 06+ |
| BABAR: THE MOVIE | 2.8 | Fantasy | 06+ |
| WILLY WONKA / CHOC. FACTORY | 2.8 | Fantasy | 06+ |
| CHRONICLES OF NARNIA, THE | 3.0 | Fantasy | 06+ |
| SWAN PRINCESS, THE | 3.1 | Fantasy | 06+ |
| MUPPET CHRISTMAS CAROL, THE | 3.3 | Fantasy | 06+ |
| SECRET OF NIMH, THE | 3.3 | Fantasy | 06+ |
| TOM THUMB | 3.3 | Fantasy | 06+ |
| BLUE YONDER, THE | 3.5 | Fantasy | 06+ |
| INDIAN IN THE CUPBOARD | 3.5 | Fantasy | 06+ |
| WIZARD OF OZ, THE | 4.0 | Fantasy | 06+ |
| CAMELOT | 2.2 | Musical | 06+ |
| BABES IN TOYLAND | 2.3 | Musical | 06+ |
| FLOWER DRUM SONG | 2.3 | Musical | 06+ |
| IT HAPPENED AT/ WORLD'S FAIR | 2.5 | Musical | 06+ |
| PIED PIPER OF HAMELIN, THE | 2.5 | Musical | 06+ |
| HANS BRINKER | 2.7 | Musical | 06+ |
| BYE, BYE BIRDIE | 2.8 | Musical | 06+ |
| SCROOGE | 2.8 | Musical | 06+ |
| HANS CHRISTIAN ANDERSEN | 3.0 | Musical | 06+ |
| PIRATES OF PENZANCE | 3.0 | Musical | 06+ |
| SHOWBOAT | 3.0 | Musical | 06+ |
| OKLAHOMA! | 3.2 | Musical | 06+ |
| YOUNG AT HEART | 3.2 | Musical | 06+ |
| CAROUSEL | 3.3 | Musical | 06+ |
| CINDERELLA | 3.5 | Musical | 06+ |
| FUNNY GIRL | 3.5 | Musical | 06+ |

| Title | Rating | Type | Age |
|---|---|---|---|
| AMERICAN IN PARIS, AN | 3.7 | Musical | 06+ |
| EASTER PARADE | 3.7 | Musical | 06+ |
| MUSIC MAN, THE | 3.7 | Musical | 06+ |
| SOUND OF MUSIC | 3.7 | Musical | 06+ |
| POINT, THE | 3.8 | Musical | 06+ |
| THAT'S ENTERTAINMENT II | 3.8 | Musical | 06+ |
| BAND WAGON, THE | 4.0 | Musical | 06+ |
| MARY POPPINS | 4.0 | Musical | 06+ |
| CASE OF / LOGICAL i RANCH | 3.0 | Mystery | 06+ |
| CASE OF/ SEA WORLD ADVEN. | 3.0 | Mystery | 06+ |
| CASE OF/ THORN MANSION | 3.0 | Mystery | 06+ |
| MYSTERY OF FIRE ISLAND | 3.0 | Mystery | 06+ |
| BUCK ROGERS / 25TH CENTURY | 1.7 | Sci-Fi | 06+ |
| STAR TREK—MOTION PICTURE | 2.0 | Sci-Fi | 06+ |
| BATTLESTAR GALACTICA | 2.2 | Sci-Fi | 06+ |
| MAN FROM ATLANTIS | 2.7 | Sci-Fi | 06+ |
| ISLAND AT / TOP OF THE WORLD | 2.9 | Sci-Fi | 06+ |
| INVADERS FROM MARS | 3.3 | Sci-Fi | 06+ |
| AURORA ENCOUNTER | 3.5 | Sci-Fi | 06+ |
| STAR WARS | 3.7 | Sci-Fi | 06+ |
| DAY THE EARTH STOOD STILL | 3.8 | Sci-Fi | 06+ |
| CLOSE ENCOUNTERS OF 3rd KIND | 4.0 | Sci-Fi | 06+ |
| STAR TREK—THE MENAGERIE | 4.0 | Sci-Fi | 06+ |
| STAGECOACH | 1.7 | Western | 06+ |
| YUMA | 2.2 | Western | 06+ |
| LONE RANGER, THE | 2.7 | Western | 06+ |
| ROOSTER COGBURN | 2.7 | Western | 06+ |
| DESTRY RIDES AGAIN | 4.0 | Western | 06+ |

## AGE GROUP 12

| Title | Rating | Type | Age |
|---|---|---|---|
| HELLCATS OF THE NAVY | 2.2 | Adventure | 12+ |
| FIRE | 2.3 | Adventure | 12+ |
| IRON WILL | 2.3 | Adventure | 12+ |
| VOYAGE OF THE YES | 2.3 | Adventure | 12+ |
| WHITE FANG 2: MYTH/ WHITE WOLF | 2.3 | Adventure | 12+ |
| BEAR, THE | 2.5 | Adventure | 12+ |
| RUNAWAY BARGE, THE | 2.5 | Adventure | 12+ |
| SNATCHED | 2.5 | Adventure | 12+ |
| FLOOD | 2.7 | Adventure | 12+ |
| FLYING LEATHERNECKS | 2.8 | Adventure | 12+ |
| FLYING TIGERS | 2.8 | Adventure | 12+ |
| KARATE KID, PART II | 2.8 | Adventure | 12+ |
| LAND OF FARAWAY, THE | 2.9 | Adventure | 12+ |

# Appendix — Secular Movies

| Title | Rating | Type | Age | Title | Rating | Type | Age |
|---|---|---|---|---|---|---|---|
| ENEMY BELOW, THE | 3.0 | Adventure | 12+ | YOUNG EINSTEIN | 2.1 | Comedy | 12+ |
| HEAVEN KNOWS MR. ALLISON | 3.0 | Adventure | 12+ | ERNEST SCARED STUPID | 2.3 | Comedy | 12+ |
| LEFT HAND OF GOD | 3.0 | Adventure | 12+ | D2: THE MIGHTY DUCKS | 2.5 | Comedy | 12+ |
| RED ALERT | 3.0 | Adventure | 12+ | METEOR MAN | 2.6 | Comedy | 12+ |
| FAR FROM HOME:YELLOW DOG | 3.2 | Adventure | 12+ | DISORDERLY ORDERLY, THE | 2.7 | Comedy | 12+ |
| FOUR FEATHERS | 3.2 | Adventure | 12+ | DENNIS THE MENACE | 2.8 | Comedy | 12+ |
| HATARI! (DANGER!) | 3.2 | Adventure | 12+ | GRASS/GREENER / SEPTIC TANK | 2.8 | Comedy | 12+ |
| LIONHEART | 3.2 | Adventure | 12+ | LONG, LONG TRAILER, THE | 2.8 | Comedy | 12+ |
| MOGAMBO | 3.2 | Adventure | 12+ | WITHOUT A CLUE | 2.8 | Comedy | 12+ |
| PRINCESS BRIDE, THE | 3.2 | Adventure | 12+ | IZZY AND MOE | 2.9 | Comedy | 12+ |
| SNOWS OF KILIMANJARO, THE | 3.2 | Adventure | 12+ | WACKIEST SHIP IN THE ARMY, THE | 2.9 | Comedy | 12+ |
| WIND AND THE LION, THE | 3.2 | Adventure | 12+ | BABYSITTERS CLUB | 3.0 | Comedy | 12+ |
| HIGH AND THE MIGHTY, THE | 3.3 | Adventure | 12+ | BACHELOR & THE BOBBYSOXER | 3.0 | Comedy | 12+ |
| IVANHOE | 3.3 | Adventure | 12+ | BILL COSBY-HIMSELF | 3.0 | Comedy | 12+ |
| LONELY ARE THE BRAVE | 3.3 | Adventure | 12+ | FATHER'S LITTLE DIVIDEND | 3.0 | Comedy | 12+ |
| NORTH TO ALASKA | 3.3 | Adventure | 12+ | IT SHOULD HAPPEN TO YOU | 3.0 | Comedy | 12+ |
| RUN SILENT, RUN DEEP | 3.3 | Adventure | 12+ | IT'S A MAD, MAD, MAD WORLD | 3.0 | Comedy | 12+ |
| SCARLET PIMPERNEL | 3.3 | Adventure | 12+ | LADY TAKES A CHANCE, A | 3.0 | Comedy | 12+ |
| SHIPWRECKED | 3.3 | Adventure | 12+ | RUSSIANS ARE COMING, THE | 3.0 | Comedy | 12+ |
| TARZAN, THE APE MAN | 3.3 | Adventure | 12+ | SECRET LIFE OF WALTER MITTY | 3.0 | Comedy | 12+ |
| VON RYAN'S EXPRESS | 3.3 | Adventure | 12+ | SISTER ACT 2: BACK IN THE HABIT | 3.0 | Comedy | 12+ |
| WHITE FANG | 3.3 | Adventure | 12+ | UNDERGRADS, THE | 3.0 | Comedy | 12+ |
| ZORRO | 3.3 | Adventure | 12+ | WHAT'S UP DOC? | 3.0 | Comedy | 12+ |
| NEVER CRY WOLF | 3.5 | Adventure | 12+ | EFFICIENCY EXPERT | 3.2 | Comedy | 12+ |
| RUDYARD KIPLING'S JUNGLE BK | 3.5 | Adventure | 12+ | FARMER'S DAUGHTER, THE | 3.2 | Comedy | 12+ |
| SCARLET AND THE BLACK, THE | 3.5 | Adventure | 12+ | ONLY YOU | 3.2 | Comedy | 12+ |
| WATERSHIP DOWN | 3.5 | Adventure | 12+ | TO BE OR NOT TO BE | 3.2 | Comedy | 12+ |
| FAIL-SAFE | 3.7 | Adventure | 12+ | WHILE YOU WERE SLEEPING | 3.2 | Comedy | 12+ |
| SEA HAWK, THE | 3.7 | Adventure | 12+ | BACHELOR MOTHER | 3.3 | Comedy | 12+ |
| GUNS OF NAVARONE, THE | 3.8 | Adventure | 12+ | ENCHANTED APRIL | 3.3 | Comedy | 12+ |
| LONG VOYAGE HOME, THE | 3.8 | Adventure | 12+ | ENGLISHMAN WHO WENT UP HILL | 3.3 | Comedy | 12+ |
| THEY WERE EXPENDABLE | 3.8 | Adventure | 12+ | FATHER OF THE BRIDE | 3.3 | Comedy | 12+ |
| TRAIN, THE | 3.8 | Adventure | 12+ | GAMBIT | 3.3 | Comedy | 12+ |
| TWENTY THOUS. LEAGUES/ SEA | 3.8 | Adventure | 12+ | LIMELIGHT | 3.3 | Comedy | 12+ |
| AFRICAN QUEEN, THE | 4.0 | Adventure | 12+ | FATHER OF THE BRIDE II | 3.5 | Comedy | 12+ |
| BRIDGE ON THE RIVER KWAI, THE | 4.0 | Adventure | 12+ | GROUNDHOG DAY | 3.5 | Comedy | 12+ |
| KING KONG | 4.0 | Adventure | 12+ | INDISCREET | 3.5 | Comedy | 12+ |
| NORTH BY NORTHWEST | 4.0 | Adventure | 12+ | LIFE WITH MIKEY | 3.5 | Comedy | 12+ |
| STALAG 17 | 4.0 | Adventure | 12+ | MONKEY BUSINESS | 3.5 | Comedy | 12+ |
| TREASURE OF SIERRA MADRE, THE | 4.0 | Adventure | 12+ | NO TIME FOR SERGEANTS | 3.5 | Comedy | 12+ |
| SPACED INVADERS | 1.8 | Comedy | 12+ | ROOKIE OF THE YEAR | 3.5 | Comedy | 12+ |
| LOVE LAUGHS AT ANDY HARDY | 2.0 | Comedy | 12+ | SABRINA | 3.5 | Comedy | 12+ |
| SON OF THE PINK PANTHER | 2.1 | Comedy | 12+ | SABRINA | 3.5 | Comedy | 12+ |

## Secular Movies

| Title | Rating | Type | Age | Title | Rating | Type | Age |
|---|---|---|---|---|---|---|---|
| WRONG ARM OF THE LAW, THE | 3.5 | Comedy | 12+ | FRANK AND OLLIE | 2.5 | Document. | 12+ |
| BORN YESTERDAY | 3.7 | Comedy | 12+ | BRIEF HISTORY OF TIME, A | 3.5 | Document. | 12+ |
| I.Q. | 3.7 | Comedy | 12+ | ALL I WANT FOR CHRISTMAS | 2.2 | Drama | 12+ |
| LIFE WITH FATHER | 3.7 | Comedy | 12+ | ACCOMPANIST, THE | 2.3 | Drama | 12+ |
| MOUSE THAT ROARED, THE | 3.7 | Comedy | 12+ | ALAN AND NAOMI | 2.3 | Drama | 12+ |
| OPERATION PETTICOAT | 3.7 | Comedy | 12+ | BLUE KNIGHT, THE | 2.3 | Drama | 12+ |
| SUPPORT YOUR LOCAL SHERIFF | 3.7 | Comedy | 12+ | DAKOTA | 2.3 | Drama | 12+ |
| WOMAN OF THE YEAR | 3.7 | Comedy | 12+ | CHASING DREAMS | 2.5 | Drama | 12+ |
| GREAT DICTATOR, THE | 3.8 | Comedy | 12+ | GIFT OF LOVE, THE | 2.5 | Drama | 12+ |
| MAN IN WHITE SUIT, THE | 3.8 | Comedy | 12+ | IN THE CUSTODY OF STRANGERS | 2.5 | Drama | 12+ |
| PHILADELPHIA STORY | 3.8 | Comedy | 12+ | JUSTIN MORGAN HAD A HORSE | 2.5 | Drama | 12+ |
| HIS GIRL FRIDAY | 4.0 | Comedy | 12+ | SPENCER'S MOUNTAIN | 2.5 | Drama | 12+ |
| IT HAPPENED ONE NIGHT | 4.0 | Comedy | 12+ | STARS FELL ON HENRIETTA, THE | 2.5 | Drama | 12+ |
| MISTER ROBERTS | 4.0 | Comedy | 12+ | STRATEGIC AIR COMMAND | 2.5 | Drama | 12+ |
| QUIET MAN, THE | 4.0 | Comedy | 12+ | TOMORROW'S CHILD | 2.5 | Drama | 12+ |
| ALAMO, THE | 2.7 | Docudrama | 12+ | WHEN THE WHALES CAME | 2.5 | Drama | 12+ |
| EXODUS | 2.8 | Docudrama | 12+ | WOMAN HUNTER, THE | 2.5 | Drama | 12+ |
| LAST COMMAND, THE | 2.8 | Docudrama | 12+ | ALL GOD'S CHILDREN | 2.7 | Drama | 12+ |
| CHINA RUN | 3.0 | Docudrama | 12+ | NINETEEN EIGHTEEN (1918) | 2.7 | Drama | 12+ |
| JESSE OWENS STORY, THE | 3.0 | Docudrama | 12+ | TOM BROWN'S SCHOOL DAYS | 2.7 | Drama | 12+ |
| KITTY: RETURN TO AUSCHWITZ | 3.0 | Docudrama | 12+ | UNCLE TOM'S CABIN | 2.7 | Drama | 12+ |
| SISTER KENNY | 3.0 | Docudrama | 12+ | 84 CHARING CROSSRDS | 2.8 | Drama | 12+ |
| TIME FOR MIRACLES, A | 3.0 | Docudrama | 12+ | BEETHOVEN LIVES UPSTAIRS | 2.8 | Drama | 12+ |
| MANDELA | 3.1 | Docudrama | 12+ | GETTYSBURG | 2.8 | Drama | 12+ |
| BILL: ON HIS OWN | 3.2 | Docudrama | 12+ | INCRED. JOURNEY / DR MEG LAUREL | 2.8 | Drama | 12+ |
| SOS TITANIC | 3.2 | Docudrama | 12+ | PIONEER WOMAN | 2.8 | Drama | 12+ |
| SPIRIT OF ST. LOUIS, THE | 3.2 | Docudrama | 12+ | SUMMER MAGIC | 2.8 | Drama | 12+ |
| I WILL FIGHT NO MORE FOREVER | 3.3 | Docudrama | 12+ | THREE FACES OF EVE | 2.8 | Drama | 12+ |
| RAID ON ENTEBBE | 3.3 | Docudrama | 12+ | THREE COINS IN THE FOUNTAIN | 2.8 | Drama | 12+ |
| SUNRISE AT CAMPOBELLO | 3.3 | Docudrama | 12+ | TRAPEZE | 2.8 | Drama | 12+ |
| BITTER HARVEST | 3.5 | Docudrama | 12+ | WHALE FOR THE KILLING, A | 2.8 | Drama | 12+ |
| CRISIS AT CENTRAL HIGH | 3.5 | Docudrama | 12+ | RUNNING WILD | 2.9 | Drama | 12+ |
| DIARY OF ANNE FRANK | 3.5 | Docudrama | 12+ | BELIZAIRE THE CAJUN | 3.0 | Drama | 12+ |
| MAN FOR ALL SEASONS, A | 3.5 | Docudrama | 12+ | CALL TO GLORY | 3.0 | Drama | 12+ |
| SEPARATE BUT EQUAL | 3.5 | Docudrama | 12+ | CLOAK AND DAGGER | 3.0 | Drama | 12+ |
| MAN FOR ALL SEASONS, A | 3.6 | Docudrama | 12+ | COCAINE: ONE MAN'S SEDUCTION | 3.0 | Drama | 12+ |
| BILL | 3.7 | Docudrama | 12+ | COURTSHIP | 3.0 | Drama | 12+ |
| GANDHI | 3.7 | Docudrama | 12+ | DARK HORSE | 3.0 | Drama | 12+ |
| GIDEON'S TRUMPET | 3.7 | Docudrama | 12+ | EL CID | 3.0 | Drama | 12+ |
| MY BRILLIANT CAREER | 3.7 | Docudrama | 12+ | HOUSEKEEPING | 3.0 | Drama | 12+ |
| BRIAN'S SONG | 3.8 | Docudrama | 12+ | IRON AND SILK | 3.0 | Drama | 12+ |
| POPE JOHN PAUL II | 3.8 | Docudrama | 12+ | MAGNIFICIENT OBSESSION | 3.0 | Drama | 12+ |
| VIVA ZAPATA! | 3.8 | Docudrama | 12+ | MAN IN THE IRON MASK, THE | 3.0 | Drama | 12+ |

# Appendix — Secular Movies

| Title | Rating | Type | Age | Title | Rating | Type | Age |
|---|---|---|---|---|---|---|---|
| MASADA | 3.0 | Drama | 12+ | HEART IS LONELY HUNTER, THE | 3.5 | Drama | 12+ |
| OF MICE AND MEN | 3.0 | Drama | 12+ | I KNOW WHY / CAGED BIRD SINGS | 3.5 | Drama | 12+ |
| SQUANTO: A WARRIOR'S TALE | 3.0 | Drama | 12+ | I REMEMBER MAMA | 3.5 | Drama | 12+ |
| SYBIL | 3.0 | Drama | 12+ | INN OF SIXTH HAPPINESS | 3.5 | Drama | 12+ |
| LOVE LEADS THE WAY | 3.1 | Drama | 12+ | JUDGE PRIEST | 3.5 | Drama | 12+ |
| NOT MY KID | 3.1 | Drama | 12+ | KEY LARGO | 3.5 | Drama | 12+ |
| AMY | 3.2 | Drama | 12+ | LILIES OF THE FIELD | 3.5 | Drama | 12+ |
| PACK OF LIES | 3.2 | Drama | 12+ | LOOKING FOR MIRACLES | 3.5 | Drama | 12+ |
| PROUD REBEL, THE | 3.2 | Drama | 12+ | MARK TWAIN AND ME | 3.5 | Drama | 12+ |
| QUO VADIS | 3.2 | Drama | 12+ | MISS ROSE WHITE | 3.5 | Drama | 12+ |
| SHENANDOAH | 3.2 | Drama | 12+ | MR HOLLAND'S OPUS | 3.5 | Drama | 12+ |
| SKYLARK | 3.2 | Drama | 12+ | MRS. MINIVER | 3.5 | Drama | 12+ |
| TRIP TO BOUNTIFUL, THE | 3.2 | Drama | 12+ | MY SWEET CHARLIE | 3.5 | Drama | 12+ |
| WHITE MAMA | 3.2 | Drama | 12+ | OUR TOWN | 3.5 | Drama | 12+ |
| ANGEL ON MY SHOULDER | 3.3 | Drama | 12+ | PASTIME | 3.5 | Drama | 12+ |
| CHRISTMAS WITHOUT SNOW | 3.3 | Drama | 12+ | PENNY SERENADE | 3.5 | Drama | 12+ |
| COLD SASSY TREE | 3.3 | Drama | 12+ | PIANO FOR MRS. CIMINO, A | 3.5 | Drama | 12+ |
| DECORATION DAY | 3.3 | Drama | 12+ | SANDS OF IWO JIMA | 3.5 | Drama | 12+ |
| FATHER FIGURE | 3.3 | Drama | 12+ | SECRET GARDEN, THE | 3.5 | Drama | 12+ |
| FOREVER YOUNG | 3.3 | Drama | 12+ | SENSE AND SENSIBILITY | 3.5 | Drama | 12+ |
| JERICHO MILE, THE | 3.3 | Drama | 12+ | SERGEANT YORK | 3.5 | Drama | 12+ |
| JUAREZ | 3.3 | Drama | 12+ | SEVEN DAYS IN MAY | 3.5 | Drama | 12+ |
| LANTERN HILL | 3.3 | Drama | 12+ | SUMMER OF MY GERMAN SOLDIER | 3.5 | Drama | 12+ |
| LONG WAY HOME, A | 3.3 | Drama | 12+ | TESTAMENT | 3.5 | Drama | 12+ |
| ONE AGAINST THE WIND | 3.3 | Drama | 12+ | TO SIR WITH LOVE | 3.5 | Drama | 12+ |
| PRINCESS CARABOO | 3.3 | Drama | 12+ | TUCKER: THE MAN AND HIS DREAM | 3.5 | Drama | 12+ |
| SARAH, PLAIN AND TALL | 3.3 | Drama | 12+ | TWO BITS | 3.5 | Drama | 12+ |
| SHELL SEEKERS, THE | 3.3 | Drama | 12+ | CAINE MUTINY | 3.7 | Drama | 12+ |
| THIRTY SECONDS OVER TOKYO | 3.3 | Drama | 12+ | GIANT | 3.7 | Drama | 12+ |
| TO RACE THE WIND | 3.3 | Drama | 12+ | GOING MY WAY | 3.7 | Drama | 12+ |
| TRIBES | 3.3 | Drama | 12+ | GREEN EYES | 3.7 | Drama | 12+ |
| TWO OF A KIND | 3.3 | Drama | 12+ | MARTY | 3.7 | Drama | 12+ |
| WILD HEARTS CAN'T BE BROKEN | 3.3 | Drama | 12+ | MY FATHER'S GLORY | 3.7 | Drama | 12+ |
| WORLD WAR III | 3.3 | Drama | 12+ | SAN FRANCISCO | 3.7 | Drama | 12+ |
| I HEARD THE OWL CALL MY NAME | 3.4 | Drama | 12+ | SECRET OF ROAN INISH | 3.7 | Drama | 12+ |
| ADAM | 3.5 | Drama | 12+ | SONG OF BERNADETTE | 3.7 | Drama | 12+ |
| AIRPORT | 3.5 | Drama | 12+ | TALE OF TWO CITIES | 3.7 | Drama | 12+ |
| BEST LITTLE GIRL IN/ WORLD | 3.5 | Drama | 12+ | TO KILL A MOCKINGBIRD | 3.7 | Drama | 12+ |
| CHOSEN, THE | 3.5 | Drama | 12+ | TWELVE O'CLOCK HIGH | 3.7 | Drama | 12+ |
| COUNTRY GIRL | 3.5 | Drama | 12+ | BAD DAY AT BLACK ROCK | 3.8 | Drama | 12+ |
| FAREWELL TO ARMS, A | 3.5 | Drama | 12+ | BEN-HUR | 3.8 | Drama | 12+ |
| GATHERING, THE | 3.5 | Drama | 12+ | BREATHING LESSONS | 3.8 | Drama | 12+ |
| HAMLET | 3.5 | Drama | 12+ | CHIEFS | 3.8 | Drama | 12+ |

## Secular Movies

| Title | Rating | Type | Age |
|---|---|---|---|
| CYRANO DE BERGERAC | 3.8 | Drama | 12+ |
| DRIVING MISS DAISY | 3.8 | Drama | 12+ |
| FALLEN IDOL | 3.8 | Drama | 12+ |
| GOODBYE MR. CHIPS | 3.8 | Drama | 12+ |
| HEIRESS | 3.8 | Drama | 12+ |
| KING'S ROW | 3.8 | Drama | 12+ |
| LAST HURRAH, THE | 3.8 | Drama | 12+ |
| RAISIN IN THE SUN, A | 3.8 | Drama | 12+ |
| REBEL WITHOUT A CAUSE | 3.8 | Drama | 12+ |
| ROMAN HOLIDAY | 3.8 | Drama | 12+ |
| SEARCHING FOR BOBBY FISCHER | 3.8 | Drama | 12+ |
| SOUTHERNER, THE | 3.8 | Drama | 12+ |
| TWELVE ANGRY MEN | 3.8 | Drama | 12+ |
| WINSLOW BOY, THE | 3.8 | Drama | 12+ |
| BEST YEARS OF OUR LIVES | 4.0 | Drama | 12+ |
| BOOMERANG | 4.0 | Drama | 12+ |
| CASABLANCA | 4.0 | Drama | 12+ |
| EAST OF EDEN | 4.0 | Drama | 12+ |
| FRIENDLY PERSUASION | 4.0 | Drama | 12+ |
| GONE WITH THE WIND | 4.0 | Drama | 12+ |
| GOOD EARTH, THE | 4.0 | Drama | 12+ |
| GRAPES OF WRATH, THE | 4.0 | Drama | 12+ |
| I AM / FUGITIVE FROM / CHAIN GANG | 4.0 | Drama | 12+ |
| LITTLE WOMEN | 4.0 | Drama | 12+ |
| MR. SMITH GOES TO WASHINGTON | 4.0 | Drama | 12+ |
| ON THE WATERFRONT | 4.0 | Drama | 12+ |
| PLACE FOR ANNIE, A | 4.0 | Drama | 12+ |
| PRIDE AND PREJUDICE | 4.0 | Drama | 12+ |
| RETURN OF THE KING | 4.0 | Fantasy | 12+ |
| HELLO DOLLY | 2.0 | Musical | 12+ |
| NEWSIES | 2.2 | Musical | 12+ |
| KISMET | 2.3 | Musical | 12+ |
| BUNDLE OF JOY | 2.5 | Musical | 12+ |
| TILL THE CLOUDS ROLL BY | 2.5 | Musical | 12+ |
| HAPPIEST MILLIONAIRE, THE | 2.7 | Musical | 12+ |
| SOUTH PACIFIC | 2.7 | Musical | 12+ |
| WHITE CHRISTMAS | 2.7 | Musical | 12+ |
| BELLS ARE RINGING | 2.8 | Musical | 12+ |
| GUYS AND DOLLS | 3.0 | Musical | 12+ |
| STATE FAIR | 3.0 | Musical | 12+ |
| THAT'S DANCING | 3.0 | Musical | 12+ |
| THIS IS THE ARMY | 3.0 | Musical | 12+ |
| UNSINKABLE MOLLY BROWN | 3.0 | Musical | 12+ |

| Title | Rating | Type | Age |
|---|---|---|---|
| HIGH SOCIETY | 3.2 | Musical | 12+ |
| BRIGADOON | 3.3 | Musical | 12+ |
| FIDDLER ON THE ROOF | 3.3 | Musical | 12+ |
| GIRL CRAZY | 3.3 | Musical | 12+ |
| INSPECTOR GENERAL | 3.5 | Musical | 12+ |
| SHALL WE DANCE | 3.5 | Musical | 12+ |
| FUNNY FACE | 3.7 | Musical | 12+ |
| HOLIDAY INN | 3.7 | Musical | 12+ |
| JOLSON STORY, THE | 3.7 | Musical | 12+ |
| MY FAIR LADY | 3.7 | Musical | 12+ |
| GREEN PASTURES | 3.8 | Musical | 12+ |
| KING AND I, THE | 3.8 | Musical | 12+ |
| LILI | 3.8 | Musical | 12+ |
| THAT'S ENTERTAINMENT III | 3.8 | Musical | 12+ |
| THAT'S ENTERTAINMENT | 3.8 | Musical | 12+ |
| WEST SIDE STORY | 3.8 | Musical | 12+ |
| YANKEE DOODLE DANDY | 3.8 | Musical | 12+ |
| GIGI | 4.0 | Musical | 12+ |
| MEET ME IN ST. LOUIS | 4.0 | Musical | 12+ |
| OLIVER! | 4.0 | Musical | 12+ |
| ON THE TOWN | 4.0 | Musical | 12+ |
| SEVEN BRIDES FOR 7 BROTHERS | 4.0 | Musical | 12+ |
| SINGIN' IN THE RAIN | 4.0 | Musical | 12+ |
| APPOINTMENT WITH DEATH | 1.8 | Mystery | 12+ |
| NANCY DREW : GHOSTWRITER | 2.0 | Mystery | 12+ |
| CAROLINE? | 3.2 | Mystery | 12+ |
| MURDER ON ORIENT EXPRESS | 3.5 | Mystery | 12+ |
| PRIVATE LIFE / SHERLOCK HOLMES | 3.5 | Mystery | 12+ |
| THIN MAN, THE | 3.8 | Mystery | 12+ |
| TOPKAPI | 3.8 | Mystery | 12+ |
| FOREIGN CORRESPONDENT | 4.0 | Mystery | 12+ |
| LAURA | 4.0 | Mystery | 12+ |
| MALTESE FALCON, THE | 4.0 | Mystery | 12+ |
| REAR WINDOW | 4.0 | Mystery | 12+ |
| STRANGERS ON A TRAIN | 4.0 | Mystery | 12+ |
| VERTIGO | 4.0 | Mystery | 12+ |
| BLACK HOLE, THE | 1.8 | Sci-Fi | 12+ |
| PROTOTYPE | 2.2 | Sci-Fi | 12+ |
| SUPERMAN IV: QUEST FOR PEACE | 2.5 | Sci-Fi | 12+ |
| VOYAGE TO THE BOTTOM OF SEA | 2.8 | Sci-Fi | 12+ |
| SUPERMAN | 3.3 | Sci-Fi | 12+ |
| TIME MACHINE, THE | 3.3 | Sci-Fi | 12+ |
| MYSTERIOUS ISLAND | 3.5 | Sci-Fi | 12+ |

# Appendix — Secular Movies

| Title | Rating | Type | Age |
|---|---|---|---|
| STAR TREK VI | 3.5 | Sci-Fi | 12+ |
| WAR OF THE WORLDS, THE | 3.5 | Sci-Fi | 12+ |
| FORBIDDEN PLANET | 3.7 | Sci-Fi | 12+ |
| STAR TREK: GENERATIONS | 3.7 | Sci-Fi | 12+ |
| RARE BREED, THE | 2.5 | Western | 12+ |
| SEPTEMBER GUN | 2.5 | Western | 12+ |
| WILD WOMEN | 2.5 | Western | 12+ |
| RIO LOBO | 2.7 | Western | 12+ |
| SACRED GROUND | 2.7 | Western | 12+ |
| SHADOW RIDERS | 2.8 | Western | 12+ |
| WAR WAGON, THE | 3.0 | Western | 12+ |
| BEND OF THE RIVER | 3.3 | Western | 12+ |
| HOW THE WEST WAS WON | 3.3 | Western | 12+ |
| TRUE GRIT | 3.3 | Western | 12+ |
| ANGEL AND THE BADMAN | 3.5 | Western | 12+ |
| HOMBRE | 3.5 | Western | 12+ |
| WAGONMASTER | 3.5 | Western | 12+ |
| GREY FOX | 3.6 | Western | 12+ |
| RIO BRAVO | 3.7 | Western | 12+ |
| MAN WHO SHOT LIBERTY VALENCE | 3.8 | Western | 12+ |
| HIGH NOON | 4.0 | Western | 12+ |
| RED RIVER | 4.0 | Western | 12+ |
| RIDE THE HIGH COUNTRY | 4.0 | Western | 12+ |
| SEARCHERS, THE | 4.0 | Western | 12+ |
| SHANE | 4.0 | Western | 12+ |
| STAGECOACH | 4.0 | Western | 12+ |

## AGE GROUP 17+

| Title | Rating | Type | Age |
|---|---|---|---|
| ALIEN FROM LA | 1.8 | Adventure | 17+ |
| DEERSLAYER, THE | 2.3 | Adventure | 17+ |
| EMPIRE OF THE SUN | 2.7 | Adventure | 17+ |
| GLORIA | 3.0 | Adventure | 17+ |
| BEYOND RANGOON | 3.5 | Adventure | 17+ |
| LAWRENCE OF ARABIA | 3.5 | Adventure | 17+ |
| MR. NORTH | 3.0 | Comedy | 17+ |
| BAREFOOT IN THE PARK | 3.5 | Comedy | 17+ |
| BILL COSBY : 49 | 3.5 | Comedy | 17+ |
| HUDSUCKER PROXY | 3.5 | Comedy | 17+ |
| HOUSE ON GARIBALDI STREET | 2.5 | Docudrama | 17+ |
| LIFE & ASSASSINATION / KINGFISH | 3.2 | Docudrama | 17+ |
| CASE OF LIBEL, A | 3.5 | Docudrama | 17+ |
| MISSILES OF OCTOBER | 3.5 | Docudrama | 17+ |
| ROMERO | 3.5 | Docudrama | 17+ |
| SAKHAROV | 3.5 | Docudrama | 17+ |
| AUTOBIOGRAPHY/ JANE PITTMAN | 3.8 | Docudrama | 17+ |
| DEAR AMERICA: LTRS/ VIETNAM | 3.8 | Document. | 17+ |
| CIVIL WAR, THE | 4.0 | Document. | 17+ |
| GREAT DAY IN HARLEM, A | 3.0 | Document. | 17+ |
| DAD | 2.0 | Drama | 17+ |
| PURSUIT | 2.2 | Drama | 17+ |
| BURNING SECRET | 2.5 | Drama | 17+ |
| ELENI | 2.5 | Drama | 17+ |
| ON VALENTINE'S DAY | 2.5 | Drama | 17+ |
| PERSUASION | 2.5 | Drama | 17+ |
| UNSTRUNG HEROES | 2.5 | Drama | 17+ |
| NOT WITHOUT MY DAUGHTER | 2.8 | Drama | 17+ |
| ROSENCR. & GUILDEN. ARE DEAD | 2.8 | Drama | 17+ |
| AND BABY MAKES SIX | 3.0 | Drama | 17+ |
| ANOTHER WOMAN | 3.0 | Drama | 17+ |
| BARABBAS | 3.0 | Drama | 17+ |
| CRY THE BELOVED COUNTRY | 3.0 | Drama | 17+ |
| EAGLE HAS LANDED, THE | 3.0 | Drama | 17+ |
| JOURNEY OF AUGUST KING, THE | 3.0 | Drama | 17+ |
| MASS APPEAL | 3.0 | Drama | 17+ |
| MISSION, THE | 3.0 | Drama | 17+ |
| MONTH BY THE LAKE, A | 3.0 | Drama | 17+ |
| SUMMER SOLSTICE | 3.0 | Drama | 17+ |
| WHERE ANGELS FEAR TO TREAD | 3.0 | Drama | 17+ |
| AGE OF INNOCENCE | 3.2 | Drama | 17+ |
| DESERT BLOOM | 3.2 | Drama | 17+ |
| FAMILY UPSIDE DOWN, A | 3.2 | Drama | 17+ |
| JANE DOE | 3.2 | Drama | 17+ |
| KATHERINE | 3.2 | Drama | 17+ |
| MEMORIAL DAY | 3.2 | Drama | 17+ |
| MR. JOHNSON | 3.2 | Drama | 17+ |
| PICTURE BRIDE, THE | 3.2 | Drama | 17+ |
| ADVISE AND CONSENT | 3.3 | Drama | 17+ |
| COLONEL CHABERT | 3.3 | Drama | 17+ |
| GLASS MENAGERIE | 3.3 | Drama | 17+ |
| ORDEAL OF DR. MUDD, THE | 3.3 | Drama | 17+ |
| REHEARSAL FOR MURDER | 3.3 | Drama | 17+ |
| SCENT OF GREEN PAPAYA | 3.3 | Drama | 17+ |
| STRANGERS: MOTHER & DAUGHTER | 3.3 | Drama | 17+ |
| TEN (10) RILLINGTON PLACE | 3.3 | Drama | 17+ |
| TO THE LIGHTHOUSE | 3.3 | Drama | 17+ |
| TOM AND VIV | 3.3 | Drama | 17+ |
| WAR, THE | 3.3 | Drama | 17+ |

## Secular/Christian Movies — Appendix

| Title | Rating | Type | Age |
|---|---|---|---|
| PASSAGE TO INDIA | 3.4 | Drama | 17+ |
| DAY AFTER, THE | 3.5 | Drama | 17+ |
| DEAD, THE | 3.5 | Drama | 17+ |
| FIRST KNIGHT | 3.5 | Drama | 17+ |
| HEARTLAND | 3.5 | Drama | 17+ |
| MANCHURIAN CANDIDATE, THE | 3.5 | Drama | 17+ |
| SECOND BEST | 3.5 | Drama | 17+ |
| UNNATURAL CAUSES | 3.5 | Drama | 17+ |
| WALK IN THE CLOUDS, A | 3.5 | Drama | 17+ |
| HANDFUL OF DUST | 3.7 | Drama | 17+ |
| HENRY V | 3.7 | Drama | 17+ |
| JULIA | 3.7 | Drama | 17+ |
| BLIND SPOT | 3.8 | Drama | 17+ |
| DR. ZHIVAGO | 3.8 | Drama | 17+ |
| ELEPHANT MAN, THE | 3.8 | Drama | 17+ |
| LORENZO'S OIL | 3.8 | Drama | 17+ |
| REMAINS OF THE DAY | 3.8 | Drama | 17+ |
| SHADOWLANDS | 3.8 | Drama | 17+ |
| TO LIVE | 3.8 | Drama | 17+ |
| BABETTE'S FEAST | 4.0 | Drama | 17+ |
| CITIZEN KANE | 4.0 | Drama | 17+ |
| HOWARD'S END | 4.0 | Drama | 17+ |
| JUDGEMENT AT NUREMBERG | 4.0 | Drama | 17+ |
| SUNDOWNERS, THE | 4.0 | Drama | 17+ |
| THOUSAND PIECES OF GOLD, A | 4.0 | Drama | 17+ |
| STILL OF THE NIGHT, THE | 2.7 | Mystery | 17+ |
| SUTURE | 3.0 | Mystery | 17+ |
| WHISTLE BLOWER | 3.3 | Mystery | 17+ |
| CHARADE | 3.8 | Mystery | 17+ |
| IN THE HEAT OF THE NIGHT | 4.0 | Mystery | 17+ |
| STARGATE | 2.7 | Sci-Fi | 17+ |
| ANDROMEDA STRAIN, THE | 3.3 | Sci-Fi | 17+ |
| FAHRENHEIT 451 | 3.5 | Sci-Fi | 17+ |
| SON OF THE MORNING STAR | 3.3 | Western | 17+ |

## LISTING OF CHRISTIAN MOVIES BY AGE GROUPS

### AGE 04+

| Title | Rating | Type | Age |
|---|---|---|---|
| ADVENT/ OF THE FLYING HOUSE | 3.0 | Adventure | 04+ |
| PETER AND THE MAGIC SEEDS | 3.0 | Adventure | 04+ |
| STORYBOOK TREE, THE | 3.0 | Comedy | 04+ |
| CHRISTMAS IS... | 3.0 | Drama | 04+ |
| DOOG'S GARAGE THEATER - VOL. I | 3.0 | Drama | 04+ |
| DOOG'S GARAGE THEATER - VOL. II | 3.0 | Drama | 04+ |
| QUIGLEY'S VILLAGE- BE KIND | 3.0 | Drama | 04+ |
| FILLING STATION TEACHING SERIES | 3.0 | Educational | 04+ |
| HUMPTY | 3.0 | Fantasy | 04+ |
| COLBY'S PLACE- SKATEBOARD/ SALE | 2.5 | Musical | 04+ |
| COLBY'S MISSING MEMORY | 3.0 | Musical | 04+ |
| MUSIC MACHINE, THE | 3.0 | Musical | 04+ |
| QUIGLEY'S VILLAGE- /NOT FAIR | 3.0 | Musical | 04+ |
| GINGERBROOK FARE | 4.0 | Musical | 04+ |
| GERBERT- GOD KNOWS / FEELINGS | 3.5 | Variety | 04+ |
| GERBERT- THE WORLD AROUND US | 3.5 | Variety | 04+ |
| GERBERT- HOP TO IT | 4.0 | Variety | 04+ |
| GERBERT- SAFE IN HIS ARMS | 4.0 | Variety | 04+ |
| GERBERT- THE CAT'S MEOW | 4.0 | Variety | 04+ |

### AGE 06+

| Title | Rating | Type | Age |
|---|---|---|---|
| RESCUER, THE | 2.5 | Adventure | 06+ |
| ADVENTURES IN ODYSSEY | 3.0 | Adventure | 06+ |
| CROSS CURRENTS | 3.0 | Adventure | 06+ |
| GREAT ROCK RIVER RAFT RACE | 3.0 | Adventure | 06+ |
| LIFE FLIGHT | 3.0 | Adventure | 06+ |
| SUPERBOOK BIBLE STORY SERIES | 3.0 | Adventure | 06+ |
| TUNNEL, THE | 3.0 | Adventure | 06+ |
| WOLFHUNTER | 3.0 | Adventure | 06+ |
| YEARS OF THE BEAST | 3.3 | Adventure | 06+ |
| FOR PETE'S SAKE | 3.5 | Adventure | 06+ |
| GREATEST ADVENT BIBLE STORY SERIES (Hanna Barbera) | 3.5 | Adventure | 06+ |
| LAST CHANCE DETECTIVES: ESCAPE/FIRE LAKE | 3.5 | Adventure | 06+ |
| LAST CHANCE DETECTIVES: LEGEND OF / DESERT BIGFOOT | 3.5 | Adventure | 06+ |
| LAST CHANCE DETECTIVES: MYSTERY LIGHTS | 3.5 | Adventure | 06+ |
| SECRET ADVENTURE SERIES | 2.5 | Comedy | 06+ |

# Appendix — Christian Movies

| Title | Rating | Type | Age |
|---|---|---|---|
| WHITCOMB'S WAR | 2.5 | Comedy | 06+ |
| SPORTS CAPERS! | 2.8 | Comedy | 06+ |
| BIG MONEY MIX UP | 3.0 | Comedy | 06+ |
| GREAT BANANA PIE CAPER | 3.0 | Comedy | 06+ |
| MITCH AND ALLEN | 3.5 | Comedy | 06+ |
| PENELOPE GANG, THE | 3.5 | Comedy | 06+ |
| CASH, JOHNNY - THE GOSPEL ROAD | 2.2 | Concert | 06+ |
| CAMP, STEVE - SOLD OUT | 3.0 | Concert | 06+ |
| CARMAN - COMIN' ON STRONG | 3.0 | Concert | 06+ |
| CARMAN - THE STANDARD | 3.0 | Concert | 06+ |
| CARMAN LIVE - RADICALLY SAVED | 3.0 | Concert | 06+ |
| DUNCAN, BRYAN - MERCY ALIVE | 3.0 | Concert | 06+ |
| GRANT, AMY - AGE TO AGE CONCERT | 3.0 | Concert | 06+ |
| GRANT, AMY - FIND A WAY | 3.0 | Concert | 06+ |
| GRANT, AMY - HEART IN MOTION | 3.0 | Concert | 06+ |
| GREEN, STEVE - FOR GOD / ALONE | 3.0 | Concert | 06+ |
| HOLM, DALLAS - AGAINST THE WIND | 3.0 | Concert | 06+ |
| IMPERIALS - 20TH ANNIV. CONCERT | 3.0 | Concert | 06+ |
| MOORE, GEOFF AND THE DISTANCE | 3.0 | Concert | 06+ |
| NEWSONG - ALL AROUND / WORLD | 3.0 | Concert | 06+ |
| SMITH, MICHAEL W. - BIG PICTURE | 3.0 | Concert | 06+ |
| STONEHILL, RANDY - LOVE BEYOND REASON | 3.0 | Concert | 06+ |
| TAKE FIVE | 3.0 | Concert | 06+ |
| TROCCOLI, KATHY - LIVE CONCERT | 3.0 | Concert | 06+ |
| WALSH, SHEILA - SHADOWLANDS | 3.0 | Concert | 06+ |
| FRONT ROW: MICHAEL CARD | 3.5 | Concert | 06+ |
| PARIS, TWILA - SANCTUARY | 3.5 | Concert | 06+ |
| PATTI, SANDI - LET THERE BE PRAISE | 3.5 | Concert | 06+ |
| PHILLIPS, CRAIG & DEAN - CONCERT OF THE AGE | 3.5 | Concert | 06+ |
| SPARROW TV DINNERS | 3.5 | Concert | 06+ |
| PATTI, SANDI - "LIVE" CONCERT | 3.8 | Concert | 06+ |
| FRONT ROW: CHARLIE PEACOCK | 4.0 | Concert | 06+ |
| SMITH, MICHAEL W. - CHANGE YOUR WORLD | 4.0 | Concert | 06+ |
| WATSON, WAYNE - IN CONCERT - WATERCOLOR PONIES | 4.0 | Concert | 06+ |
| CROSS AND THE SWITCHBLADE | 1.5 | Docudrama | 06+ |
| MOSES | 2.5 | Docudrama | 06+ |
| ANCIENT SECRETS OF THE BIBLE II | 3.0 | Docudrama | 06+ |
| HEAVEN'S HEROES | 3.5 | Docudrama | 06+ |
| JONI | 3.5 | Docudrama | 06+ |
| KING OF KINGS | 3.5 | Docudrama | 06+ |
| STORY OF RUTH, THE | 4.0 | Docudrama | 06+ |
| GOD'S GAME PLAN | 3.0 | Document'y | 06+ |
| GRANT, AMY - CIRCLE OF LOVE | 3.0 | Document'y | 06+ |
| GOLDEN DOLPHIN, THE | 2.0 | Drama | 06+ |
| LIFETIME CONTRACT | 2.0 | Drama | 06+ |
| CAUGHT IN TIME | 2.5 | Drama | 06+ |
| FATHER, SON & THREE MILE RUN | 2.5 | Drama | 06+ |
| JUST LAST SUMMER | 2.5 | Drama | 06+ |
| NITE SONG | 2.5 | Drama | 06+ |
| CLIMB A TALL MOUNTAIN | 2.8 | Drama | 06+ |
| MOUNTAIN MAN GO HOME | 2.8 | Drama | 06+ |
| BELONGING GAME | 3.0 | Drama | 06+ |
| CITY THAT FORGOT / CHRISTMAS | 3.0 | Drama | 06+ |
| FRIENDSHIP'S FIELD | 3.0 | Drama | 06+ |
| JIMMY AND THE WHITE LIE | 3.0 | Drama | 06+ |
| MCGEE AND ME- NOT SO GREAT ESCAPE | 3.0 | Drama | 06+ |
| PRIZE, THE | 3.0 | Drama | 06+ |
| SAMMY | 3.0 | Drama | 06+ |
| SECRET OF / SECOND BASEMENT | 3.0 | Drama | 06+ |
| TIME TO RUN | 3.0 | Drama | 06+ |
| ANGEL ALLEY | 3.5 | Drama | 06+ |
| COACH | 3.5 | Drama | 06+ |
| HAPPINESS IS . . . | 3.5 | Drama | 06+ |
| HARLEY | 3.5 | Drama | 06+ |
| MCGEE AND ME- A STAR/ BREAKING | 3.5 | Drama | 06+ |
| PROSECUTOR, THE | 3.5 | Drama | 06+ |
| SHEPHERD, THE | 3.5 | Drama | 06+ |
| STORY KEEPERS SERIES | 3.5 | Drama | 06+ |
| LITTLE TROLL PRINCE | 3.8 | Drama | 06+ |
| MCGEE & ME- SKATE EXPECTATIONS | 4.0 | Drama | 06+ |
| MOMS, DADS, & OTHER ENDANGERED SPECIES | 2.8 | Educational | 06+ |
| CHRISTIAN MUSIC DIET | 3.0 | Educational | 06+ |
| HOOMANIA | 3.0 | Fantasy | 06+ |
| LION, THE WITCH & THE WARDROBE | 3.0 | Fantasy | 06+ |
| WENDY AND THE WHINE | 3.5 | Fantasy | 06+ |
| BIBLEMAN SHOW: THE BIG BIG BOOK | 2.5 | Musical | 06+ |
| GAITHERS - DREAM ON | 3.0 | Musical | 06+ |
| KID'S PRAISE 4 | 3.0 | Musical | 06+ |

## Christian Movies

| Title | Rating | Type | Age |
|---|---|---|---|
| KID'S PRAISE 5 | 3.0 | Musical | 06+ |
| NATHANIEL THE GRUBLET | 3.0 | Musical | 06+ |
| REBA - HE GAVE ME MUSIC | 3.0 | Musical | 06+ |
| HITOPS | 3.5 | Musical | 06+ |
| MUSIC BOX | 3.5 | Musical | 06+ |
| GOOSEHILL GANG & / MYSTERY OF /HOWLING WOODS | 3.0 | Mystery | 06+ |
| GOOSEHILL GANG & /MYSTERY OF / TREEHOUSE GHOST | 3.0 | Mystery | 06+ |
| MYSTERY OF WILLOUGHBY CASTLE | 3.0 | Mystery | 06+ |
| GOOSEHILL GANG & GOLDRUSH TREASURE MAP | 3.5 | Mystery | 06+ |
| GOOSEHILL GANG & / MYSTERIOUS STRANGERS | 3.5 | Mystery | 06+ |
| GOOSEHILL GANG & / VANISHING SCHOOLMATE | 3.5 | Mystery | 06+ |

### AGE 12+

| Title | Rating | Type | Age |
|---|---|---|---|
| SURVIVAL | 3.0 | Adventure | 12+ |
| REZ VIDEO | 2.5 | Concert | 12+ |
| TWO X 4 | 2.5 | Concert | 12+ |
| DEGARMO & KEY - VISION / LIGHT BRIGADE | 3.0 | Concert | 12+ |
| GOSPEL MUSIC LIVE - PUBLIC PERFORMANCES | 3.0 | Concert | 12+ |
| PETRA - WAKE-UP CALL | 3.0 | Concert | 12+ |
| TAYLOR, STEVE - LIMELIGHT | 3.0 | Concert | 12+ |
| DEGARMO & KEY - DESTINED TO WIN | 3.5 | Concert | 12+ |
| BEYOND THE NEXT MOUNTAIN | 2.5 | Docudrama | 12+ |
| DRAVECKY: STORY OF COURAGE AND GRACE | 2.5 | Docudrama | 12+ |
| HIDING PLACE, THE | 2.8 | Docudrama | 12+ |
| BIBLE, THE | 3.0 | Docudrama | 12+ |
| JESUS OF NAZARETH (Parts 1, 2, 3) | 3.0 | Docudrama | 12+ |
| JOHN HUS | 3.0 | Docudrama | 12+ |
| NO LONGER ALONE | 3.0 | Docudrama | 12+ |
| PLACE CALLED HOME, A | 3.0 | Docudrama | 12+ |
| SAMSON AND DELILAH | 3.0 | Docudrama | 12+ |
| ST. JOHN IN EXILE | 3.0 | Docudrama | 12+ |
| TEN COMMANDMENTS | 3.0 | Docudrama | 12+ |
| BROTHER SUN, SISTER MOON | 3.2 | Docudrama | 12+ |
| MIRACLE OF FATIMA | 3.2 | Docudrama | 12+ |
| ALL THE KINGS HORSES | 3.5 | Docudrama | 12+ |
| CHINA CRY | 3.5 | Docudrama | 12+ |
| MOLDER OF DREAMS | 3.5 | Docudrama | 12+ |
| SHADOWLANDS (C.S. LEWIS: THROUGH / SHADOWLANDS) | 4.0 | Docudrama | 12+ |
| TWICE GIVEN | 4.0 | Docudrama | 12+ |
| WARLORD MEETS CHRIST: CONVER. OF COLONEL BOTTOMLY | 4.0 | Docudrama | 12+ |
| LEARN TO DISCERN | 3.0 | Document'y | 12+ |
| PSYCHIC CONFESSIONS | 3.0 | Document'y | 12+ |
| REFLECTIONS OF HIS LOVE | 3.0 | Document'y | 12+ |
| SCARS THAT HEAL: DAVE ROEVER STORY | 3.0 | Document'y | 12+ |
| UNHOLY HOLLYWOOD | 3.0 | Document'y | 12+ |
| GODS OF THE NEW AGE | 3.5 | Document'y | 12+ |
| MINE EYES HAVE SEEN THE GLORY | 4.0 | Document'y | 12+ |
| SPLIT INFINITY | 2.0 | Drama | 12+ |
| GOD ON TRIAL | 2.5 | Drama | 12+ |
| WELCOME HOME | 2.5 | Drama | 12+ |
| AGONY AND THE ECSTASY, THE | 3.0 | Drama | 12+ |
| COME THE MORNING | 3.0 | Drama | 12+ |
| DISTANT THUNDER, A | 3.0 | Drama | 12+ |
| FACE IN THE MIRROR | 3.0 | Drama | 12+ |
| FIESTA | 3.0 | Drama | 12+ |
| GOLD THROUGH THE FIRE | 3.0 | Drama | 12+ |
| GUESS WHO'S COMING TO AMERICA | 3.0 | Drama | 12+ |
| HEALING, THE | 3.0 | Drama | 12+ |
| HOLDING ON | 3.0 | Drama | 12+ |
| IMAGE OF THE BEAST | 3.0 | Drama | 12+ |
| IN MY WILDEST DREAMS | 3.0 | Drama | 12+ |
| INTRUDER, THE | 3.0 | Drama | 12+ |
| JOAN OF ARC | 3.0 | Drama | 12+ |
| MOMENT OF TRUTH | 3.0 | Drama | 12+ |
| ORDINARY GUY | 3.0 | Drama | 12+ |
| PILGRIM'S PROGRESS | 3.0 | Drama | 12+ |
| SAFE AT HOME | 3.0 | Drama | 12+ |
| SEASONS OF THE HEART | 3.0 | Drama | 12+ |
| TAKE TWO | 3.0 | Drama | 12+ |
| THIEF IN THE NIGHT | 3.0 | Drama | 12+ |
| TWO A PENNY | 3.0 | Drama | 12+ |
| RUN TO THE SEA | 3.2 | Drama | 12+ |
| HOUSE DIVIDED, A | 3.3 | Drama | 12+ |
| ANGEL OF SARDIS | 3.5 | Drama | 12+ |
| BEHIND THE SUN | 3.5 | Drama | 12+ |

# Appendix — Christian Movies

| Title | Rating | Type | Age |
|---|---|---|---|
| CROSSFIRE | 3.5 | Drama | 12+ |
| EARLY WARNING | 3.5 | Drama | 12+ |
| ENTER AUNT JENNY | 3.5 | Drama | 12+ |
| FINISH LINE | 3.5 | Drama | 12+ |
| JESUS FILM, THE | 3.5 | Drama | 12+ |
| PRODIGAL, THE | 3.5 | Drama | 12+ |
| RISE & WALK: DENNIS BIRD STORY | 3.5 | Drama | 12+ |
| ROBE, THE | 3.5 | Drama | 12+ |
| SAND CASTLES | 3.5 | Drama | 12+ |
| PRODIGAL PLANET | 3.8 | Drama | 12+ |
| BAMBOO IN WINTER | 4.0 | Drama | 12+ |
| CLIMB, THE | 4.0 | Drama | 12+ |
| GREATER THAN GOLD | 4.0 | Drama | 12+ |
| PARADISE TRAIL | 4.0 | Drama | 12+ |
| FOURTH WISE MAN, THE | 2.5 | Drama | 12+ |
| DATING MOVIE, THE | 3.0 | Educational | 12+ |
| DATING - TURNING YOUR LOVE LIFE OVER TO JESUS | 3.0 | Educational | 12+ |
| EDGE OF EVIL, THE | 3.0 | Educational | 12+ |
| TOUGH QUESTIONS ABOUT SEX | 3.0 | Educational | 12+ |
| RIGOLETTO | 3.0 | Musical | 12+ |

## AGE 17+

| Title | Rating | Type | Age |
|---|---|---|---|
| FURY TO FREEDOM | 3.0 | Docudrama | 17+ |
| FALSE GODS OF OUR TIME: IN THE BEGINNING | 3.0 | Document'y | 17+ |
| HOLLYWOOD VS. RELIGION | 3.0 | Document'y | 17+ |
| HOLLYWOOD: LIGHTS, CAMERA, BLASPHEMY | 3.0 | Document'y | 17+ |
| COLSON: RELUTANT PROPHET | 3.5 | Document'y | 17+ |
| REFORMATION OVERVIEW | 3.5 | Document'y | 17+ |
| LAST RODEO, THE | 2.8 | Drama | 17+ |
| DARK VALLEY | 3.0 | Drama | 17+ |
| INNOCENT AGAIN | 3.0 | Drama | 17+ |
| IN SEARCH OF MORGAN AVERY | 3.5 | Drama | 17+ |
| JUDAS PROJECT, THE | 3.5 | Drama | 17+ |
| POWERPLAY | 4.0 | Drama | 17+ |
| REVIVAL | 4.0 | Musical | 17+ |

---

# FAMILY MOVIE REVIEW CARD

**UP-TO-DATE MOVIE REVIEWS BY PHONE 24 HOURS PER DAY REVIEWS FROM A FAMILY VALUES PERSPECTIVE**
Prepared By Movie Morality Ministries

- 30-Second Reviews Of All Major Currently Showing Movies
- Specific Information On Offensive And Commendable Elements In Films
- Updated Weekly With New Releases
- Special Review Section On Movies Recommended For Families

**$10 CARD BUYS 20 MINUTES OF MOVIE REVIEWS**

TO ORDER CALL 1-800-479-3820 or
Send Check/Money Order for $12.50 ($10 plus $2.50 Shipping and Handling) To: P.O. Box 12371, Dallas, Texas 75225

# Let's Go to the Movies ...or Watch TV!

## But do you really know what's in store for you ... and your children?

There is uncertainty about most films these days, even G and PG rated films, and definitely about PG-13 and R rated movies. You may find yourself and your children immersed in a deluge of obscene language, profanity, violence, nudity, sex and occultic phenomena.

The **PREVIEW FAMILY MOVIE & TV REVIEW** makes it possible for parents and young persons to know what to expect before they view a movie or TV series. Our staff previews all of the popular films before they are shown in the theaters throughout the U.S. We prepare a summary of each film's plot along with an analysis of the movie from a Christian and family perspective. We also include a tabulation of the frequency and intensity of crude and obscene language, sex, nudity, and violence. Also, any undesirable messages are pointed out as well as the positive elements in the film. You will have this information before or at the time the films are showing in your town. We also publish reviews of new TV series with special emphasis on those we feel are desirable.

So that you can keep right up-to-date with movies and TV shows, we publish **PREVIEW** twice a month and send it by first class mail. To receive the reviews for a year, we suggest a gift of $33.00 **If you would like to subscribe to PREVIEW, call us at 1-800-807-8071 or write to us at the address below.**

---

**PREVIEW FAMILY MOVIE & TV REVIEW**
1309 Seminole Dr., Richardson, TX 75080-3736
A publication of Movie Morality Ministries, Inc.